GLOBALISED INDIA AND DEVELOPMENT ISSUES

GLOBALISED INDIA AND DEVELOPMENT ISSUES

Editor:
K.N. JENA

ABHIJEET PUBLICATIONS
DELHI 110094

ABHIJEET PUBLICATIONS
2/46 Tukhmeerpur Extension
Delhi-110 094
Phone: 011-22960492, 65698474
E-mail: abhijeetpublication@gmail.com

GLOBALISED INDIA AND DEVELOPMENT ISSUES

First Published 2009

ISBN 978-93-80031-19-4

PRINTED IN INDIA

Published by J.K. Singh for Abhijeet Publications, Delhi-110 094, Lasertypeset by Gaurav Graphics, New Delhi and Printed at Himanshu Printers, Delhi.

Foreword

It is a privilege for me to go through the volume 'Globalised India and Development Issues' edited by Dr. K. N. Jena. Before writing the Foreword for this volume as I was well versed with Dr. Jena's way of looking at globalization-related issues, I am not at all surprised at the kind of care and concern, Dr. Jena has put in editing this volume. The most important aspects of it is that Dr. Jena with the differential approach has successfully established seamlessly correlation among diverse issues and challenges of development in the perspective of Globalised India.

I am reasonably confident this well edited volume would stir many a mind, to look at the issues of globalization and development in a happening country like India with fresh concern and queries.

Prof. S.N. Tripathy
Prof. of Economics,
Gokhale Institute of Politics and Economics,
Pune

Editorial

Globalisation as a process has touched the market, polity, and society of India in more than one way. It has charmed and sneaked into our drawing room, bedroom and even our toilets in a such a way that now we love it better, hate it better and gel with it better. It has become in separable from our collective mind and psyche. Whether it is the societal ethics, cultural basics, economic dynamics or nuances of politics nothing has remained un affected. In a word, it has become a hot potato which we can not hold it long nor let it go. Its dictats and dynamics have become irreversible and irrevocable. In such a situation, the best course of action is not how to break it rather how to make it more humane. Thus the present time is a trying time that goes begging for alternative approaches to adopt and adapt globalization from below and make India a safe and secured place to live in. Since the culmination of Uruguay Round of GATT and birth of WTO, the world has been enamored with 'top down' theories and practices with expectations that the nectar of globalization would trickle down and percolate to the last layer of the societal pyramid. But both the process and project of globalization from the top has seriously betrayed all expectations. While a miniscule of India has been shining, the majority of it is whining and crawling at the periphery of so called global existence. The under belly of globalization has been badly exposed and 'state' that has been relegated to the back ground, is again being appealed to come to the fore. With such realities staring us, it is high time to declare enough is enough and this far and no further. Now instead of being dazzled at the glare of pseudo sophisticacy of globalization, we have to set our priorities right with the real issues of development that includes all and excludes none. This edited volume is an honest attempt to stitch together some of the differential approaches to the issues of development in the so called Globalised India.

K.N. JENA

Acknowledgements

As the editor of this volume, I am profoundly thankful to all the contributors but for whose timely cooperation, my effort would have gone waste. I am equally thankful to all my colleagues and well wishers in Tripura University for their constant encouragement for embarking upon this modest exercise. I am also grateful to our honorable Vice-Chancellor, Tripura University, Prof. Arunoday Saha, whose constant refrain 'Publish or Perish' has a tonic effect in challenging my sense of academic imagination to undertake such an exercise. I am sincerely indebted to my wife Moushumi Jena and my daughters Monmita and Monprit for their encouragement and sacrifices that made me focused till the culmination of this humble effort. My line of acknowledgement would never be full and final without thanking Mr. J.K. Singh, Managing Director, Abhijeet Publications, Delhi, for his dedication and care in publishing this book in shortest possible time.

Dr. K. N. Jena

Acknowledgements

Contents

1

Intellectual Property Rights in India and Global Equations

K.N. JENA*

Indian Foreign Relations: A Historical Perspective

It is not at all easy task to account for how much of foreign relations of India is the result of a conscious design of the policy makers, an how much of the same is the result of emerging situations. Factors like ideological leaning, international economic, military situations and equations and current domestic as well as external processes, have played their vital role in shaping the form and text of India's foreign relations. But a clinical assessment will reveal that certain factors had a powerful impact on her relations with other countries. By the time India became independent in 1947, the modern European States had moulded international politics into a legacy and an environment for both new and old states of the world.[1] More than that, the tools of power and diplomacy that India could use to adjust her relations with other states were those which were bequeathed to her as a colony by her former masters. However, with the independence India, under the leadership of Late Pundit

* Reader and Head, Department of Political Science, Tripura University.

Jawaharlal Nehru, tried to navigate in the choppy and cold waters of post World War-II international relations, with the bows of non-alignment, that subsequently became the trademark of India's foreign policy. Government after government and Prime Minister after Prime Minister in India had to toe the path of non-alignment, throughout the cold war era, with minor deviation here and there depending upon, the political ideology of the personality, party of parties in power, border tensions, domestic political and economic situations and international compulsions. However basically basically it had been all through foreign policies and relations structured by the principles of non-alignment with a moderate touch of liberal socialism. The compelling reasons behind India's such track record, can be very well identified in her desire for that matter Nehru's desire to establish India's credentials as a seeker of world peace, lover of humanity, and her endeavour for her nation building. However, notwithstanding the western criticism that India's non-alignment policy is an opportunistic policy of enjoying the best of the both worlds, India tried to maintain her relations with the members of the Soviet and the US block.

Factors like domestic instability, a weak military, huge economic complex, philosophical inclinations of Jawaharlal Nehru, and above all pull of the super powers under the cold war, influenced Indian non-alignment foreign policy to a great extent. One fact, however was apparent that the shape of Indian foreign policy in its final analysis was determined by Nehru's judgment as to country's needs and her proper role in world affairs. Accordingly India with her policy of non-alignment desired to play an effective role in the polarized world politics. But at this juncture pragmatically, India's leadership should have concentrated its attention on domestic economic scene. Unfortunately instead of analyzing in economic terms, Jawaharlal Nehru thought of India in terms of her past glory and unmatched spiritual heritage. Thus non-economic factors and personal conviction, led Nehru to indulge in world politics, without the necessary military and economic ability. India plunged into international political exercises, justifying her actions in the name of morality and world peace. Nehru thought to lead the Asian states away from alliances of the Western or Eastern block of nations and at the same time, he attempted to exert influence on the policies of the USA and USSR, all in the name of prevention of third world war and the principle of self determination. He did not hesitate to request and receive economic assistance from America and Russia, but when these nations attempted to tie strings to the aid, he protested. What is interesting is that vagaries of international events for a brief period seemed to indicate that India was achieving her objectives successfully. But it was not long before the deteriorating economic situations in India, military engagements with China, in 1962 and with Pakistan in 1965, 1971, domestic turbulence and certain changes on the international scene proved the impossibility of success of her experiment with non-alignment. As an Asian Power, India wished to be consulted whenever the future of any part of Asia was being debated. With little economic standing and military strength to back her, India could not do much to directly influence the course of international events and India's foreign policy was forced to change its inputs. In the subsequent years particularly in 1971 with the treaty with USSR and in 1974 with nuclear explosion, India distinctly accepted the fact that she has not been effective in creating a united front of Third World countries. Experience in three wars made her highly security conscious and she has at last become convinced that her security must be built on a foundation of economic growth and military maturity and not on international goodwill that she chased for more than two decades.

With the end of cold war, the pragmatism of India's foreign relation based on ethics of non-alignment got diluted with the hurrah of marketocracy in nation after nation. With the market failure of socialism all over the world and disintegration Soviet Russia the Mecca of socialism, the colour, content and context of India's foreign relations and foreign policy options got visibly redefined, redirected and reinvented towards evolving her self into a regional economic power in the immediate future.

Indian Foreign Policy in Pre- and Post Globalisation Era

With gradual dominance of international economics over world politics, the idealistic platform of India's foreign policy based on high moral tone of Nehruvian legacy, started loosing ground and proving inadequate to deal with the fast changing space and pace of world politics. Towards the end of 1980's the GATT wind had started blowing towards every nook and corner of the globe. The buzz word doing the round, was dismantlation of economic insulation's around the different economies of the world. Free market economy and borderless international trade catching the fancy of the governments and policy makers all over the world. The World Bank, IMF and other international financial institutions began to be more effective, assertive and penetrative than the UNO and its agencies. Ideologies started taking backseat in favour of hard economies and pure commerce. The world started shrinking to become a global village, political and economic systems turned colourless and the countries virtually appeared borderless, the histories of hot and cold war started vanishing from the minds of the world leaders as they were preparing themselves for an encounter of the third kind called E. War (Economic War). The question of security, which was dominant in post world war period and in cold war era, with militaristic connotation, started assuming economic significance in terms of favourable balance of trade and balance of payments, better technology and knowledge based economy. Towards late 80's the premises of International relations and foreign policy, had already become commerce centric. The efficacy of military stratagems, nuclear deterrations, ideological convictions, and cold war machinations etc. as determining factors of foreign relations were stretched to limits and their relevance as the tools of foreign policy had lost much of their sheen. The top powers of the world had realized that in the changed circumstances it is the market power, not military power which will ensure them a decisive role in international relations. Hence, the lading countries of the world like the USA, UK, Canada, Japan, Countries of European Union started flexing their market muscles in preference to military muscles, to win away as many foreign markets (nations) to buttress their own national interests. The end result was that, exercise of foreign policies became more commerce oriented. With this backdrop the long history of GATT that started in 1947 culminated in WTO in the year 1994, at Uruguay round of GATT. The WTO with its other sister entities like TRIPs, TRIMs, and FDI became the new 'mantras' of globalization and new axis around which international relation and foreign policy exercises started revolving. The countries, started realizing the importance of economic growth, stability, capability and self sufficiency in the sphere of international relations. They began to assert their economic interests vis-à-vis others, to enjoy better bargaining powers in world politics in general and bilateral and multilateral negotiations in particular. In the past, countries in Asia and Africa could not influence the course of world politics, because economically they were not stable and sound enough to take care of their own domestic economic complexes and exert pressure in the world politics. As mentioned earlier in this chapter, a country like India, being in the forefront of non-alignment movement still could not position herself as the most effective actor in the international and even in the Asian theatre. The reasons of such Indian experience are not very far to seek. Weak military capability and economic standing made India vulnerable in her attempt to position herself with the movers and shakers of world politics. India's weak military capability was a logical corollary of her weak economic capability. In the initial years of her independence, India opted for non-militaristic way to world affairs not exclusively due to her obsession with world peace and cooperation, but due to the fact that at that particular juncture, India was economically not in a position to afford a full fledged militaristic alignment with any particular power block. This proved that in the past, India's policy of non-alignment could not deliver the desired result because of her own economic complexes as well as the economic weaknesses of the countries that India expected to lead vis-à-vis the power block politics of the United States and the Soviet Union. However, the past is not always past as it can enlighten the future, provided the past omissions are taken care of, in the future scheme of things. One of such serious omission on the part of Indian foreign policies is non-inclusion of domestic economic interest of India as a major determining factor in the formulation of India's foreign relations. However, with the changed scenario of international relations. However, with the changed scenario of international relations and radical alteration in the ground realities of world affairs, every country including India has to look at the exercise of foreign relations through economic prisms and lenses. India being in the forefront of technological revolution among developing countries and being a leading economic power in the South, can hardly afford to look at the issue other way round without compromising with her strong wind of globalization and economic liberalization, blowing in all directions, India can't expect to chalk out a course of foreign relations without advancing her economic interests.

In the era of globalization, each country is virtually going to loose the exclusive right over her domestic market and to compensate that sacrifice each country will be trying to have a piece of the pie in other countries markets. In this game of apparent market swapping, there is a possibility of emergence of a genre of proverbial foxes and cranes in the theatre of international economics and politics to hoodwink the gullible. Thus, political and economic survival of developing nations like India in this rat race for market, E. Power (Economic Power) now largely depends upon how best a nation plays her political and economic variables vis-à-vis other nations.

World Trade Organisation (WTO) came into force in 1995 and since then it has virtually become storehouse of globalization process. The treaty on intellectual property rights known as TRIPs agreement also came into existence with the creation of WTO. Almost all the developing countries including India became the members of WTO and signed the TRIPs agreement. The basic understanding was WTO will facilitate free international trade and TRIPs agreement will ensure smooth flow of intellectual properties in the forms of new idea, technical know-how, better technology etc. from the developed states to the poor and developing countries. However the developing countries including India found to their surprise that the TRIPs agreement instead of facilitating free flow of technical know-how and technology has been proving to be modus operandi for exploitation of the markets of the poor and developing countries by the developed states owning monopoly over intellectual property rights in wide spectrum of commodities and services. Moreover the developed countries started claiming IPRs over the use of products belonging to bio-diversity of the underdeveloped and developing countries, without sharing the benefits accruing out of such IPRs. In some cases the new technical know-how developed by the research and development centres of the developed states, infact could be possible by using the skilled manpowers, like doctors, engineers, and scientists of the developing countries, for whom it was nothing but brain drain. Rationally, the countries suffering from such brain drain and bio-resource drain must have a due share in the economic prosperity resulting out of such exercises. But unfortunately that is what exactly not happening. On the other hand such lopsided applications of TRIPs Agreement and inefficiency of dispute settlement mechanism in WTO, have caused a kind of economic insecurity among the developing and poor nations. This peculiar situation is strong enough to cause an imbalance in the policy making processes of both the developed and developing nations. The pertinent question is which area of policy making of a state will be affected the most? The answer comes always in economic terms as it is the economic policies, market conditions, economic interests of a country, that immediately come under the influence of such situations. In the globalize era, as a state is never free from the market compulsions a state will have no way out except chalking out a kind of foreign policy which will serve its political as well economic interests better. The marketization of the states and globalization of national economies have pushed the policy making authorities, particularly in developing state like India for market sustaining foreign policies and external relations, to maintain a balancing act between national economic interests and transnational market integration.

Hence, now the question is not low a developing state like India is going to redefine her foreign policy objectives vis-à-vis others, but how to design foreign policy in the current form of "State market condominium".[2]

To make her sustainable in the face of increased relevance of the global intellectual property rights markets? In the present tug of war between state and market, the policies of the state should be such that the market, will sustain the state. The point is that we can't have one without the other. While determining the relations with other states, the focus should not be only on the cultural and military interests of the state but on the interaction of political and the market interests of the states. The market in the present time is propelling force behind stability of governance and intellectual property rights (IPRs) over the products and services are the invisible force behind market, and economic development. Thus, in the ultimate analysis, each and every state particularly belonging to the south of the global village, has to realize this truth that its right over new ideas hand new technology which will make their market economy and state sustainable. Therefore while determining the relations among themselves the policy makers must not loose sight of this basic truth. Unfortunately India right after being independent, pursued a policy of non-alignment towards one and sundry mostly on the basis of her past glory, high moral thinking and personal judgment and conviction of her leaders and parties in power, without considering her material and market status in the eyes of the world community. The net result was India ended with having so-called friendly foreign relations with almost everybody without having real friend in anybody. (Till the pact with USSR 9 August, 1971).

Events in the last few years have forced India to comprehend a world in which the cold was has ended, communism has collapsed, the Soviet empire has withered away, the USA has turned world's sole policeman and WTO, TRIPs, TRIMs, FDI etc., have posed foreign policy challenges to virtually all countries in the world.[3] This is true of developing countries in general and India in particular. As a poor country like India scramble to make sense of the new economic world order and to avoid of being caught offside of the WTO norms and TRIPs rules, the resulting turbulence in hitherto settled patterns of third world interactions with the nations enriched with intellectual property powers introduced additional uncertainties and complications in her foreign policy options. In contrast to a triumphant technologically powerful nation on the ascendant, India, in spite of her vast skilled manpower, huge bio and natural resources, large market potentiality and enormous middle class purchasing power, has not been able to make full use of her potentials and present herself as a real power in the international political and economic theatre. "By the end of the Rajiv Gandhi government (1984-89) India had achieved the dubious distinction of being on bad terms with all its neighbours. The successor, V.P. Singh government (1989-90), by pitting Indian against India, managed to destroy Indian society more effectively than any enemy could have effectively dared to hope. The Government under Chandrasekhar (1990-91) floundered and flip-flopped embarrassingly to respond to the Gulf crisis. In the process it succeeded in alienating both Baghdad and Washington without winning any friends."[4] Thus, from mid 80s to early 90's the essence of India's foreign relations were neither politically directed nor economically determined. However, with coming of Narsimha Rao government, in the early 90's, India for the first time, tried to give an economic orientation to her foreign relations. The economic policies formulated by Manmohan Singh the then finance minister in essence provided the basic inputs and directions of Indian foreign policy options. In principle India for the first time accepted the global reality i.e., economic liberalization and global integration are indispensable realities that India might dislike but can not avoid. Secondly, India like all other countries accepted the fact that protective economy has to be phased out and international trade has to be free from unsuitable tariff barriers. But unfortunately, what India could not foresee is the ultimate repercussions of different provisions of WTO and TRIPs agreement on the national economics, politics, social ethics and cultural basics of India. The inadevertent omission and commission on the part of the economic policy makers of India, should have been ideally taken care of by the foreign policy makers of India. The most practical course before India was to open channel of political relations with the developed states on the one hand the developing states on the other, to make them see the reason behind the uneasiness of India and other developing countries vis-à-vis various disadvantageous aspects of TRIPs agreement. This would have resulted in proper review of the TRIPs agreement in the subsequent meets on the TRIPs agreement. The resultant benefits to India would have two folds; First India could have taken an effective leadership of the developing countries, in the matter of TRIPs and its related issues in the WTO and in other forums. In the second place India being in the threshold of technological revolution in the field of biotechnology, information technology and other allied fields, could have better working relations with the major IPR owning countries. But unfortunately after signing the TRIPs agreement, India hardly tried to interact immediately with the developed states, nor maintained any dialogue with other developing countries, on the issues. .Thus in the years of Narasimha Rao government, Indian went forward for liberalization and played the game of globalization without fully comprehending the ins and outs of the rules of the game. These economically strategic lapses could have been redressed to some extent by foreign political strategies on the part of foreign policy makers of India. But, the highly complicated issues relating to TRIPs were allowed to float in the domestic political sea and assume emotive dimensions to take care of electoral politics of India.

The coming and going of two short tenured United Front Governments (from July 96 to March 96), under the leadership of Mr. Devegowda an Mr. I.K. Gujaral, had hardly the time and temper to decipher and deal with the invisible IPRs problems and chalk out foreign relations with the developed and developing countries, to make best bargain out of worst deal i.e. TRIPs agreement. On the other hand, instead of initiating any pro-active political measures in the external front to protect India's interest under WTO and TRIPs regime, both Mr. Devegowda and Mr. Gujaral governments tried to make the issue of domestically more emotive, to extricate maximum political mileage in the election times. The left parties being an outside partner of United Front dispensation left no stone unturned to express their total disapproval of previous Congress government's signing of WTO and TRIPs agreement. But this was only for domestic public consumption. The United Front Government's in this period had hardly done anything externally through strategic foreign relations exercise to protect India's IPRs interests. It is in this period only, the American and Canadian corporations, taking advantage of the TRIPs provisions were silently patenting different things belonging to Indian agriculture, geographical indications, and bio-diversity. The famous patent cases relating to 'Basmati Rice', 'Haldi' (turmeric) and Neem. The last two are well known cases relating to intellectual property right (patents) involving American corporations and Indian government. These issues ultimately turned to highly expensive cases in foreign courts. This resulted in bitter and expensive lesson for India.

With the coming BJP led (march 1998) coalition government at the centre in 1998, with Prime Minister Mr. Atal Bihari Vajpayee as the Prime Minister, the foreign economic and political relations of India, with the developed states, particularly the USA were on ascendancy. BJP being right wing political party, naturally saw virtues in cultivating good and favourable relations with the European Union, and the USA. So far so good but the foreign policy makers in India remained oblivious of the fact that strong foreign relations with the developed nations as well the developing nations don't solely depend upon imaginative political diplomacy. The relevance of futuristic economic diplomacy counts a lot in making the political relation more stable and favourable. In the present day international system as the neoclassical realists predict, an increase in relative material power will enventually lead to a corresponding expansion of scope of a country's foreign relations and that a decrease in such power will eventually lead to a corresponding contraction. However, the pattern is not necessarily symmetrical or uniform because it depends not solely on objective material trends but also on how political decision makers subjectively perceive them.5 And that countries, with weak political authorities will take longer time to translate an increase in material power into expanded foreign policy activity or will take a more circuitous route there. That is because sometimes small, insignificant, even invisible economic choices or lack of choices can have big consequences on foreign policy behaviour of the nations concerned.[6]

Unfortunately, India's external relations exercises under the past and present governments, have hardly on the line of the cardinal principle of enriching the material power, to pursue successful and most effective foreign relations with other nations. Speaking from the theoretical premises of neoclassical realists, the best course of India's foreign relations must spring from and conditioned by the factors that directly or indirectly contribute to the development of India's material power. Material power however is not a static, condition. It is as dynamic variable as foreign relations. Material power of India can't be enriched by moralistic stand based on high sounding ideals, past glory, and self trumpeted importance. It is a dynamic process conditioned by hard core scientific discoveries, inventions, new ideas, futuristic research and development etc. which are ultimately put to implementation at the users end. However, that is not to suggest that all these components of material power have to be necessarily of indigenous origin. The material powers are identified in the forms of availability of financial aids technical know-how, technology transfer, patent rights, copyright, licenses, trademarks, etc. Out of all these micro components of material power, finance capital is most visible and contribute instantly to the construction of material power, but its long term efficiency is shorter than those of others mentioned above. It is the non-financial components that contribute most in the making of material power, which are inevitable in nature but makes a nation's power renewable and long sustainable. This category of components in the ultimate analysis make up the real material power of a nation.

Applying the above analysis, in the context of India it can be well argued that whatever invisible ingredients (intellectual property powers) or material powers are indigenously available can be used as effective countervailing inputs, in the analysis and determination of India's foreign policy response or initiation vis a vis other nations (both developed and developing). More so because countries, would like to take advantage of India's expertise and intellectual property powers in the varied field of economics, commerce, science and technology, that ultimately would help those countries to develop their own material power. On the other hand the intellectual property powers or invisible ingredients that help in the making up material power of India, if not indigenously available and India has to procure, it from other countries (developed countries) then India will have to use its foreign policy expertise to achieve the same without compromising or sacrificing her domestic economic interest beyond a justifiable limit.

Thus, in the both types of situational models 'material power' as a determining factor of foreign relations pay a vital role. In the first situational model material power (intellectual power) plays the determining catalyst role in the making of foreign relations. To explain the situation further, let us imagine a situation where India has beter intellectual property powers which are needed by other developing countries in South Asia or beyond South Asia. In that case India can very well mix its economic interests in her foreign policy determination process and thereby secure long term national interests.

Such a strategy will go long way towards evolving a cooperative framework for regional cooperation, as long as it retains linkages with mutual interest in the field of economics and politics of the concerned countries.[7] Moreover, the countries taking intellectual property powers from India, due to their own internal political dynamics and economics under development underscoring their dependence on India, will prove handy for India in her endeavour to play active role in different world forums like UNO, World Bank, IMF and WTO and even in different conflicting world situations. Again India's foreign policy propelled by its knowledge based economic processes will help in creating a climate conducive to regional cooperation. Such cooperative ventures may also reduce the leverage exercised by the extra-regional powers in counting south Asia countries, among whom India desires to have a decisive say. Thus, India can compensate her limited ability to provide material and financial capital to her potential friends, by extending the intellectual capital aids, in which India In the present world is a well recognised power. To make it more attractive for the developing countries, India can very well offer liberalized package of intellectual capitals in comparison to that of developed countries, which are invariably fraught with open conditionalities and hidden catches. To cap it all, India's intellectual property package to the developing countries particularly in Asia will be much sought after as it will be more cost effective and compatible with local economic conditions.

Thus from the point of view of India's foreign relations conditioned by economic determinants like intellectual properties, always stand a fair chance of success in the immediate neighbourhood and region. An economically strong India and a 'friendly India' for the immediate region 'will pave the way' for strong Indian in the global village. Hence, in the long run what is more important is not foreign policy based on transfer of material resources, but the foreign policy encouraging cooperation in South Asia as well as South East Asia to avoid indiscriminate import of technology through greater cooperation and exchange of technologies among the member countries. India has a very successful record of fruitful cooperation and exchange of technologies with other countries by sharing of her experience in industrial development, deputation of technical and managerial experts in various fields, the organization of training for developing countries, preparation of feasibility reports for industrial projects.[8] However, what India at this juncture needs is that India should aggressively pursue this economic aspects of her foreign relations, so that in the near future, she can play the role of full fledged Asian major in the international political and economic theatre. However, in the present time India's activities in the SAARC are not fully upto mark to hit the bull's eye India has to depend on more economic diplomacy in the SAARC.

The most glaring irony of the present globalization process is that the relevance of regional cooperation has not lost its sheen. In fact the foreign relation of the nations in the past belonging to different regional arrangements like, North American Fee Trade Association (NAFTA), The Caribbean Economic Community (CARICOM), the council for Arab Economic Unity (AEU) the Organisation of Arab Petroleum Exporting Countries (OAPEC), the Organisation for Africa Unity (OAU), the Association of South East Asian Nations

(ASEAN), have always been conditioned by their economic and material imperatives. To be more particular, the countries like Malaysia, Thailand, Indonesia, Singapore, Hongkong, which belong to ASEAN have always interacted with one another more on economic issues which subsequently formed the very basis of their foreign relations.

So far India's efforts and all her political gestures towards ASEAN to become its member have gone in vain due to economic looseness of India as perceived by the ASEAN. Therefore, India to make her more viable and acceptable in any sort of regional cooperative arrangement, has to make her economic net worth more alluring. This is possible, by harnessing developing and packaging her intellectual property powers.

However in the second type of situation, where India has to depend on the intellectual capital of the developed states for enrichment of her own material power, India's efforts through her foreign political and economic relations need to be most imaginative and futuristic. In the areas like information technology where India is a leading intellectual capital provider to the developed states like, the USA, Japan, Australia, Canada etc., India is required to expect more than just foreign exchange earning. India must have to use this favourable position to bargain and barter for the technology which is badly required by her. Moreover Indian foreign economic and political policy dealing with the transnational and multinational Corporations having their origin in the developed states, in the field of bio-technology and pharmaceutical industries using Indian bio-diversity for raw materials, needed to be very critical and pragmatic. But some how Indian foreign policy makers are yet to fully understand the ramifications of invisible intellectual property powers in the realm of international politics and economics. The reason is that some times it is difficult to comprehend seemingly small choices which can have big consequences and foreign policy behaviour may look "clocklike" only from a distance and over the long term, on close inspection and over to short to medium from "cloud like" activity may be the norm.[9]

In the Indian perspective it can be said that it is better late than never. No doubt India took time to realize, the importance of IPRs as economic boosters and their relevance to international relations but now India fully realize the positive aspects of IPRs and IPRs propelled knowledge based material strength of a nation. This knowledge based economic power of India, in all probability, is going to determine, shape and effect her future interaction, rapport and terms of relation with other nations. On the basis of such understanding Mr. Jaswant Singh, the ex-external affairs Minister, viewed that the economic matters, now form the integral part of Indian foreign policy in the light of changed world economic order. Speaking in a seminar "vision 2010 & Indian Diaspora" in New Delhi, Mr. Singh told that due to overflow of globalization processes, political clauses are being attached to international business which have to be dealt with ministry of external affairs (MEA).[10] Colonialism was born as a result of quest for markets, in today's world markets are dominated and controlled by new inventions, technologies, processes and ideas. These developments belong to the domain of Intellectual Property Rights (IPRs). More a country owns IPRs, more is the possibility of its dictating terms to other nations. IPRs are the unlimited and inexhaustible sources of material power. Therefore Mr. Jaswant Singh, the ex-external affairs minister in the NDA ministry believed that the Ministry of External Affairs has to involve the economy aspect in the determination of country's foreign relations. But unfortunately as he pointed out in the said seminar, "India is now so much consumed with domestic politics that enough attention is not being paid to important issue like IPRs that constitutes a new agenda of foreign policy in the present day situations."

Indian foreign policy in the future is unlikely to succeed unless the IPRs related issues are adequately addressed in the determination of foreign relations. The importance of IPRs as a critical component of future foreign relation is already visible to the discerning policy makers. India's equations with the U.S. in the post WTO and TRIPs agreements period are mostly being qualified by knowledge based economic issues and intellectual capitalism. India and USA have crossed swords quite a number of time over IPRs related issues. The litigations involving American corporations and Govt. of India, are over the ownership of patents on products of Indian bio-diversity and Indian traditional knowledge. Some of the famous cases involving patent and IPRs are *neem, haldi* (turmeric), *basmati* rice, jack fruit, *sharifa,* ginger, *karela* etc. These cases involve a lot of technical aspects which sometimes are incomprehensible not only to the common man but also to the policy makers and technocrats. But the simple truth is that the cases relating to IPRs and patents involving India, in reality are the vital areas of country's economic interests and independence. India has own some isolated cases involving *HALDI & NEEM,* but these are costly propositions which India can hardly afford every time. Therefore the exact need of the hour is that India should determine and formulate her foreign relations (both political and economic) in such way that her IPRs interests are well protected vis-á-vis developed countries like USA, Japan, European Union (EU) & Canada.

A few cases involving India's vital economic interests and IPRs related problems can be focused to bring home the relevance of IPRs in the making of foreign relations. In the field of pharmaceuticals and health care industry, the traditional medicines of Indian origin continue to be patented by multi-national pharmaceutical giants in the name of new research and developments and inventions. For example a patent has been granted in the United States in the use of jamun (black berry), karela and brinjal as anti diabetic agents. These properties of the foresaid plants have been well documented in the ancient Indian texts.

In the field of agriculture, which is the backbone of Indian economy, IPRs and patents of different products and plants by the foreign companies will play havoc to Indian economic interest. On the other hand without proper IPR protection and futuristic patent regimes relating to Indian agriculture and bio-diversity India cannot ensure her position as a major agricultural producer and foreign exchange earner. Hence India can hardly afford to deal with IPR related issues and bio-diversities as it dealt in the past with the basmati rice. It is only because of unsystematic and unorganized patent regime and IPRs policies, India was pushed to wall in her fight against the Rice Tec Corporation which have attempted to patent the basmati rice at the cost of Indian agriculture. This has created a lot of chaos and confusion in and out of Indian parliament.[11] It soon became an emotive issues in India. The opposition in India took the govt. to task, due to latter's casual approach to patent issue in India. The political understanding is that unless India streamline her IPR priorities and fit it into her foreign policy agenda, India has to fight costly litigations involving foreign multinational companies. If India would have strictly and objectively negotiated the patent issue over basmati rice, with the govt. of USA and prevailed upon latter with her foreign policy mechanism, the Rice Tec would not have been in position to fiddle with the patent of basmati rice in the name of texmati. Although the govt. of India consoles itself that the patenting of texmati which is different from basmati and it has not affected India's economic interests, yet for all practical purposes India's economic interest have been greatly compromised on this count. Similarly the cases involving chemically and genetically engineered seeds patented by Monsanto corporation infamously known as Terminator seeds, is most likely to affect the vital interest of Indian agriculture and India has to fight more and more similar costly court cases in foreign lands. Therefore India has to pursue a long-term action plan through IPRs oriented foreign political and economic relations, with developed countries. It may sound bit impractical and wishful thinking in the light of present day trend of corporate governance and influence of TNC's and MNC's. However, the truth is that the present world politics based on economic logic, has a better chance of delivering positive results than that of traditional and classical foreign policies determined on the basis of geographical contiguity, culture, ideology, military objectives etc. If India can package her IPRs interest in the broad format of foreign relation, India will not only buttress her interest better but also unveil new genre of foreign policy practices which other developed and developing countries will treat as alternative policy models.

Even in the field of pharmaceutical, biotechnology, genetic engineering, space research, traditional knowledge, like yoga, mantra, tantra etc. India has to do her IPR related homework in the field of IPRs to enjoy the emerging economic situations. India being god gifted in bio-diversity, the patent scenario in India has specific relevance to her bio-diversity. Even India has to push the IPR logic to her traditional knowledge in medicine, art, architecture, construction technology etc. In built in the epics like the *Mahabharat,* the *Ramayan,* the *Bhagwat Gita,* and the Vedas. Most of the ideas that constitute the very core of the above mentioned creations infact are the invisible and inexhaustible sources of future creations in the field of medicine, science, technology, art literature, and architecture. A proper culture of their IPRs can ensure great economic windfall for India. Therefore India has to not only treat IPRs as a legal issue, it should also treat IPRs as the political and economic vehicles to protect her national interests. The world has already adopted tight patent and IPR regime. In such a situation if India does not go for a pragmatically structural IPR policy exercise it would fail to protect the intellectual properties in the above mentioned fields. India, in such a situation, would be like a man who argues everything is owned in common and therefore allows his possessions to be stolen. The most important reason why India must bring its IPR policy to the core of her general international policy is that without a structured and strategic IPR policy, India will be taken seriously by the IPRs holding developed states. And India will be always lagging in the field of science, technology, research and development. The bulk of the scientific output in the west comes from the private sectors, especially the type of knowledge with tangible economic benefits. But in India and in almost all third world countries, science and technology are a govt. monopoly. This means it is largely haphazard and starved of funds. This will remain so if India lacks an IPR regime and India's foreign relations lack IPR orientation. However the present IPR scenario in India and its linkage with her international political and economic policies are so discouraging that if an Indian invents something of consequence his first act is to fly away to the US and patent it there. His home country cannot guarantee that his idea will not be immediately stolen. The flow of knowledge from the overseas is equally stymied by the lack of a proper patent regime. India will always get obsolete technology because it can not secure the rights of the owner of that technology.[12]

The IPR policy regime in India is so outdated that while a person filing for a patent in USA, can get it in about two eyars and globally in three years, in India the applicant could find himself making circles for up to 7 years. As a result of which 1,53,000 patent were granted in the USA in 1999, 1,50,000 in Japan. In India a total of 1,844 patents were granted in 1997-98. Out of which 619 were granted to Indian and rest 1255 patents to foreigners.[13]

India's status is particularly glaring in the field of Info-Tech. Indians are said to have hold one-third of patents in Silicon Valley, but only 104 IT patents were filed in India last year against 70,000 patents in the US. Again a large number of patents filed in India were by IT multinationals. Many of the patentees choose to bypass the Indian patent regime and apply directly in the US or Europe where they face neither antiquated laws nor grossly under staffed offices. With such a depressing patent scenario in India what is urgently required is that there should be immediate change in the Patent Act that date back to 1970. The second Amendment Bill 1999 is expected to reduce the process to three to four years once its comes to force. But unfortunately it is still in parliamentary cold storage. However, India being a signatory to the WTO, is obliged to change its law in line with the TRIPs agreement. Thus compliance with global practice on IPRs has to be ensured by India before the year 2005. However before India does that it had the option of allowing exclusive marketing right (EMR) for these years. The situation became more acute because India lost its case against the US on the pharmaceutical issue before the Dispute Settlement Body (DSB) of WTO. As result of which India had to opt for EMR route. However the decision to grant EMR to foreign multinational companies created a lot of political problems in India. Strong opinion was formed both in the political and economic front that India buckled on IPR issue because of foreign pressure channelised through MNCs and TNCs. It was also viewed as compromising the economic sovereignty of India noted academician like Arun

Ghosh was of the view that instead of capitulating to unjust condition of TRIPs agreement India could have taken the advantage of the escape clause in the agreement (TRIPs) on moral and ethical grounds. Again on the issue of IPR period, there is great concern among the Indian academicians, economists, technocrats and legal experts. The Associated Chambers of Commerce and Industry (ASSOCHAM) has called for shortening the validity of patents from 20 years to 10 years in the view of the compressed life cycle for all products including drugs and pharmaceuticals. The world needed a socially managed enclosure movement for IPR, otherwise there would be scramble among the powerful nations to grab valuable pieces of intellectual property. Therefore, India's endeavour must be to make to developed countries realize that the fundamental shifts in the technology and economic landscape are making the current global IPR system unworkable and ineffective as the existing system is tilted towards the technologically developed nations. This is possible through effective foreign economic and political relations.

In the failed Seattle Conference on TRIPs in December 1999, India adopted the right approach in its effort to bring a consensus among the developing countries through it's economic diplomacy, sought to make the poor and developing states to see the logic behind the dissemination of technology to prevent possible abuse of patent holders. India also rightly pointed out in the Seattle Conference that international competitiveness to a large extent is determined by access to advanced technologies. As the fast world science report of UNESCO highlighted that the gap between the developed and developing countries is now not so much a resource gap as it is a knowledge gap. Industrialised countries, for instance hold 97% of all the patents worldwide.

However, transfer of technology, which is implicit in the TRIPs agreement, is not easily forthcoming. Therefore, it is essential that measures must be taken at the level of external relations to make the IPRs holding developed countries realize the concerns of the developing countries like India on IPR issues.

Therefore no more IPRs should be considered to be part of legal and economic platforms. It must be recognized as a catalyst and determinant of future global relations. India being in the vanguard of technological revolution in the south end of the global village, will do a great service to her own cause and that of the other developing countries, if India fits in IPR economics in its external relation vis-à-vis other nations.

The people at the helm of external relation making and dealing with political and economic diplomacy must realize that IPR is one of the impending challenges that Indian policy faces, has ben underscored by the unfolding relevance of IPRs in the transnational relations. Moreover a vital justification for IPR becoming a determinant of global relations, emerge out of the fact that, if not only transcends the national economy of India, but also national constitution and the spirit of India policy. The constitution of India is supreme, even over majority public opinion in the country. No other document or agreement can be contrary to that effect. But unfortunately the signing of the TRIPs agreement and various provisions of the agreement are directly in collision with the provisions of Indian constitution. IN fact the TRIPs has become the new password 'open sesame' to transcend with our constitutional provisions. The agendas of transnational business cartels are fast becoming unwritten economic constitution of India.

For all practical purposes the transnational corporate power are dominating the national financial, military and foreign policies. It has been bending India's economic policies and successfully seeking to reverse all that was gained following the attainment of independence.

Thus Indian foreign policy has to highlight the above-mentioned dangers that are rising from the interventionist impulse in the name of transnational integration and economic globalization courtesy intellectual property rights. With its fast emerging status as a global economic power especially in the field of information technology (IT) and other knowledge-based economy, India cannot afford to loose the opportunity by accepting the one-sided dictates of TRIPs agreement. Hence India has to integrate its economics with her external relations with the developed as well as developing countries. With its vast market potentiality and increasing purchasing power, India can reorient her foreign policy objectives. Thus for the determination of foreign policy, India can no more depend solely upon the judgment of professional policy makers. India has to follow the example of the US where more and more technocrats, corporate professionals representing big business houses, economics and legal experts constitute the core of the foreign policy making processes. Thus in the changed world situation, it is economics and commerce that are going to determine the parameters and subject mater of global relations. India cannot be an exception. Sooner India realize this truth beter will be her chance to consolidate her position in the international community.

In the recent years, India's relations with the US, UK, Japan, EU, France, Germany and Canada, have gone for positive change, mostly due to the increasing importance of India's growing economy and market. Even the positive thinking on the part of the countries belonging to ASEAN, about India, can be singularly attributed to economic factors. In future, if India desired to play an effective role in South Asia, it has to present a robust, stable and sustainable economy. It has been already proved beyond doubt that no amount of military power can guarantee a nation's relevance in the international arena, if it is not backed by a super and fast-growing economy. The disintegration of the USSR is the best example to bring home the point noted above. The formation of European Union (EU) and its ever growing strength, the merger of the two Germanies with the collapse of Berlin Wall, the gradual coming closer of two Koreas are some of the big events of the last century that can be best explained and interpreted in economic terms only. Again Japan's importance in the present world politic is another pertinent example in this direction. After collapse of the USSR, the role of sole policeman that the US has been playing, at best can be attributed, in addition to its military power, to its super economic status in the world community. All these trends and facts should be the best eye openers for India. India has to streamline her economic priorities, to present itself as a nation of strength and substance before the world community. The naked truth is that in this age of 'marketocracy' without adequate economic strength, no nation will be taken seriously by other nations. The fate of non-alignment lost its relevance not only due to the end of Cold War but also because of the economic weaknesses of almost all the countries belonging to this movement. India being the torchbearer of this movement, has also learnt this lesson hard way. Therefore, India has to highlight her economic priorities in the determination of her foreign relations. However, as India is deficient in financial capital, it has to neutralize this deficiency only through intellectual capital in which India is fortunately far ahead of many other nations. Hence India has to take the issue of intellectual capitalism and intellectual property rights to boost her economic countervailing power. The determination of foreign relation qualified by the intellectual property rights and other economic parameters, is one of the most practicable and viable vehicles to carry forward India's concern and interest. This is also equally true for other nations with India like experiences and situations.

REFERENCES

1. Chawala, Sudershan, *The Foreign Relation of India,* Dickenson, California, 1976, pp. 1-4.
2. Underhill, Goffry R.D.: "State, Market, and Global Political Economy", *International Affairs* (Blackwell, London 1999-2000), Vol. 76, No. 4, pp. 823-824.
3. Thakur, Ramesh: *The Politics and Economics of India's Foreign Policy,* (Oxford University Press, Delhi, 1999), p. 1.
4. *Ibid.*
5. Rose, Gideon, "Neoclassical Realism and Theories of Foreign Policy" Review Article, *World Politics* (Johns Hopkins University Press, USA; 1998) Vol. 51, October, 1998, No. 1, pp. 167-68.
6. *Ibid.*
7. Baral and K. Raj "Towards a Regional Foreign Policy" in the *Regional Cooperation in South Asia: Problems and Prospects,* ed. Bimal Prashad (Vikas Publishing House, New Delhi, 1989), p. 188.
8. Rasgotra, M.K. "New Era of Economic Cooperation in South

Asia", in the *South Asian Cooperation in Industry, Energy and Technology,* ed., Arif A. Wakif (Sage, New Delhi, 1987), pp. 30-32.

9. Kenneth, N. Waltz, Man, *The State and War,* (Columbia Press, New York, 1959), p. 238.
10. See, *The Pioneer,* New Delhi, dt. 25.11.2000.
11. See, *The Times of India,* New Delhi, dt. 21.08.2001 and 23.08.2001.
12. See, Editorial, *The Telegraph,* Calcutta, dt. 25.12.1998.
13. See, *The Times of India,* New Delhi, dt. 27.08.2001.

2

Globalization and Development Interventions: The Experiences of the Chakmas of the Chittagong Hill Tracts of Bangladesh

BINDU RANJAN CHAKMA*

Introduction

The concept of globalization is not new, *albeit*, it has created a new impetus in development debate academic literature in the 1990s following formation of the multilateral trade body, the World Trade Organization (WTO) in 1995. There were multilateral trading organizations like the European Economic Community, which reorganized per se as European Union (EU) later on, Association of South East Asian Nations (ASEAN), G-7, G-77 etc, but these organizations were either regional or tarns-regional in character. Whereas, the WTO, the principal organization of the globalization process, is an organization where most of the 21st century's nation states including the Peoples Republic of China (PRC) and Vietnam (150 member) are signatories to and member of it. Bangladesh

---

* Lecturer, Department of Political Science, Netaji Subhas Mahavidyalaya, Udaipur, Tripura.

as a country initiated economic liberalization program from 1975 onwards. It is a signatory of the WTO and various multilateral agreements such as the Agreement of Agriculture (AoA), Trade Related Intellectual Property Rights (TRIPs), Trade Related Investment Measures (TRIMs), agreements on Trade and Environment etc. under the WTO regime. As a least developing country, it has to primarily depend on donor countries and other multilateral donor agencies for macro economic stabilization and undertaking and implementing development activities.

Objectives of the Study

The objectives of this research paper are:

(i) To study the implications of development activities of the government of Bangladesh in the CHT funded by multilateral donor agencies on economic and socio-cultural lives of the Chakmas of the CHT of Bangladesh;

(ii) To reorient in the approach of development interventions of the multilateral donor agencies in the CHT;

(iii) To look and suggest for an all inclusive development regime.

Methodology

The study has been carried on analysis of both primary and secondary sources of data and information although secondary sources are looked at most cases. Some vital documents and interviews with some eminent Chakma leaders like Chakma Raja Barrister Devasish Roy of the CHT either through direct or a mail questionnaire method have been considered as the primary sources in the study. In the secondary sources, review of literature is paid utmost importance. The study critically examines some existing reports, policy papers, books on globalization and development interventions in the CHT of Bangladesh. Internet sources have also been dully considered to carry on this study. Information and data that include research paper, reports and outcomes of seminars and workshops related to this study published in websites are also collected, complied and critically studied and analyzed.

Location of the Study

The CHT is situated in the South Eastern part of Bangladesh covering a total physical area of 5.093 sq. miles. It is the ten percent of the total land area of country. The government of Bangladesh formed a Development Board in the name of CHT Development Board (CHTDB) in 1976 to look, initiate, monitor and implement development projects and activities in the CHT. The CHT consists of three districts-the Rangamati, the Khrgrachari and the Banderban. There is a Hill District Council (HDC) in each of these district headquarter. Besides, the CHT Regional Council (CHTRG) was formed in the CHT following conclusion of the CHT Peace Accord in December 1997. There are eleven ethnic indigenous groups in the CHT. Among them, the Chakma community is the largest and their concentrations are found in all the three districts, although majority of them reside in the Rangamati and Khagrachari districts of the CHT. Therefore, the study primarily focused on the developmental programs of the Rangamati and Khagrachari districts of the CHT.

Globalization as a Development Regime

It refers to an increasing integration of economies around the world, particularly through trade and financial flows. It also sometimes refers to movement of people (labour) and knowledge (technology) across international borders. This gradually leads to an increased economic interdependence and the integration of all national economies into one economy within the framework of a capitalist market. The European Commission defined globalization 'as the process by which markets and production in different countries are becoming increasingly interdependent due to the dynamics of trade in goods and services and flows of capital and technology'.[1] According to Robert Cox, "The Characteristics of globalization includes the international division of labour, new migratory movement from the South to the North, the new competitive environment that accelerates these processes and internationalizing of the states...making states into agencies of globalized world".[2] In the words of David Held, "Globalization can be thought as a process (set of processes) characterized by increasing inflow of trade, capital and information, as well as mobility of individuals, across the borders. It is not a new phenomenon. Globalization has progressed throughout the course of recorded history, although not in a steady or linear fashion."[3]

The concept of pursuing economic development through economic cooperation resulting from economic interdependence and integration is appreciating. The problems like poverty, environmental degradation, spread of hazardous diseases like HIV AIDS, international terrorism with possible application of weapons of much destruction etc are global in character that demand global cooperation to contain and neutralize these threat to global security. Moreover, every state has some inadequacies and limitations for which it has to depend on others. For instance, the developing countries are still significantly lagging behind in scientific innovations, access to modern technology, capitals of both financial and human to experience rapid industrialization for economic growth. The developed countries are generally developed in these areas. But they need market for investment for their capitals and human resources, raw materials and labour to sustain continuity and consistency in their economic progress. The developing countries are the important destinations which are well equipped with abundant raw materials and cheap labour and where both financial and human capitals can be invested. Therefore, the scope for global cooperation for containing and solving the global challenges is wide. Therefore, if the concept of globalization is developed and operationalized along this noble objective, there is nothing to be pessimistic about the positive outcome of globalization. But the question is: does the present form of globalization possess such an inclusive development character?

As a regime of development, the present form of globalization is basically based on the liberal or modernization perspective of development. The neo-liberal economic principles are currently dominating the globalization regime of development. This perspective of development argues that globalization will bring progress through gradual expansion of market and therefore it is the key to future economic development. But to experience economic development, transformation of the old social order through introduction of new values, norms, institutions and organizations is sine-quo-non. Therefore, in the words of the modernization theorists:

Economic development success involves more than simply instituting economic changes: new values, norms, institutions and organizations had to be introduced to transform the old social order. Elements of traditional societies that constitute obstacles to modernization had to be replaced. (Brahman)[4]

Vincent Tucker explains the modernization perspective of development in the following language:

> Development was conceived of as economic growth, industrial development and the establishment of complementary social and economic institutions on the mode of the USA. Other cultural formations were viewed as forms of resistance to modernization which had to be overcome.[5]

These two explanations tell us that the modernization perspective of globalization is prescriptive and institutionally biased towards the Western conception of development that considers the values of traditional societies as barriers to economic progress. Therefore, the modernization paradigm of development is assimilationist in orientation in its attempt to develop a global economic development regime. Under this circumstance, its prescriptions, as it will reflect in the following analysis, are bound to collide with the traditional cultural values of many traditional societies which believe that inclusion of such values to play an important role in the developmental discourse.

Globalization and Development Interventions and Implications on the Socio-Economic Life of the Chakmas in the CHT

The administration in the CHT has so far taken many development activities like generation of hydroelectricity, logging, commercial or industrial plantations. All these development activities have been generally funded by various multilateral investment agencies like ADB, UNDP, FAO, UNICEF, SIDA, and ICIMOD etc. The government of Bangladesh, as noted earlier, established the CHTDB in 1976 for the purpose of formulating development policy, coordinating and implementing the development programs. Let us now look at how these development initiatives funded by the multi national agencies have affected forests and wild life, and eco system of the CHT and their immediate implications on the social and economic life of the Chakmas.

The Kaptai Hydroelectric Dam Project (1959-63) on the Karnafuli River located in the present Rangamati district of the CHT was the first major development project that the Chakmas had to experience. The project was funded by the US Development Agency, the USAID. Electricity is essential for industrialization and economic development and modernization of socio-cultural life of the people of a country. It was for that purpose, the contemporary government of East Pakistan had chosen the Karnafuli River at Kaptai area as an idle destination for generating hydroelectricity. The development project had brought devastating implications on the socio-cultural and economic life of the Chakmas. It inundated over 54,000 acres accounting 40% of the total agricultural land of the whole CHT. It also displaced 100,000 tribal belonging to mostly Chakmas.[6] Over 40000 of these displaced Chakmas left for Indian and settled in parts of the Northeast region, including Arunachal Pradesh.[7]

This development project provided a number of benefits to the country as a whole such as electricity, employment opportunities, fisheries and an improved water transportation system, but the benefits of the indigenous people (including Chakmas) were minimal. In practical terms, out of the total number of displaced people, less than 0.1% had access to electricity, and in term of employment, less than 1% of the indigenous people (Chakmas) were employed directly or indirectly by the project.[8]

An informal impact assessment survey was conducted in 1979 among the people displaced by the dam reported the following: [9]

i. 89% were displaced by inundation of their homes and land;

ii. 87% had faced difficulties in rebuilding new homes;
iii. 69% had received inadequate compensation due to corruption of government officials;
iv. 78% did not get any employment opportunities in the project;
v. 69% felt that their present food and economic crisis was caused by the Kaptai dam;
vi. 93% felt that their general economic condition had deteriorated as a result of the dam and believed that their standard of living and overall situation had been much better prior to the construction of the Kaptai dam.

The largest development project undertaken by the CHTDB was the CHT Development Project that was commenced in 1979 at an estimated cost of US $41.86 millions. The lion's share of this amount was funded by the ADB and UNDP.[10] The project was multi-purpose in nature as it covered different areas such as upland settlement, afforestation and rehabilitation, development of road network, agricultural research, agricultural extension, nursery development, and construction of go down for fertilizer and seed etc.

Under this multi purpose development project, the first initiative of the CHTDB was that it adopted a horticulture based development scheme called *Joutha Khamer* which claimed to resettle 1540 families during 1976-1983.[11] The principal objective of this scheme was to encourage the Jhumias to adopt rubber and wood-tree plantation and fruit gardening as an alternative source of Jhum cultivation. The project failed to produce desired result mainly for the following reasons:

1. In reality, the actual Jhum cultivators were not included in the scheme; [12]
2. The significant part of the Unclassified State Forests (USF) of the CHT was allocated to private sector (mostly influential non-indigenous individuals) for rubber plantation. For instance, out of the total 45,000 acres of land under rubber plantations, the government allocated 33,000 acres of land to private parties (25 acres each for 387 recipients) and only

12,000 acres to the CHTDB accounting only 25 acres each for a Jhumia family.[13]

3. After the termination of the projects many members, who were included in the projects, had either sold and left the allotted plots, in search of the alternatives.[14]
4. Moreover, according to the report of a recent study on rubber plantation in the CHT suggests that in the last 3 years, over 6000 tons of rubber have remained unsold and the multinational companies which have successfully established over 8,000 acres of rubber plantations, are reported to have been facing 'an uncertain future'.[15] Therefore, under the existing national and global situation, the economic feasibility of rubber cultivation has raised serious concerns.
5. The most problem which the Jhumias who are included in the scheme is that the lands allotted to them under the project are yet to be registered officially against their name due to administrative and legal duality.[16]
6. In many cases, the indigenous people (including the Chakmas) opposed the project because the 'beneficiaries' were hardly selected from the indigenous communities of the CHT.[17]

The CHTDB initiated another program *called Sloping Agriculture Land Technology* (SALT) in 1992 at an estimated expenditure of 35.5 lakh taka. But the CHTDB failed to get any positive result from this program because it was completely an imported technology from Thailand with which the Jhumias were not acquainted and comfortable without arrangement of any training program by the CHTDB or any government or non government agency. Therefore, the technology was also proved to be not suitable for the condition of the CHT.[18] Beside these developmental activities, the CHTDB also undertook another development scheme called *'The Upland Settlement Scheme'* under the financial assistance of ADB. The project was designed basically as an afforestation program. The indigenous peoples criticized the program as it had been detrimental to not only the natural environment of the CHT due to commercialization of forest products but also it had resulted in uprooting the indigenous people from their traditional homesteads and destroying their way of life.[19]

It appears that none of the development program of the CHTDB funded by various multinational agencies has become successful. The CHT Commission in its report on the CHT situation in 1994 stated that the indigenous people of the CHT did not welcome and criticize the development interventions of the CHTDB mainly because they were very much suspicious towards its development activities as the government planned these programs in the CHT without any involvement of their knowledge in planning.[20]

Forests policy of Bangladesh and its implications on socio-economic life of the Chakmas

According to the customs of the indigenous people of the CHT, forests were considered as common property. These customs were all unwritten rules institutionalized in the forms of social codes which were naturally upheld by the community. The Chakmas on the basis of these customs enjoyed the right to a particular forest area either for Jhum cultivation or for a homestead and the right to extract forest produce as well as hunting and the right to access to common grazing lands.[21]

When the British administration annexed the CHT in 1860, it soon introduced the concept of forest governance in the CHT. It promulgated Act VII of 1865 to ensure forest governance in the CHT. Under section 2 of this Act, the British administration created "Government Forests.[22]" In the 1870's, one forth of the total land of CHT was categorized as "Reserve Forests" under direct administration of the Forest Department that outlawed all previous rights of access to and use of forest resources in these areas.[23] The British administration promulgated another Forest Act of 1920 according to which no one could claim right to private property within the reserve forests. The forest governance of the British administration was aimed at commercial exploitation of forest resources for increasing their revenue.

Bangladesh has signed, ratified, accepted and acceded to various multilateral treaties and agreements related to conservation of biodiversity and environment such CITES, World Heritage Convention, CBD, Climate Change

Convention and Convention to Combat Desertification. Thus it adheres and commit to the conservation of biodiversity and the environment.

It has prepared National Conservation Strategy (NCS) and the National Environment Management Action Plan (NEMAP) and introduced the Social Forestry Rules 2000 that has provided sweeping powers to the Forest Department of Bangladesh to have exclusive and overriding jurisdiction in the management of forests affairs. Thus the forest legislation Act of 2000 strongly emphasizes on 'state control over forest land' and protection of forests through 'regulatory and policing mechanism'. All the subsequent governments of independent Bangladesh attempted to present forest governance in the CHT. But while do, they have followed basically the British forest laws in forming forest governance in the CHT. Therefore, a part from other forest laws, it has imposed the 2000 Forest Legislation Act in the CHT. This new law enlarged the area of reserved forests by including another 220, 000 acres of lands situated outside the reserve forests which were mostly inhabited by the indigenous people displaced following the construction of the Kaptai Hydroelectric dam.[24] The indigenous people of the CHT criticized the forest legislation Act of 2000 because it harmed their interests (Chakma 1999, Chowdhury 1998, Gain 1995, 1998, 2000). Once a certain area is classified as reserve forest, the inhabitants of this area are prohibited from using the forest completely, and therefore unable to maintain their livelihood through forest products.

But forest governance in the CHT is criticized not only on that ground. The critics argue that although forest governance in the CHT is aimed at conserving biodiversity and the environment, such policy has encouraged commercialization of forest products in the CHT leading to significant deforestation. Although there is stringent ban on timber extraction, large-scale injudicious commercial felling of trees has been a regular feature in the CHT causing major depletion of forest resources. It was reported that influential businessmen in collaboration with forest Department and other concerned officials started illegal felling of the forests and sold timber and bamboo on loaded truck illegally.[25]

There is a general decline in the rich biodiversity of the region. Human aggression on forests has been the major cause for the decrease of tree and bamboo varieties over the last ten to fifteen years. The erosion of forest resources vis-à-vis environmental degradation has triggered long term ecosystem damage in the CHT. Many springs and aquifers that were traditionally used for source of drinking waters began to dry up during the dry seasons. Major rivers of the CHT such as the Chengi, the Maini, and the Kasoalong etc remain dry during dry season. The ground water level also goes down during this season causing huge scarcity in water resources. Majority of the households in the rural area have to walk on an average a distance between 100 and 500 meters to collect drinking water.[26] The decline of animal and plant life, and wild fruits, which once formed an important nutritional supplement for the indigenous communities, is resulting in nutritional deficiencies. Due to decline of natural herbaria, the traditional know how of disease prevention and cure is now in the verge of extinction. Deforestation is also resulted in loss of many traditional occupations for e.g. the village medicine men who use natural herbs, local artisans who use canes and bamboos etc.[27]

Global ecological imbalance which has further been aggravated in the era of globalization has also affected and threatened the life the Chakmas of the CHT in another way. Over the last of couples of decades, there has a gradual rise in the water level of coastal area of Bangladesh. It has also become repeated victims of natural calamity like cyclone, heavy flood due to overflows of its major rivers. Thousands of people specially belonging to the poorest section of the Bengalis have become worst victims of such natural disaster. The government of independent Bangladesh implanted thousands of those natural disaster victims in different places of the CHT from 1975 onwards, the process of which is still going on causing a serious threat to the cultural and political identity of the Chakmas.[28]

Governance and Development Administration in the CHT

There is a strong institutional linkage between development and good governance, for without good governance, there can not be either development, or if there is development, its benefits will not inclusive in character. Therefore, good governance is paid utmost priority in nowadays developmental strategy. What is good governance?

It generally refers to a process of administration which is characterized by rules of democratic laws, respects for human rights and greater transparency and efficiency in public administration. According to P. R. Chari, an administration is said to be governed by good governance only when it includes the following characteristics:[29]

(i) Promotion of efficiency and transparency in public administration,

(ii) Respects for human rights and rules of laws,

(iii) Greater of the civilian bodies in managing and monitoring the security sector.

The World Bank[30] has identified several characteristics while defining good governance. These are

(i) Political accountability, including the acceptability of political system by the people, and regular elections to legitimize the exercise of political power,

(ii) Freedom of association and participation by various religious, social, economic, cultural and professional groups in the process of governance,

(iii) Bureaucratic accountability ensuring a system to monitor and control the performance of government offices and offices an officials in relations to quality of quality of service, inefficiency and abuse of discretionary power. The related determinants include openness and transparency in administration,

(iv) An established legal framework based on the rule of law and independence of judiciary to protect human rights, secure social justice and guard against exploitation and abuse of power,

(v) A sound administrative system leading to efficiency and effectiveness,

(vi) Cooperation between government and civil society organizations.

According to the Organization for Economic Cooperation

and Development (OECD) countries, the key components of good governance with which they sought to link development assistance, are the following:[31]

(i) Legitimacy of government,
(ii) Accountability of political and official elements of government,
(iii) Competence of government to make policy and deliver services,
(iv) Respects for human rights and rule of laws.

None of the features of good governance, as noted above, is found in the development administration of the CHT. The development administration of the CHT can be explained with help of following dominant features:

(i) Divisiveness

The history of development administration in the CHT has been divisive as it continues to be administered along ethnic communal lines. As stated earlier, there are different administrative bodies such as the Hill District Council in each of the three districts, the CHTRC and the CHTDB in the CHT. These administrative bodies are not found in other parts of Bangladesh. The other administrative bodies which are present in other parts of Bangladesh are the Office of Deputy Commissioner (DC) in each district and the Office of Thana (Police) Nirvahi Officers (TNO). Beside these bodies, the military as an institution still plays a predominant role as an administrative institution, if not in other part, at least in the CHT of present Bangladesh. Although there is a closer administrative coordination between the DCs, TNOs and the Military officials on hierarchical basis, such administrative cooperation between the CHTRC and the Hill District Council is absent. According to Article 9(A) of Part C of the CHT Peace Accord, the development activities in the CHT are to be controlled and monitored by the CHTRC in coordination with the CHTDB and the three Hill District Councils. But the CHTRC is yet to be empowered with this supervisory power. Under Article 10 of Part C of the Peace Accord, no non Hill People[32] could be appointed as Chairman of the CHTDB. But, Md. Wadud Bhuiyan, a non Hill People was appointed as Chairman of the CHTDB in total contravention of the Peace Accord. The DCs, TNOs and Army are still the most powerful institutions in the development administration of the CHT. The Hill People criticized this policy of the government of Bangladesh and took it in hostility.

(ii) Lack of Transparency and Accountability

There is hardly any transparency and accountability in the development administration of the CHT. It is manned mostly by corrupt elements. Evasion of taxes, money laundering, bribing, smuggling and other economic offences are the common features of the development administration in the CHT. This has also led to criminalization of politics. The nexus between the criminals and anti social elements and the ranks and pillars of the government is a major problem to present good governance in the CHT.

(iii) Absence of Rule of Law and Respects for Human Rights

There is virtually no rule of law and respects for human rights in the CHT. The CHT remained under tight militarization for a prolonged period of time for anti insurgency operation. Human rights during those days remained at peril in the CHT. Although the military rule has been partially relaxed following conclusion of the CHT Peace Accord in 1997, yet military as an institution, as noted above, continues to maintain its strong influence in the CHT and military related gross human rights violations are still routinely reported from different corners of the CHT.

Conclusion

The study reflects that the CHT received huge amount of foreign aids for development works, although there has been virtually no good governance in the CHT, an important pre condition which the developed countries and multinational financial institutions and donor agencies link for development assistance. But, despite such distorting picture in presenting good governance, the donor agencies of the developed countries provided huge development aids, from time to time, to the government of Bangladesh to undertake development projects in the CHT in contravention of their principles that govern extension of development aids. As a consequent, such development aids could not produce desired results in the CHT. Instead, in many cases, as the study reveals, such development works brought nightmare to the Chakmas threatening their subsistence economic and socio-cultural life in many aspects. The major reason for the emergence of such a hostile environment was non inclusion of local opinion, knowledge, resources and values. The donor agencies framed their development vision on the basis of the expert opinion of the governmental officials of the government of Bangladesh.

The study further reveals that being a signatory to trade related environment agreement and other multilateral environment related agreements, the Government of Bangladesh promulgated different forests rules and introduced laws to comply with its environmental commitments. Such forests laws, instead of presenting good forest governance, rather encouraged commercialization of forest products resulting in huge deforestation and destruction of environmental habitat of the CHT. It also infringed on the economic, social and cultural life of the Chakmas in many ways. The developed countries and the donor agencies did not look at this issue seriously before deciding to provide financial aids to initiate projects for afforestation in the CHT.

Need for Reorientation in the Development Approach in the CHT

To be successful and result oriented in inclusive manner, the development works funded by the multinational donor agencies need for a reorientation in the development approach. To be so, it must consider the following three fundamental issues:

(i) The present form of globalization must be restructured and redesigned in inclusive manner instead of its predominant exclusive feature. The local values and knowledge should be given due consideration before initiating development projects and activities so that local interests are not overlooked, ignored and instead of opposition, and such works are overwhelmingly welcome. The same approach can be followed for development activities in the CHT in future.

(ii) Good governance is an essential precondition of development. The donor agencies must emphasize on improving governance in the CHT. Instead of being selective, this should be applied in inclusive manner. To do so, the donor agencies must exert pressure on the government of Bangladesh to implement the CHT Peace Accord, reduce the influence of the Army in the administration of the CHT and allow the civilian institutions such as the CHTRC, Hill District Councils to play grater role in managing and controlling the development administration in the CHT.

(iii) Natural resources in the CHT should be exploited on sustainable basis. The present trend destruction and depletion of natural resources should be discontinued curtailing afforestation activities like illegal felling and logging of trees, bamboos in order to improve ecological habitation of the CHT. In other words, development must be environment friendly among human beings.

(iv) Social integration based on group cohesiveness, social harmony, cooperation is also essential as without it development will remain a far cry. Therefore, the development activities funded by multinational donor agencies must play a negotiated and accommodative role in bringing down communal disharmony between the Hill People and the non Hill People in the CHT. The donor agencies should seriously address this issue before extending financial supports for development projects in the CHT.

NOTES

1. Vandana Upadhyay, "Globalization and Development in North East India: Challenges and Opportunities" in M.C. Behera (ed.), *Globalization and Development Dilemma: Reflections form North-East India*, New Delhi: Mittal Publications, 2004, p. 34.
2. Robert Cox, as quoted in John Baylis and Steve Smith (ed.), *The Globalization of World Politics: An Introduction to International Relations*, Oxford: The Oxford University Press, 2001, p. 15.
3. *Ibid.*

4. John Brahman, *Popular Development: Rethinking the Theory and Practice of Development*, Oxford: Blackwell Publishers Ltd., 1996, p.20. Also visit http//www.newcastle.edu.au/faculty/bus-law/news/comment_sym/anderson_keynote.pdf.
5. Vincent Tucker, as stated in Munck and Denis O' Hearn (ed.), *Critical Development Theory: Contribution to a New Paradigm*, London: Zed Books, 1999, p. 3.
6. Kashinath Jena and Bindu Ranjan Chakma, *Ethnic Unrests and India's Security Concerns*, New Delhi: Abhijeet Publications, 2008, p. 33, Rajkumari Chandra Kalindi Roy, *Land Rights of the Indigenous Peoples of the Chittagong Hill Tracts, Bangladesh*, Copenhagen: International Working Group on Indigenous Affairs (IWGIA) Document No. 99, 2000, p. 95.
7. Mahendra P. Lama," Poverty, Migration and Conflict: Challenges to Human Security in South Asia" in P.R. Chari and Sonika Gupta (ed.), *Human Security in South Asia: Gender, Energy, Migration and Globalization*, New Delhi: Social Science Press, 2003, p. 133.
8. Roy, *op. cit.*, p. 102.
9. *Ibid.*, pp. 102-103.
10. Mahbub Alam, *Victims of Unsustainable Development Interventions: Experience of Indigenous People of Chittagang Hill Tracts in Bangladesh*, a paper presented in the ICIP 2008 conference on Indigenous people arranged by CPDS (Department of Poverty and Development Studies), University of Malaya, Malaysia.
11. *Ibid.*
12. *Ibid.*
13. *Ibid.*
14. M. Tripura, *Indigenous Society and Development*, a journal of Zabarang Kalyan Samity, Rangamati, 2001, p. 35.
15. Alam, *op. cit.*
16. *Ibid.*
17. *Ibid*, Tripura, *op. cit.*, p. 35.
18. Alam, *op. cit.*
19. *Ibid.*
20. The Chittagong Hill Tracts Commission, *Life is not ours: Land and Rights in the CHT*, 1994.
21. Mr. Biplob Chakma, Mr. Bihita Bidhan Khisa and Ms. Senti Chakma, "Conflict into Opportunities: Towards Forest Governance in Chittagong Hill Tracts (A case study from

Bangladesh)" in *http://www.mtnforum.org/oldocs/1474.pdf*. This has also been confirmed by Mr. Behita Bidhan Khisa in an interview through mail questionnaire method with the author on 19/04/09.

22. Muhammed Ishaq *Bangladesh District Gazetteers: Chittagong Hill Tracts*, Dhaka: Ministry of Cabinet Affairs, 1975, p. 107.
23. Roy, *op. cit.* p. 151.
24. Alam, *op. cit.* This is also based on my personal interactions with Chakma Raja Barrister Devasish Roy on 16.04.2009 in Agartala. Barrister Roy has been adviser of the Interim Government of Bangladesh on CHT Affairs and Forest Department during 2008-09.
25. http://www.mtnforum.org/oldocs/1474.pdf.
26. Alam, *op. cit.*
27. http://www.mtnforum.org/oldocs/1474.pdf.
28. This is based on a documentary film, *Karnafulli*, produced by Laser Vision, Dhaka, 2006.
29. P.R. Chari, "Security and Governance in South Asia: Their Linkages", in P. R. Chari (ed.), *Security and Governance in South Asia*, New Delhi: Monohar, 2001, p. 14.
30. World Bank, *Governance: The World Bank Experience*, Washington D. C: the World Bank Publication, 1994.
31. OECD, *Multilateral Agreement Paper*, October 1997.
32. The thirteen ethnic minority groups such as the Chakma, Marma, Tripura, Murang, Khiang, Bhowm, Phankua, Chak etc. are the indigenous people of the CHT. They call them sometimes as Hill People, for they live in the hilly areas and sometimes as Jummas as most of them depend on Jhum cultivation for their livelihood. They generally consider the other people, more apparently the Bengalis as non-Hill People.

BIBLIOGRAPHICAL REFERENCES

1. Alam, Mahbub (2008), *Victims of Unsustainable Development Interventions: Experience of Indigenous People of Chittagang Hill Tracts in Bangladesh*, a paper presented in the ICIP 2008 conference on Indigenous people arranged by CPDS (Department of Poverty and Development Studies), University of Malaya, Malaysia.
2. Bank, World Bank, (1994), *Governance: The World Bank Experience*, Washington D. C: the World Bank Publication.
3. Baylis, John and Smith, Steve (2001) (ed.), *The Globalization of World Politics: An Introduction to International Relations*, Oxford: The Oxford University Press.

4. Chari, P.R. (2001), "Security and Governance in South Asia: Their Linkages", in P.R. Chari (ed.), *Security and Governance in South Asia,* New Delhi: Monohar.
5. Commission, the Chittagong Hill Tracts, (1994), Life is not ours: Land and Rights in the CHT.
6. Ishaq, Muhammed, (1975), *Bangladesh District Gazetteers: Chittagong Hill Tracts*, Dhaka: Ministry of Cabinet Affairs.
7. Lama, Mahendra P., (2003)," Poverty, Migration and Conflict: Challenges to Human Security in South Asia" in P.R. Chari and Sonika Gupta (ed.), *Human Security in South Asia: Gender, Energy, Migration and Globalization,* New Delhi: Social Science Press.
8. Munck and Hearn, Denis O' (1999) (ed.), *Critical Development Theory: Contribution to a New Paradigm,* London: Zed Books.
9. Jena, Kashinath and Chakma, Bindu Ranjan, *Ethnic Unrests and India's Security Concerns,* New Delhi: Abhijeet Publications.
10. *Karnafulli,* (2006), a documentary film produced by Laser Vision, Dhaka,
11. OECD, *Multilateral Agreement Paper*, October 1997.
12. Roy, Rajkumari Chandra Kalindi, (2000), *Land Rights of the Indigenous Peoples of the Chittagong Hill Tracts, Bangladesh,* Copenhagen: International Working Group on Indigenous Affairs (IWGIA) Document No. 99.
13. Tripura, M., (2001), *Indigenous Society and Development,* a journal of Zabarang Kalyan Samity, Rangamati.
14. Upadhyay, Vandana, (2004) "Globalization and Development in North East India: Challenges and Opportunities" in M.C. Behera (ed.), *Globalization and Development Dilemma: Reflections form North-East India,* New Delhi: Mittal Publications.
15. http://www.mtnforum.org/oldocs/1474.pdf
16. http//www.newcastle.edu.au/faculty/bus-law/news/comment_sym/anderson_keynote.pdf.
17. Interview with Chakma Raja Barrister Devasish Roy on 16/04/09.
18. Interview with Behita Bidhan Khisa, the founder of HILL (Hill Institute for Live and Livelihood), a policy and research NGO based in the CHT on 19/04/09.

3

Issue of Child Labour in Globalized India

SANGITA CHAKRABORTY*

The issue of child labour is hardly an issue in a country that houses the largest numbers of child labourers in the world! But it is less of a surprise when one learns that the official position of the country has been insouciant, accepting it as a 'harsh reality', intrinsic to its status as a developing country. Among the many implications of such a position, the most obvious one is that poverty as the prime casual factor that perpetuates the supply of labour. As long as there is poverty, it is expected that there would be an unrelenting supply of child labourers. This also muffles the lurking status of the Constitutional provision of universal elementary education. The Directive Principles of the Constitution enjoyed upon the Government to provide free and compulsory education to all children up to age of 14 by 1960. It is a sad commentary on the progress of elementary education that even after the lapse of nearly five decades, there is no hope of the fulfillment of this Constitutional Directive. Child educations like 'kichree', is a composite product. While preparing kichree, the cook has to be aware of the characteristics of the different ingredients and how they have to be treated differently. By

* Research Scholar, Burdwan University, Burdwan, W.B.

first keeping them separate and giving them a different treatment, a wonderful end result can be obtained. The school draws different types of children and still leaves many children out. In order to develop education into universal education, these latter children will have to be added. Adding them necessitates knowledge of the characteristics of these children the reasons why they are not enrolled or why they have dropped out. Adding them to the school system, and producing universal education as the end product, thus requires a rigorous analytical framework lest one muddles different categories. Unless the 'ingredients' which enter (or not enter) education are analysed and categorized separately, universal education will remain elusive.

In their drive for universal education, many activist and NGOs have muddled the different categories of out of school children into one: the category of Child labour. All children not in school are subsumed as working children.

Millions of children in India enter the labour market at an early age and in significant numbers, as part of their family's subsistence strategies. Despite divergent estimates of the magnitude of child labour in India, It cannot be denied that in India the problem of child labour is a serious one, especially in the hazardous occupations/processes. The Child Labour Act, 1986 banned child labour in India in many processes/occupations and regulated working conditions in other occupations. Under this act, no child should be employed or permitted to work under the age of 14 years. It includes all preparatory and incidental processes there of.

In India, several protective and promotional constitutional safeguards exist for women and children. But they were not implemented effectively, until recently. If the authority wants to implement, the common people does not want because poverty compel them to send their children into the labour market. Forty percent of the Indians live below the poverty line. In the morning, they think that how they will fill their stomach. Several economists and organizations have conducted studies on the extent of poverty in India. They also recommended several paths to take up the poor from the poverty line. Mr. P.D. Ojha, Dr.V.M. Dandekar, Dr. P.K. Bardhan, Montek Singh Ahluwlia studied the trends in incidence of rural poverty in India for the period 1956-57 to 1973-74. They estimated the poverty line on the basis of calorie intake per day (2250 per capita per day). Attempts had been made to protect the poor, but the action was not so prompt. We know that the benefit of economic development must accrue more and more to the relatively less privileged classes of society, and there should be a progressive reduction of the concentration of incomes, wealth and economic power. Two accounts for this high incidence of poverty among rural labour households. Firstly, there is a considerable degree of unemployment and underemployment among rural labourers. It has been established that incidence of unemployment is the highest among casual labourers. Even during periods of employment, their weak bargaining power results in low wages being paid to them. The market forces are so strong that minimum wage legislation is observed more in breach than in compliance. Another major cause of rural poverty is the low asset base of the poor. Standard of living of the rural masses is very poor due to absolute poverty. The objectives of the planning commission in India were to raise the standard of living of the masses, but the Planning Commission has failed to keep his word. The Second Plan talked of creating a 'milieu' for the small man. The Fourth Plan talked of improvement in the condition of the common man and the weaker sections, especially through provision of 'employment and education'. It also emphasized the attainment of a 'national minimum' as an essential pre-requisite to improve the conditions of the 'lower income groups'. It recognized that the small farmers and the landless labourers constitute the bulk of the agricultural proletariat 'having no productive base and depending for its livelihood on wage employment'. The fourth plan categorically stated: "In the implementation of the programme, the weakest are looked after and the benefits of development are made to flow by planned investment in the underdeveloped regions and among the more backward sections of the community".

Empowerment of family especially the women is an essential precondition for socio-economic development and for the eradication of social scourges like child labour. The Copenhagen Declaration of the World Summit on Social

Development (1995), "recognizes that the empowerment of women is a precondition to social development, and pledges action to achieve equality and equity between men and women" (ILO 1995:12). Eradication of child labour is indispensable to promote human resource development. "As the incidence of poverty falls and education improves, the child labour will decline" (World Bank 1995:73). Studies have found that with increase in income the incidence of child laour has also declined (UNICEF 1997:62). Hence, it is expected that empowerment of women would help reduce the problem of child labour. In addition, feminist movements have also played a significant role in the struggle to exterminate various forms of exploitation and discrimination against women and children. As a consequence, many countries have brought forth several safeguards and initiated measures for their protection and development.

According to V.K.R.V. Rao "External aid is like a sulpha drug. We must know when to use it, when to stop it, and we should always have a B-complex to neutralize its effects". So self-reliance and self-sufficiency is inevitable to eliminate child labour, the social sin. Self-reliance should be an extremely important objective of child labour reduction in India.

The Indian farmers, generally speaking, are poor illiterate, ignorant, superstitious, conservative and bound by outmoded customs and institutions such as the caste system and the joint family. Superstition and belief in fate or the curses which keep the farmers fully satisfied with their primitive system of cultivation. Except the small group of enlightened farmers who adopted quickly modern techniques of production, vast majority of farmers are not motivated by considerations of economic progress. Besides, they are so poor that they did not have the means to improve their economic condition. However, this changes is much slower in the BIMARU states, to use the term coined by Prof. Ashish Bose, Bihar, MP, Rajasthan and UP. All these states suffer from low levels of literacy.

Poverty, low level of literacy, social taboos, belief in fate, big family size, low return on agriculture, bonded labour, minimum wage and low family income are the main causes of creating child labour. The parents are interested in sending their children to schools; their poor economic conditions forced them to discontinue the education. The school-going children being urged by most of the parents to assist in their work, this leads to poor performance in their studies. Consequently, the student get detained in the class, and eventually become child labour.

Child labour has cropped up as an issue of widespread concern in the last quarter of the 20th century. There has been, in recent years, growing interest in the subject of child labour among academics, public officials and the media. There are few topics in the core of the development literature today that enjoy as much importance and evoke as much passion as that of child labour. The subject has moved from the national to the international arena. Many dramatic case studies have appeared to illustrate the heinous conditions under which children have to work. The report women and child labour of the study group commissioned by the Labour Commission (Study Group 2001) marshals a number of such cases to illustrate many thing:

Children are working unacceptably long hours a day; Children are working in narrow trenches in mines; children in the carpet industry elsewhere have been bonded; children are severely punished and tortured if they attempt to escape; also in agriculture many children work as bonded agriculture labour; home based industries with child labourers working under abominable conditions are quite typical in a number of industries; children working in unhygienic and crowded conditions suffer from many occupation-related diseases; they become old and unproductive citizens at a time when most other people are just beginning to participate in a full life. Being minors, the membership of trade unions is not open to child labour and hence it is a advantage to the employer. Employers find children more amenable to discipline and control. Child labour is very cheap and trouble free since they can't organize agitations against employers.

According to World Bank, "India has sound child labour laws, yet millions of children are working, often in hazardous conditions" (World Bank 1995:6). In other woulds, neither had the women benefited nor had the problem of child labour been eradicated. Child labour continues to persist in various occupations, particularly in the informal sector. In recent years, both the union government and state governments have enacted several acts besides providing various incentives to eradicate child labour. Several acts prohibiting child labour in industries where enacted, and educational advancement is being extended through specific schemes. Further, several schemes and programmes have been initiated for the economic development of households, because the problem of child labour is associated with the living conditions of the family as well as availability of school facilities. "A high prevalence of child labour is linked to poverty and to poor quality or availability of education" (World Bank 1995:72).

Casteism, poverty, family size, low level of income, level of education etc. are some of the major factors that have intensified the problem of child labour in India. Gurupadaswami Committee has revealed in its report that the child labour problem is a result of poverty and elimination of poverty in itself a great problem. Therefore, this committee has justified prevalence of child labour in cases where children are made to work according to their physical capacity for a fixed number of hours and with sufficient arrangement of education, recreation and relax and with the condition that the said employment shall not cause insecurity to health of the children.

It is imperative to have a discussion on the evaluation of child rights before delving into the problem of child labour. The expansive nature of the concept of child rights clubbed with the realization that without guaranteeing economic, social and cultural rights, full enjoyment civil rights was not possible and led to inclusion of economic, social and cultural rights. These rights place a more positive duty on governments to act in order to ensure the realization of these rights. Growing realization of governments, activists, elite, opinion builders and Constitutionalists that constitution of most of the feminist movement, movement for environment protection and sustainable development, movement for protection of minorities and indigenous people and their culture, movement for abolishing of child labour and all forms of exploitation contributed to taking recourse to human rights concept and its language more frequently. In fact, these movements have contributed in a great measure to the increasing reliance on child rights concept in national concepts.

Realisation of child rights requires evolving a culture that is more sensitive to the basic needs of every human being. It respects the need for ensuring to everyone, social and economic justice and provides fair and equal opportunities for growth and development to every individual and group of people. Due to lack of recognizing the significance and importance of education as a key instrument for bringing changes in social and cultural attitudes and that too in a country like India which has a history of feudal and colonial past and where impoverishment, ignorance and illiteracy pervade all around, it is only in the last few years that the importance of education in relation to child labour has allocated the attention of national policy-makers, educationists and education planners.

To solve such type of social acute problem, rigorous extension work is necessary by the every level of society as well as from the government and non-government sectors. Extension's specific philosophy is furnishing the inspiration, supplying specific advice and technical help, and counseling to see that the people as individuals, families, groups and communities work together as a unit to achieve their objective.

The goal of evolving child labour problem requires operating at various levels such as:

- Spreading awareness amongst masses.
- Not only creating awareness amongst masses particularly amongst weaker, poor and vulnerable groups but also imparting capacities and confidence in them to stand for protection and preservation of their rights.
- Creating different knowledge, involving or reforming structures, methods and normative regimes, and imparting new skills and competencies so that policy making, its enforcement and for solving the child labour problem.
- Strengthening the economic condition of that family of child labour and also the others poor family by taking various poverty eradication programmes.

- Women employment, which can reduce child labour through generating income such as women entrepreneurship, SHG, home based industry, social forestry etc.
- Women can change the scenario of any problem. Rural woman is not equipped with any skill, knowledge, education and information. The kind of socialization she receives from child hood denies her the traits such as self-confidence, need for achievement, inclination to take risk independent outlook which are essential for any venture. Woman development essential for solving the problem.
- Youth are active in mobilizing around issues such as child rights, land rights, bonded labour and wages. Club, NGOs and Youth can take initiative to eradicate this problem, and the elite class of the society could participate.
- (The parents are interested in sending their children to schools, their poor economic conditions forced them to discontinue the education. The school-going children being urged by most of the parents to assist in their work, this leads to poor performance in their studies. Consequently, the student get detained in the class, and eventually become dropouts.)
- Giving education to the working children at theirs convenience time.
- Fully developing the sense of dignity.
- Promoting understanding, tolerance, gender equality and friendship among them.
- Enabling everyone to participate effectively in a free society.

No doubt, the child labour problem is an intense socio-economic problem in the country that requires a long term multi-pronged strategy to be carried out on a continuous basis. This strategy should include enforcement of Child Labour Acts., strengthening of primary education in the rural areas, rehabilitation of the child labour, improvement of economic conditions of the parents of the child labour through various poverty alleviation and employment generation programmes as well as prevention of children joining the work. It is also necessary that a strong evaluation and monitoring be done for the various child labour elimination programmes and projects.

Children are the most precious assets of any nation. A happy child is a symbol of the development of society and the progress made by mankind. The survival and uplift of children in a developing country like India is a great challenge, as children constitute the real wealth of a country. The future of any society depends on the attention that is provided at any given moment to its children. "As the twig is bent, so will the tree grow". A happy childhood is the basis for a stable and strong adulthood. Hence, right type of physical and mental care, guidance, assistance and opportunities are required for their well being and proper growth.

References

(i) David, Rationalisation of housework, in Dbarker and S. Allen (eds). *Dependence of Exploitation in Work and Marriage,* (Harlow: Longman, 1991).

(ii) Raman, A.V., Entrepreneurship and Economic Development, *Kurukshetra,* (nov,1999).

(iii) Antony, Piush, Gayathri, V., Child Labour: A perspective of Locate and Context, *EPW,* Dec 28- Jan 3, 2003, No. 52.

(iv) Lieten, G.K., Child Labour in India : Disentangling Essence and Solutions *EPW.*

(v) Sarvanan, Velatutham: Women's Employment and Reduction of Child Labour : Beedi Workers in Rural Tamil Nadu; *EPW.*

(vi) Datt Ruddar, K.P.M Sundaram; *Indian Economy;* S.Chand and Company ltd. Ramnagar New Delhi-55.

(vii) Census of India 2001.

(viii) Planning Commission, Ninth Five Year Plan (1997-01), Vol. 1, Feb, 1999. Ministry of Rural development, Annual Report (1996-97)

(ix) Ministry of Rural Development, Annual Report (1996-97).

(x) Weiner, Myron (1991); *The Child and the State in India,* Oxford University Press, Delhi.

(xi) Study Group (2001): Report of the Study Group on Women and Child Labour, National Commission on Labour, New Delhi.

(xii) Mishra, Lakshmidar (2002): *Child Labourers in India,* Oxford University Press, New Delhi.

(xiii) UNICEF (1997): *The State of the World's Children 1997,* Oxford University Press, New York.

(xiv) World Bank (1995): *Workers in an Integrating World, World Development Report,* Oxford University Press, New York.

(xv) *Employment News;* 29th Nov, 2002.

(xvi) Dr. Chowdhury Aparajita, Dr. Rath Arundhati, Dr. Chowdhury Rita: *Children in Rural Orissa.*

(xvii) *Kurukshetra: A Journal of Rural Development;* May, 1999.

4

Self Help Tribal Groups (SHTGs) in Globalised India

RAJESH CHATTERJEE*

Concept of Globalization

We now live in an era of globalization. The 'New World Order' has made the LPG model of development almost irreversible with no escape for any country or region at least in the present context. It simply refers to the point that what is good for a person or a society is not determined by boundaries of the nation states. Strictly speaking such processes and dynamics are not new in human society. People exchanged goods and knowledge across boundaries in ancient societies. Globalization is a buzzword in the World, making people to think in new ways and work on new methods. World has become a global village in the sense that whatever happens in a village is easily known all over the World. Globalization means many things so many people. Positive thinkers view it as an opportunity to grow to higher level and negative person picturise it as a devil pregnant with destructive and

* Lecturer, Rural Development, Department of Rural Development and Management, Tripura University.

exploitative qualities, particularly undermining the developing economies. India is part and partial of this Globalization process. It has both positive and negative impacts on the emerging and developing economies. India has the capacity to convert negative characteristics into positive force. This has been proved by extra ordinary growth path India has entered into since the economic reforms implemented in the country.

Why Nationalizing & Globalization SHGs?

The Indian rural market with its vast size and demand base offers great opportunities to marketers. Our nation is classified in around 450 districts, and approximately 630000 villages, which can be sorted in different parameters such as literacy levels, accessibility, income levels, penetration, distances from nearest towns, etc.

Nearly 3/4th of India's population resides in rural areas where approximately 64% are related to village level agrarian works and above 30% live below the poverty line. It was felt that without elevating the rural masses, the economy of the state cannot be accelerated and sustainable development will be beyond reach. Therefore, contribution of rural people in the planning process was felt to be necessary because rural people are the one who could better understand their own existing problem. As such, it was felt unless women are empowered and taken into account in the planning process, development of the nation and the state will be beyond reach. Again if the rural masses do not participate in the process of development, the country will be failure to enjoy the economic and social effect of globalization.

About fifty per cent of 50% sales come from the rural sector. A lot of rural supplies are actually routed through the urban areas. This is because people from villages prefer making their purchases from neighboring cities.

Most of the groups are formed with woman members where they can take any role for the development of their entrepreneurship. Considering the entrepreneurial environment, women's activities are very interesting as they offer a great source of knowledge and innovation. For example: there is no single type of female micro-entrepreneur, they differ in social background, educational level, experience and age. Another interesting factor is their strong social coherence that allows them to maintain strong communications-channels at all levels.

Congruity with human nature enhances the relevance and utility of human development initiatives. The core of SHG bank linkage in India has been built around an important aspect of human nature—the feeling of self worth. Over the last ten years, it has come to symbolize an enduring relationship between the financially deprived and the formal financial system, forged through a socially relevant tool known as Self Help Groups (SHGs). Self-help Group is a voluntary group formed to attain common goal and provide self-sufficiency and moral support including monetary aid to each other among the groups in times of difficulties. Conceptually, SHG is a homogenous group formed to earn mutually and agree to contribute to the common fund from which the members will be given or lent for productive and emergent credit needs. The concept of SHG evolved form women organization from women voluntary organization during 1990s. SHGs are motivated to function as an element of social change, gender awareness, social education, training and improved human resource. The SHGs usually target the grass root people to increase their knowledge and skills as well as elevation in decision making power. SHG is one of the greatest self-help aid which acts both as voluntary and as a unit. SHG is always considered as an important institution for improving the life of women in various economic and social components such as health, education, sanitation, child care, human rights, etc. Now the SHGs of the country are treated as the component of entrepreneurship development. However in reality, it does not happen without any specific inputs or direction.

While entrepreneurship is being discussed in the academic community and in state and national policy circles, definitions of the term vary widely.

Work becomes part and parcel of one's life. People involve themselves in some work or the other. Some work for others and some are self-employed. The people who work for themselves are called "Entrepreneurs". Entrepreneurship is a purposeful activity indulged in initiating, promoting and maintaining economic activities for the production and distribution of wealth. The individual as an entrepreneur is a critical factor in economic development and an integral part of socio-economic transformation. Therefore, the basic concept of entrepreneurship connotes effectiveness, an urge to take risks in the face of uncertainties and intuition. However, emergence of an entrepreneur in the society depends closely upon the interlinked social, economic, cultural, religious and psychological variables. Entrepreneurship is an economic activity emerges and functions in sociological and cultural settings. It could be conceived of as an individual's free-choice activity or a social group's occupation or profession.

Each type of entrepreneur may need different types and levels of services.

- Startups—exploring and planning a new business or within the first three years of operation.
- Small businesses—in operation three or more years, trying to survive or expand.
- Growth entrepreneurs—commercializing new technology and/or expanding rapidly to capitalize on major opportunities.
- Social entrepreneurs—creating and growing enterprises those are primarily for public and community purposes.

Why SHGs in the Entrepreneurship Development?

Businesswomen in SHGs share the following general characteristics for their entrepreneurship development:

- They are concentrated in market sectors that have low barriers to entry and low levels of outside communication (transfer to other markets).
- They focus on trade, services, and light manufacturing activities.
- Their businesses are smaller than others, employing less than five employees.
- The owners have relatively little previous working experience.

- They use traditional technologies.
- Most employees are family-related.
- They are often home based.
- Business growth strategies are affected by household responsibilities.
- Owners tend to have lower levels of education and literacy.
- Women start their enterprises with less professional work experience and knowledge of their sector than their male counterparts.

SWOT analysis of the SHGs of North-East with special reference to Tripura:

Strengths

Successes of SHGs vest in women, which will prevail in future:

- ☞ Savings habit developed & fund accumulated
- ☞ Each and every group has started inter-lending
- ☞ They depend on themselves i.e. on the group
- ☞ Already started every kind of income generation activities
- ☞ Decision making power and leadership quality developed
- ☞ Social activities started successfully like pulse polio programme, road repairing, making and cleaning drain
- ☞ Good liaison with the Bankers
- ☞ Good recovery rate of inter-lending
- ☞ Each member uses their petty cash (lending form groups) for their economic activity
- ☞ Rate of interest is much lower
- ☞ Attaining fair to sell their product
- ☞ Most of the group members are literate
- ☞ Participate in decision making process of family
- ☞ Leadership developed

Responsibility & accountability are the crucial factors of entrepreneurship development where the SHG members specially the women members have developed these two qualities by the following way:

- Homogeneous membership
- No discrimination
- Small membership (comprising with 11 to 13 members)
- Regular Attendance & Meeting
- Set of Byelaws
- Thrift (Small Savings)
- Utilizing savings for loaning
- All-women group

Weaknesses

- A sense of isolation, both from other entrepreneurs and from the larger business and political community. Many felt ignored and unappreciated by local economic development agencies and chambers of commerce that focus on larger employers.
- Lack of knowledge about emerging markets.
- Lack of access to capital.
- Limited understanding about available business support services and how to use them. They weren't sure where to go for help or could not find services relevant to their needs.
- Need for more training and education programs tailored for different levels of entrepreneurial experience.

Opportunities

Two-thirds of countries consumers live in rural areas and almost half of the national income is generated here. The rural India offers a tremendous market potential. A mere one per cent increase in India's rural income translates to a mind-boggling Rs. 10,000 crore of buying power. Nearly two thirds of all middle-income households in the country are in rural India. And close to half of India's buying' potential lies in its villages. Realizing this Corporate India is now investing a sizeable chunk of its marketing budget to target the rural consumers.

The penetration of consumer durables has seen a substantial increase in the Indian rural sector. One thirds of the premium luxury goods are now sold in the rural market. Two thirds of the middle-income households are now in the rural market. According to one study, if the rural income in India goes up by 1 %, there would be a corresponding increase of about Rs. 10,000 crores in the buying power.

Threats

The general bottle-necks in the development of village industries are financial constraints, lack of technical know-how, lack of training and extension services, management problems, lack of quality control, high cost of production due to high input cost, lack of communication and market information, poor quality of raw materials, lack of storage and warehousing facilities, obsolete and primitive technology, lack of export and lack of promotional strategy.

Why Innovations or Adaptations

The lure of rural market fascinates many a company but the challenges presented by the rural market are enormous. To conquer rural landscape companies have to surpass many challenges. Some of them are:

Lack of proper communication facilities;

Transport;

Many languages and Dialects;

Highly dispersed market;

Low per capita income;

Low level of Literacy;

Prevalence of spurious brands;

The key to success in rural market thus lie in adapting and innovating according to the local situations. It may be in the area product modification, simplification or at all the new application of product, new type of packaging, promotion or distribution or channel members.

Measuring Entrepreneurship

Despite the above, there is remains a powerful impulse, particularly amongst enterprise development practitioners, to measure entrepreneurship in some way. These measurement attempts can range from simple checklists through to complex and detailed computer programmes. This need for a definition and measure of entrepreneurship is because, however defined, the entrepreneur is the key to the successful launch of any business.

He or she is the person who perceives the market opportunity and then has the motivation, drive and ability to mobilise resources to meet it. The major characteristics of entrepreneurs that have been listed by many commentators include the following.

- Self confident and multi-skilled. The person who can 'make the product, market it and count the money, but above all they have the confidence that lets them move comfortably through unchartered waters.
- Confident in the face of difficulties and discouraging circumstances.
- Innovative skills. Not an 'inventor' in the traditional sense but one who is able to carve out a new niche in the market place, often invisible to others.
- Results-orientated. To make be successful requires the drive that only comes from setting goals and targets and getting pleasure from achieving them.
- A risk-taker. To succeed means taking measured risks. Often the successful entrepreneur exhibits an incremental approach to risk taking, at each stage exposing him/herself to only a limited, measured amount of personal risk and moving from one stage to another as each decision is proved.
- Total commitment. Hard work, energy and single-mindedness are essential elements in the entrepreneurial profile.

However, two warnings need to be attached to this partial list of entrepreneurial qualities.

Firstly, select individuals for enterprise development

training by such a set of attitudes and skills in no way guarantees business success. Secondly, the entrepreneurial characteristics required to launch a business successfully are often not those required for growth and even more frequently not those required to manage it once it grows to any size. The role of the entrepreneur needs to change with the business as it develops and grows, but all too often he or she is not able to make the transition.

Tie up the SHGs with Small Scale Industries

Small industry sector has performed exceedingly well and enabled our country to achieve a wide measure of industrial growth and diversification.

By its less capital intensive and high labour absorption nature, SSI sector has made significant contributions to employment generation and also to rural industrialisation. This sector is ideally suited to build on the strengths of our traditional skills and knowledge, by infusion of technologies, capital and innovative marketing practices.

The opportunities in the small scale sector are enormous due to the following factors:

- Less Capital Intensive
- Extensive Promotion & Support by the Government
- Reservation for Exclusive Manufacture by small scale sector
- Project Profiles
- Funding
- Finance & Subsidies
- Machinery Procurement
- Raw Material Procurement
- Manpower Training
- Technical & Managerial skills
- Tools & Tools utilisation support
- Reservation for Exclusive Purchase by Government
- Export Promotion
- Growth in demand in the domestic market size due to overall economic growth

- Increasing Export Potential for Indian products
- Growth in Requirements for ancillary units due to the increase in number of Greenfield units coming up in the large scale sector.

So this is the opportune time to set up projects in the small scale sector. It may be said that the outlook is positive, indeed promising, given some safeguards. This expectation is based on an essential feature of the Indian industry and the demand structures. The diversity in production systems and demand structures will ensure long term co-existence of many layers of demand for consumer products/ technologies/ processes. There will be flourishing and well grounded markets for the same product/process, differentiated by quality, value added and sophistication. This characteristic of the Indian economy will allow complementary existence for various diverse types of units.

The promotional and protective policies of the Govt. have ensured the presence of this sector in an astonishing range of products, particularly in consumer goods. However, the bug bear of the sector has been the inadequacies in capital, technology and marketing. The process of liberalisation will therefore, attract the infusion of just these things in the sector.

Future objectives, which will be implemented by the SHGs for the economic and social development of themselves, are as follows:

I) Formation of SHGs irrespective of APL/BPL & to enhance the Capacity Building ability of the SHG

II) Micro-finance scheme to build up the habits of saving.

III) Forest conservation and bio-diversity to reduce forest degradation with the help of SHGs.

IV) Income generation activities through encouraging poultry, goatery, training to the SHGs.

V) Management of local pond, distribution of agriculture seeds, medicinal plants and use of bio-fertilisers and vermicompost through SHGs.

VI) Alternate source of fuel energy, bio-diversity, effects of deforestation and aforestation etc. will be attached with the groups.

VII) Agricultural awareness camp to the SHG members.

Entrepreneurship strategies in our country have not been adopted as a legitimate political objective. Every rural development program has been taken as target oriented programme rather development oriented programme by the ruling party in the country as well as state government. Practically all the states in India are trying to make sizeable investments in entrepreneurship development program but more initiatives are required for nationalizing and globalizing the SHG movement rapidly. Larger investment in infrastructure has helped the states in their quest of entrepreneurship development, even when the rate of growth of state domestic product was low. This was mainly because better infrastructure facilitated the spread effect of growth. Finally the country can make satisfactory progress in the globalization of SHGs with more efficient implementation of PPP, involvement of grassroots organization in programme formulation and implementation.

There should be a Village Mobiliser in every village, which is indispensable and noteworthy for entrepreneurship development throughout the country. Field organizers will only organize the SHG meeting but Animators will monitor the groups regularly, where the political members will not be involved as organizers, monitors or animators in this process.

REFERENCES

Aneja, Rajendra (2000), *Impact of Liberalization on Marketing and Distribution in India,* Assocham, Delhi.

Kashyap, Pradeep and Raut (2005), *Rural Marketing in India,* Dream Track, Delhi.

Krishnamacharlu et, al., (2002), *Rural Marketing,* Pearson Education, Delhi.

NCAER, *Indian Marketing Demographics,* NACER, Delhi, 1998.

Saimuddin et, al., (ed.) (1997), *Rural Marketing: Thrust and Challenges,* National Publishing Corp., Delhi.

Singh, A.K. and Pandey, S.P. (2005), *Rural Marketing: Indian Respective,* New Age International, Delhi.

Singh, Sukhraj (2004), *Rural Marketing,* Vikas Publication, Delhi.

Velaudhan, S.K. (2002), *Rural Marketing: Targeting Non-urban Consumers,* Response Books, New Delhi.

Bardhan, P.K. (1984), *Political Economy of India's Development,* New Delhi: Allied Publishers.

Ganguly, S. (1978), *What Motivates Mr. Small Entrepreneur,* Indian Management.

Khanka, S.S. (1990), *Entrepreneurship in Small Scale Industries,* Himalayan Publishing House, New Delhi.

Khanka, S.S. (2007), *Entrepreneurial Development,* S. Chand & Company Ltd., New Delhi.

Murthy, Beveln, (1989), *Entrepreneurship Development in India,* Mittal Publications, New Delhi.

Cochran, T. C. (1949), *Change and the Entrepreneur,* Harvard University Press, Cambridge.

Suri, K.B. (Ed.) (1988), *Small Scale Enterprises in Industrial Development,* Sage Publications, New Delhi.

S.K. Sharma (ed.) (1978), *Dynamics of Development,* Vol. II. Concept, Delhi.

5

Informal Trade between India and Bangladesh: India's Security Dilemma

MOHOR CHAKRABORTY*

India and Bangladesh—the historical neighbours in the South Asian region—with their adjacent borders and convergence of geopolitical, strategic, and economic interests, influence each other in diverse perspectives of international relations. Mutual interdependence between the two states in the economic sphere is attested by the huge investments of Indian companies in Bangladesh, in a plethora of sectors, namely, services, textiles, ready-made garments, pharmaceuticals, power, and Information Technology, to name a few. In this context, mention may be made of India's leading industrial conglomerate, the TATAS' proposed investment in iron and steel, fertilizer and power generation sectors in the tune of US$ 2.5 billion in Bangladesh. On the other hand, Bangladeshi commodities like raw jute, jute twine and yarn, chemical fertilizer, leather products, ceramic tableware and jamdani sarees are imported by India. Consequently, a resurgence in Indo-Bangladesh bilateral trade has been visible, which has graduated to US$ 2.15 billion in the 2004-05 fiscal from US$ 900 million in the fiscal of 1999-2000.[1] Moreover, Bangladesh

* Junior Research Fellow, Department of International Relations, Jadavpur University, Kolkata.

has been keen to sign a Free Trade Agreement (FTA) with India since the middle of 2005. Unfortunately enough, this portrait of financial optimism has been clouded by the emergence of unrecorded, illegal and informal trading practices between the two countries, including gun-running, arms and drug trafficking, money laundering, and child and women trafficking, which pose a serious security dilemma for India, particularly across its contiguous borders with Bangladesh. It is also noteworthy that the economically deprived and disadvantaged groups like the 'refugees', indigenous people, underworld criminals and local gangsters have been drawn into this diabolic nexus, and have axiomatically been ostracized by and diverted from the societal mainstream. Taken in its holistic corpus, the unabated growth of such cross-border informal trade practices has generated a predominant spill-over effect in the politico-economic and security scenarios of the entire South, Southeast and East Asian regions. Thus, in the amalgamated structure of legal and illegal economic communication, the problems and prospects of regionalism have become evident in inherently shaping bilateral and multilateral policies.

Under such circumstances, this paper attempts to scrutinize the budding relations between India and Bangladesh through the architecture of bilateral trade—both formal and informal—and the effects of such transactions on the border security of India. It may be conceded without any embers of doubt that, notwithstanding political intricacies and complexities in regional affairs of the states, the pragmatic impetus on economic cooperation and its allied benefits has fascinated the policy makers of both the countries. Prior to embarking on a detailed discussion of the nature and effects of informal trade between India and Bangladesh, it would be imperative, at this juncture, to script the meaning of the terms 'Informal/Illegal' trade. The 'informal' facet of it is characterized by illegal economic activities, the existence of parallel markets, unregulated by the government and extra-legal activities that continue unabated. Moreover, since informal trade is propped up by the loss of potential government revenue, trafficking in drugs, narcotics, arms and human beings, and smuggling of goods across borders by circumventing tariff and non-tariff barriers, it is connoted as 'illegal'. The flourishing of indirect trading behaviour has been stimulated by three factors, namely, institutional, economic and non-economic. While institutional determinants may be listed as the absence of procedural delay and quantitative restrictions or paper work; marginal access of less-qualified traders to formal channels of transaction; and good market distribution network, the economic dynamics are represented by the presence of high duties in official channels; inadequacy in transport/transit systems and banking facilities; quick realization of payments and low transaction costs; and lower rent-seeking activities of public agents. Furthermore, the absence/shortage of storing/ warehousing facilities for tradable commodities; the scope of lesser time to reach destinations for perishable items; and the ill-conceived nexus, coupled with the historical, ethnic and traditional links between traders and informal agencies stimulate the blossoming of informal trade in the manifestation of its non-economic aspects.[2]

While formal trade is characterized by established rules of behaviour and regulations, has well defined products and markets, is enforced by the government, so that transactions occur within legal, recorded framework besides accounting for in the nation's Gross Domestic Product (GDP), with transparent and unrestricted market information, and the attachment of the related financial system to the Central Bank of the respective country, its informal counterpart lacks the afore-mentioned aspects, thereby making its execution illegal and surreptitious. With respect to the magnanimity of the system of informal trade that exists between India and Bangladesh, it has been estimated that, it almost equals the magnitude of bilateral formal trade. If such trade statistics are brought within the ambit of official trade data, these would account for a significant increase in total trade between New Delhi and Dhaka. The elements underlying the vitality of informal trading arrangements provide valuable inkling towards policies of rejuvenating the potential of bilateral trading as well as in identifying the bottlenecks of formal trading measures between the two sub-continental neighbours.

On an investigation of the geographical distribution of Bangladesh's informal channels, it has been established that, within the district centres of Jiban Nagar, Jessore, Benapole, Kushtia, Pragpur, Khulna, Darshana, Rajshahi, Godagiri, Dinajpur, Lalmonirhat, Burimari, Nawabgunj, Sonamasji, and Hilli,[3] there exist 3-10 informal traders on an average, who facilitate the implementation of their activities in a coordinated manner. Interestingly enough, the items traded by these illicit networks widely range from foodstuff (rice, pulses, onion, and excess PDS supplies); textiles (sarees and readymade garments); consumer goods (salt, sugar, and Phensydil) to a plethora of other objects (stone, cement, coal, machinery, guns, ammunition, narcotics); and even living beings (cattle, women and children). In the execution of informal trade between India and Bangladesh, authorized channels, personal trips, distribution networks, official media and trade fairs act as valuable sources of information for the benefactors. The method of dealing may follow payment in advance or through collateral sources, prior dealing, third party references, and even credit arrangements. For instance, a major proportion of informal trade is financed in Bangladeshi Taka, while a minor part is done in Indian Rupee. Moreover, the remittances of legal or illegal Bangladeshi migrants, domiciled in India, and the techniques of 'Hawala' (as is known in India) and 'Hundi' (as is known in Bangladesh), which do not involve any physical transfer of currency, are means of patronizing informal trade as well. Cognizant of the augmentation in informal trading behaviour, running almost parallel to the formal means of commercial transaction between Dhaka and New Delhi, the economic impact of this well-articulated 'business' deserves emphasis. Illegal migrants from Bangladesh, who do not have access to the formal channels for remitting their earnings, do so via the informal option, thereby facilitating the entry and circulation of the Bangladeshi currency into the Indian territory and bringing the issue of balance of payments between the two states to the crux. As a matter of fact, some of the legal migrants from the other side of the Indian border also use the informal channel for allowances as it is more expeditious than the official one. Taken in its entirety, this apparently simple exercise hinders the progress of the formal economic sector of both the concerned states.

The arrangements of informal trade between India and Bangladesh continue to thrive despite the attempts at regional trade liberalization mechanisms under the South Asian Preferential Trading Arrangement (SAPTA). Needless to say, unless the transacting environment of formal traders improves, informal trade will continue to coexist, even if free trade is institutionalized between the two countries, either at the bilateral level, or within the scaffold of sub-regional organizations like SAARC and BIMSTEC. There is a whole corpus of features that instigate the smooth execution of Indo-Bangladesh informal trade, which may be categorized into the following:

- *Illegal Migration and Porous Border:* In the face of the dense population residing near the border between India and Bangladesh, illegal cross-border movement gets severely compounded in the riverine and 'Char' areas where patrolling is difficult. The availability of a large market and railway facilities near the border makes it easier and attractive for the informal traders to carry out activities mostly on headloads, rickshaws, vans and boats. In the late 1980's, India sought to build a fence on the international border to stop illegal immigrants from pouring into West Bengal.[4] This issue has assumed serious proportions in the recent past as the west-bound influx has incessantly increased. Furthermore, the change in demographic patterns due to illegal migration, responsible for the ongoing insurgency in Assam and Tripura, poses threats to culture, polity, natural resources, and the very social fabric of India.
- *Legal Constraints:* The implementation of illicit trading is assisted by the absence of judicial and law enforcement infrastructure, telecommunication network, vehicles with the police, inadequate staff, ambiguous laws, and poor road network, thereby making the task of supervision extremely difficult for the border guarding forces. Moreover, the legal system has several loopholes, which are fully exploited

by the criminals. The Illegal Migrants (Determination by Tribunal) Act/IMDT Act offers a glaring example, within the paraphernalia of which, a migrant gets an opportunity to defend himself, by placing on the police the onus to prove him wrong and to allow the cases of infiltration to pass through judicial scrutiny.

- *Border Guidelines:* Consequent to the Indo-Bangladesh Border Agreement of 1974, the Joint Indo-Bangladesh Guidelines of 1975, for border authorities were framed for the border guarding forces of both the countries, in order to ensure cooperation between them over trans-border crimes and exchange of information and intelligence at appropriate levels. These guidelines, among other issues, also provide that *'neither side can have any permanent or temporary border security forces within 150 yards on either side of the International Border, and no defensive works of any nature including trenches in the stretch of 150 yards on each side of the boundary'.*[5] Under this provision, Bangladesh objects to the construction of fences within 150 yards from the International Border on the ruse that fencing violates the guidelines. It even objects to construction of roads within the stipulated distance on the same pretext.
- *Miscellaneous Factors:* Tensions surface intermittently as any permanent solution to major outstanding issues still eludes the two countries. The intricacy in Identifying Bangladeshi nationals is further compounded by the indifferent attitude of the border population towards the informal traders, as they are either dependent on the kingpins or are petrified to speak against them. Certain problems crop up regarding the issue of deporting the Bangladeshi nationals caught on the border, due to the non-receipt of lists from state police organizations in advance of the persons to be deported, who bring them in without waiting for confirmation, accompanied with the tribulations of the lack of response from Bangladesh Rifles (BDR) after handing over the lists, and so on. These issues pose considerable security threats fc India. Apart from these determinants, the enclaves[6]

(111 Indian and 51 Bangladeshi), adverse possession and disputed land, prevalent on the border become convenient points for smuggling, and are areas of entry for illegal migrants. Cultivation in adverse possession land and cutting of barbed wire by informal traders invite aggressive reactions from the other side, thereby generating tension in the relations of the border guarding forces. The limitation to applicability of law of the land in trans-border crimes (because the law of the land ceases to apply after a person crosses over to the other side) and the Government of India's allegations of Bangladesh's soft-pedaling towards Pakistan, which consequently acts as a conduit for anti-India terrorist operations, retaliated by the Dhaka Government's claims that India supports anti-Dhaka, Chakma insurgents, engender a grave situation, when cooperation on matters pertaining to illegal trading mechanisms become practically obscure.

However, notwithstanding the vibrant incarnation of the informal bilateral trading arrangements through unofficial channels between India and Bangladesh, a prescriptive analysis aimed at the reduction of such criminal endeavour may be offered under the following heads:

- *Economic Determinants:* It is contingent on both the governments of India and Bangladesh to underline the imperative of regional integration in the form of economic cooperation, political harmony, and as a mutually-reinforcing diplomatic tool, by offering bilateral support in the identification, preparation and establishment of industrial and agricultural projects, which could provide the production base for exports to other contracting states. The twin states should ensure bilateral 'special treatment' for establishing fair trade and eliminating potential tensions based on skewed economic power relations, besides addressing a more comprehensive array of trade-related issues, such as the harmonization of standards and certification, customs clearance, procedures and classification, transit and transport facilitation, rules for fair competition and foreign exchange liberalization.

- *Security-related Determinants:* It is absolutely necessary for the official circuits of New Delhi and Dhaka to address common security interests and pending unsolved mutual disputes (un-demarcated border, water rights, enclaves and adverse possessions, cross-border migration and crimes), by emphasizing bilateral Confidence Building Measures (CBMs) so that states are not forced to take any measures that compromise their national interests. It would be in mutual interest to work towards integrating the border areas with the mainland (the Government of India has initiated many programmes, which focus on their social, economic, and political development), to interpret border management in its widest sense to imply coordination and concerted action by the political leadership and administrative, diplomatic, security, intelligence, legal, regulatory and economic agencies of the governments to secure the frontiers and serve the welfare of both countries. The mandarins should also attempt to modernize the Border Security Forces (BSF) by including deployment of surveillance equipment (most significantly thermal imagers), better weaponry, hovercraft and floating platforms for riverine borders, to enhance its interception and deterrence capability, secure better intelligence coordination, strengthen border patrolling, use night vision devices and other equipments for improved border surveillance. The catchword for improvement of bilateral security relations, and axiomatically, containment of informal trade, is reciprocal trust, by making Bangladesh free from the 'realist psychoses' of fear and inferiority complexes, for which Track II diplomacy, in consonance with the conventional forms may be of advantage to both sides.
- *Commercial Determinants:* It would be prudent for the policy makers of both countries to focus on complementarities with a pro-people approach, the aim of which should not be just to sign another

bilateral Free Trade Agreement (FTA); rather, it should be focused on providing relief to the common masses and envisaging a new South Asia free from hunger and poverty. In this effort, FTAs should ideally provide 'incrementality' and value addition. Both India and Bangladesh countenance the challenge of optimizing the benefits out of their association, besides viewing the region as complementary rather than competitive. It would be worthwhile to work for greater air transport liberalization and stress linkages with other regional neighbours, as no nation, in the contemporary context of global interdependence, can afford to be an exclusive and solitary identity. However, the effectiveness of any such recommendation in this regard is obviously dependent upon its acceptability by the vision, commitment and goodwill of the respective political leadership.

- *The Human Factor:* Taking stock of the salience of the population in the border regions, it would be necessary to bring them into the societal mainstream, by providing them with ample opportunities for participation in manufacturing/processing units in local industries like agro-processing, horticulture, and textiles, in consonance with emphasizing trade in simple daily use commodities (in headloads), often through barter, which is immediately beneficial to these people. Moreover, local enterprises must be encouraged through the employment-led expansion of the regional market, replacement of outside product with home produce and servicing external demand. It would be in the interest of both the nations to streamline and institutionalize the movement of people by issuing work permits and identity cards to migrants, thereby ensuring their political satisfaction, which may be further exacerbated by the provision of adequate security, closing the cultural and communication gaps between the border people and the national mainstream and developing friendly relations with them.
- *The Border Security Forces (BSF) and the Illegal Migrants*

(Determination by Tribunal) Act/IMDT Act: The BSF, by virtue of being present along the boundary through-out the year, feels the pulse of the population. Therefore, It can not only develop cordial relations and inculcate the sense of security among the populace, but also bridge the gap between the public and government machinery, if civil authorities responsible for development of the border areas are put under its supervision. The BSF can be endowed with the responsibility of inculcating a sense of security amongst the border inhabitants by checking trans-border crimes and defending them in case of an intimidation from across the boundary. However, as long as there is no mutual trust between the border population and the BSF, this condition of optimism cannot be achieved. Apropos of the IMDT Act, since it is a verity that it has not served the purpose of detecting and deporting illegal migrants[7], this futile operation must be repealed and all illegal immigrants should be dealt with under the 'Foreigners Act', which is applicable throughout the country.

- *Infrastructural Determinants:* The territoriality of India and Bangladesh and the legacy of South Asian politics have made the transportation of goods from the Northeast to the rest of India a cumbersome process. Assamese and Tripuran goods, for instance, must currently travel 1400 and 1645 km respectively to reach the Kolkata port.[8] This distance and subsequent carrying costs could be reduced drastically if the Chittagong port could be used instead, or if goods were simply transported to Kolkata through Bangladeshi territory. It is, therefore, pragmatic for the Dhaka government to undertake the charge of developing the required infrastructure to this end. Trans-shipment would entail some reciprocity, and the opening of India's Northeast market to Bangladeshi businessmen would be an obvious one. In a gesture of goodwill and cooperation, it would also be incumbent on the Indian government to enhance infrastructural cooperation with its neighbour, taking cognizance of the Border Guidelines, so that transport costs come down.

- *Tackling Subaltern Globalization:* Subaltern globalization refers to the relationship between and amongst those 'dubious and shadowy groups'—the smugglers of goods and human beings/informal traders, producers of illicit weapons, and the like. These networks now go beyond nationality, ethnicity, race and religion. It must be noted that a national resolution of regional or post-national insecurity further empowers the dubious elements of subaltern globalization. While the puzzles relating to Bangladesh-India relations have attained new dimensions due to these various new ingredients of globalization and multilateral engagement, the response can never be national isolation or a hyper-reproduction of the state. Rather, for unlocking and resolving these conundrums, a greater hope lies in the regionalization of Indo-Bangladesh collaboration, by putting their mutual relations on stable foundations, for the fulfillment of which, both the sub-continental actors must look beyond Dhaka-New Delhi bilateralism to paradigms of SAARC/BIMSTEC multilateralism.

On a discerning analysis of whether regional trade liberalization can feature as a panacea for informal trade, the answer would be in the negative. Notwithstanding the fact that Preferential Trading Arrangements/PTAs and Free Trade Areas/FTAs indicate progress towards sectoral approach, their trade coverage has remained very low. Moreover, since FTAs require complex rules of origin to ensure that goods from third countries, passing through another member country of the FTA under consideration, meet domestic content requirement before arriving at the final market for consumption, so as to benefit from duty-free entry, such regulations provide the excuse to block official trade on the one hand, making informal trade an attractive option, on the other.

Having attempted an introspection of the maturing relations between India and Bangladesh through the architecture of bilateral trade – both formal and informal—

and the effects of such transactions on the border security of India, certain initiatives that have been undertaken by the Indian side to boost Direct Trade with Bangladesh, deserve mention in this perspective. Perhaps, the cardinal area where New Delhi needs to intervene is in correcting the balance of trade between the two countries, which has long weighed heavily against Bangladesh. For instance, in 2001-02, Bangladesh's exports to India were a meagre US $ 50.2 million, while imports from India during the same period, stood at more than US $ 1 billion.[9] That trade imbalance continues, with Bangladesh's exports to India in 2005-06 standing at US $ 251.6 million, and imports from India going up to nearly US $ 1.8 billion within the same time frame.[10] Since mid-2006, India has offered duty-free import of seven new items from Bangladesh, and promised to do away with duty on 4200 additional items within three years. New Delhi has also sought a list of all irritants, including non-tariff barriers that are currently impeding bilateral trade. In its honest undertaking, India has, from time to time, been making suggestions to help its neighbour bridge the balance of trade gap. It may be conceded that, since India's northeastern states share a common culture and lifestyle with Bangladesh, these similarities could help enhance bilateral formal trade. New Delhi has endeavoured to modernize and upgrade the existing infrastructure, including road connectivity, to further boost commercial initiatives between the two countries, especially between the northeastern states of India and Bangladesh, which have huge resources and raw materials, that can be exported to Bangladesh and after due processing, the finished products be made available to the people of the region at much cheaper rates. It was reported in July 2005,[11] that Bangladesh is keen to sign a bilateral FTA with India, which the latter should capitalize for immediate implementation. Hopes are also pinned on India's TATA group to finally negotiate its long-pending three-billion-dollar investment in Bangladesh, for the proposed power station, steel plant and fertilizer unit.

The two historical neighbours could also work sincerely on collaborative programmes in the near future, to revitalize their ties and stem the burgeoning tide of informal trade.

Apart from engaging themselves in efforts to lift non-tariff and para-tariff barriers, liberalize visa regime, allow free flow of information, relax custom procedures and remove double-taxation, to boost bilateral formal trade, in the transformed international firmament of globalization and market liberalization, both the states should seize the existing and flourishing opportunities of setting up creative economic ventures, without the prejudices of the post-Westphalian or 'modernist' nation state. On the politico-strategic front, the Joint Indo-Bangladesh Guidelines of 1975 for the border guarding forces should be revised, as some of its provisions have become irrelevant. Bangladesh needs to be convinced that fencing and roads along the border do not pose any security threat to its territorial sovereignty. Rather, it is an economic loss for India as a minimum of 150 yards of our fertile land and people between fencing and the International Border are virtually at the mercy of Bangladeshi criminals. In the wake of the brightening of relations between Dhaka and New Delhi on a quid pro quo basis, the two countries, as regional representatives of South Asia, should be in a position to envision a strategy to abort the most politically potent matter—economic migration from Bangladesh to India—by devising measures to jointly improve the economy in Bangladesh. Apart from everything else, the test for New Delhi will lie in successfully performing a delicate balancing act: between cozying up to the generals in Dhaka, and issuing a caveat on the possible consequences of straying too far from the democratic path. Although a very demanding and scrupulous enterprise, the latter cannot be accomplished without the former, and hence it becomes all the more imperative for the Government of India to sincerely address the matters of concern in the context of globalized interdependence in general, and regional cohesion and integration in particular.

REFERENCES

1. http://www.meaindia.nic
2. S.K. Chaudhari, Cross Border Trade Between India and Bangladesh, Working Paper, No. 58, NCAER, New Delhi, 1995.

3. Sanjib Pohit and Nisha Taneja, "India's Informal Trade with Bangladesh: A Qualitative Assessment", *World Economy,* Vol. 26, August 2003.
4. N.S. Jamwal, "Border Management: Dilemma of Guarding the India-Bangladesh Border", *Strategic Analysis,* January-March 2004, IDSA, New Delhi, 2004.
5. *Ibid.*
6. Ishtiaq Hossain, "Bangladesh-India Relations: Issues and Problems", in Emajuddin Ahamed (ed.), *Foreign Policy of Bangladesh: A Small State's Imperative,* The University Press Limited, Dhaka, 1984.
7. *The Hindu,* 7 September, 2007
8. N.S. Jamwal, "Management of Land Borders", *Strategic Analysis,* July-September, 2002, IDSA, New Delhi, 2002.
9. http://www.commerce.nic.in/eidb/Icntcom.asp
10. *Ibid.*
11. *The Hindu,* 9 July, 2005.

6

The Maoist Menace: Terrorism in India

R N. MISHRA* AND ANJANA MAITRA**

An organized group of social and political activists perpetrating violence and keeping the people under threats in certain parts of rural India over the past few years are variously known as the Maoists, Naxalites and the red rebels etc. The Naxalites of the sixties have been divided into several splinter groups. One of them is called the Maoists who believe in spreading terrorism. They are of recent origin. The term `Maoist' is widely used by the media and the common men. Eleven states of the country including Orissa, Andhra Pradesh, Chhatisgarh, Madhya Pradesh, Bihar, Maharastra and Uttar Pradesh, are faced with the problem of terrorism from the Maoists. Between January 20006 and October 20007 as many as 1221 persons have been killed and the incidents of violence which have taken place, have increased to 1258. The terrorists are equipped with land mines, bombs, self loading rifles (SLR), A.K-47, cartridges and other sophisticated weapons. They have their hideouts in forests and hilly areas and operate in a well organized way. The Prime Minister of India is reported to have said that the Maoist terror is the

* Former Professor of Political Science and Principal (retired), Gangadhar Meher College (Autonomous), Samblapur (Orissa).

** Lecturer, Political Science in (Government) S.G. Women's College, Rourkela (Orissa), India.

`single biggest internal security challenge'[1] that India faces now.

The Terror Strategy

The plans of action of the Maoists include hostage takings, kidnapping, blasting on railway tracks, assassinations, arson, lootings and guerrilla warfare inside the forests. Their targets are carefully chosen and they operate in a planned manner from remote and inaccessible tribal and rural areas. There are certain pockets in all these states which have witnessed the worst kind of violence. They aim at killing political leaders, key functionaries of the rural local bodies and policemen and loot arms from the police and reserve government armory. At times they kill people in the areas of their operation whom they suspect to be their enemies and informers of the police. Revenge killing and killing of people who refuse their demands for cash payment are carried on regularly to boost the morale of the terrorist squads. The civilian population is kept in a state of perpetual threat and shock Shopkeepers, rich landlords, mill-owners and contractors of village roads are compelled to pay them security money failing which they are hacked in the public. Very often the state intelligence agencies fail even to get an inkling of their operations.

The method of killing is `gruesome'. They killed 90 people in 2002, 136 in 2003, 70 in 2004 and 122 in 2005. According to Sitaram Yechuri, leader of the Communist Party of India (Marxist), it is an internecine struggle in which 80% of those who are killed are ordinary citizens and some of them were members of the other rival groups but not class enemies even judged by Maoist criteria.[2]

In June 2005 about 1,000 men and women heavily armed, attacked Madhuban town in the East Champaran district of Bihar and in November 2005, more than 500 terrorists raided Jehanabad jail and freed all the prisoners. Very recently, the Prime Minister's rural roads scheme (Pradhan Mantri Gram Sadak Yojana) has been badly affected by the demands made by the rebels. They are demanding 10% of the tender value from the contractors who are engaged in the construction work connecting 10,000 villages. Refusal for payment led to attack on men and machinery. Holding crucial projects to ransom is a new trend.[3] The result is that no agency comes forward to undertake developmental works out of fear for the terrorists. In the state of Jharkhand they hijacked the Barkakana-Barwadih train in March 2006 and kept the passengers hostage for the whole night. About three hundred of them attacked the camp of the Central Industrial Security Force at Bokaro in the same state.

The Bastar region in the state of Chhatisgarh is regarded as the bastion of the terrorists. The rebels have intensified their activities in the region comprising the districts of Dantewada, Bijapur, Narayanpur, Bastar and Kanker. In an estimate made by the Police about 5000 Maoists armed with A.K. 47 rifles, mortar, rocket launchers and land mines are active in the state, backed by another 20,000 cadres who carry self-loading rifles and traditional weapons like bows and arrows and axes. With a view to curb the growing menace of terrorism, the local tribesmen of the region started a movement called `Salwa Judum (campaign for peace) in June, 2005, supported by the state government with arms and monetary backup. Their organization was a sort of people's militia. But their efforts excited the wrath of the terrorists. The situation compelled 50,000 people, mostly tribals to desert their villages and settle in government run refugee camps. In July, 2006, a squad of 600 guerrillas armed with automatic rifles stormed into the government-run relief camp at Arabore in Dantewada district and killed at least 17 tribesmen. They opened indiscriminate fire on the tribals and abducted many of them. The rebels burnt at least 20 small houses.[4]

Not only the instances of killing security personnel have swelled up, the number of civilian people killed by the insurgents has also increased over the years. Other instances of violence include blowing up of a truck, killing 55 persons on February 28,2006, a land mine blast killing 13 persons, taking hostage of 13 persons who were beheaded in April, 2006 and looting of A.K47s, SLRs and 303 rifles from the Police in Dantewada district. In July, 2007 in an encounter between the security personnel and the Maoists in the same district, 24 police personnel and 20 Maoists were killed. The bodies of the deceased Maoists, however, could not be traced out. The incident took place while a combing operation was conducted jointly by the CRPF and Chhatisgarh police looking for an ultra Nepali Maoist camp near the forest of the Aerober police station. They had to face 300 to 400 Maoists who exchanged fire with them for about five hours. The latest incident of violence by the terrorists has taken place on December 19, 2007 in which 12 security personnel, 8 from the Chhatisgarh Armed Force and 4 from the District Police of Dantewada, were kidnapped in the course of an exchange of fires and killed later. The A.K47 rifles and cartridges in their possession were also taken away by the terrorists, leaving the dead bodies in the Gopalpalli-Krisnaram forest.[5]

In Orissa, the Maoists have been intensifying their violent activities in the tribal and backward districts of Malkangiri, Koraput, Rayagada, Gajapati, Sambalpur, Deogarh, Sundargarh and Mayurbhanj .In the district of Sambalpur the Maoists mercilessly killed the Sarpanch of Tampargarh Panchayat in Jauary, 2003, following which 17 persons were put under arrest. The incident made the state police aware of the Maoist presence in the state. Between January and July 2003, the Maoists killed at least 8 civilians, leaving about 10 wounded, kidnapped 18 persons which included one school teacher, two functionaries of the rural local bodies, 14 daily labourers and one civil contractor. They also threatened to blow up Kisinda police station. The police had two encounters with the Maoists, exchanging fires and arrested 8 terrorists during the year. During 2006 and 2007 the Maoists bombed a farm house of a local land lord and looted paddy near Dhama police station and kidnapped seven persons including a driver and a shopkeeper. The dead body of the shopkeeper was later found in the forest near Rairakhol. About 7 Maoists were killed in encounter with the police during the period.

The Finance Minister and the Minister for Scheduled Castes and Scheduled Tribes of the state, including some lower ranking policemen and civilians are included in the hit list of the Maoists at the moment. An incident of revenge killing by the Maoists was reported recently in Rayagada district. The victim Santosh Gagrana,a tribal youth of 26 years old, who was formerly active in a gang called Karlaghat Anchalika

Sangha, a Maoist outfit, laid down arms following the surrender policy of the state government announced in June, 2006 for rehabilitation of the Maoists. They suspected him of being a police informer and killed him with sharp weapons at a distance of two kilometers from his village. The murder of an ex-sarpanch (head of village level local body) of Koraput district on 30 January, 2008 was a well planned killing of suspected police informer. About 60 armed rebels dragged Markand Choudhury from his house at 3.30 am at night and sliced his neck with a sharp weapon at Langalbeda panchayat office. The rebels also ransacked the victim's house, beat some villagers and warned them of dire consequences in the event of passing on any information to the police. A few posters left by them contained writing upholding the rights of the tribals and threatening to the non-tribals.The police denied the charge that Choudhury was a police informer.[6]

One of the recent most attacks of the Maoists has been reported in the border of Orissa and Jharkhand at Biramitrapur on January 1, 2008, unleashing a reign of terror in the locality.[7] This powerful attack came at a time when the Orissa police claim to have achieved a breakthrough in containing the Maoists in Orissa. About 500 rebels launched their campaign at the mid night, surrounding the small town of Biramitrapur and launching an attack to blow up the Baunsajor police station of Jharkhand state. As stated by an eye-witness the rebels surrounded the police station and then announced in a loud-speaker giving a call to the police to surrender their arms. After a little while they opened indiscriminate fire and an encounter ensued between them and the police for nearly four hours. The rebels equipped with automatic rifles hurled petrol bombs at the police and also had a plan to bombard the nearby residential buildings. While a police man died in the firing, leaving six injured, the bodies of the dead and wounded rebels were taken swiftly by the attackers.

The Maoist attack on the wild life forest range office late at night at Badrama of Sambalpur district on January 4, 2008 proved beyond any doubt that the police have completely failed in gathering intelligence of Maoist activities. For about one and half hour the Maoists persisted in carrying on their violent activities and in the process burnt the range office and 15 motor vehicles and destroyed property worth more than one crore of rupees. Further, they snatched away one303 rifle, cash worth 15000 rupees, two cell phones, gold ornaments and dresses from the official residence of the forest official inflicting torture on his family members.[8] The attack was made by a gang of 12 persons including four women rebels. The police launched a counter offensive on the following day with two units of special operation group (SOG). Exchange of fires continued between the police and the Maoists throughout the night for about nine hours in the forest, firing 400 rounds by the police and 100 rounds by the rebels. Two Maoists of the gang aged 25 and 26 years respectively who were residents of the nearby villages were killed in the encounter and the police seized three self-loading rifles, two 303 rifle, 26 rounds of live ammunition, blank cartridges and three bags containing Maoist literature.

The Maoist offensive launched in Nayagarh on 15 February, 2008 further speaks of the failure of intelligence agencies. Around 400 to 500 Maoists raided the district headquarter town of Nayagarh at night and overran three police stations and two outposts.

They looted about 1,100 weapons including pistols, light machine guns, AK-47s, SLRs and INSAS rifles from the district and police training school armouries and left the place with the loots in a bus hijacked for this purpose. Altogether 13 police personnel and two civilians were killed in the attack which lasted for about four hours. More than 150 of them were young girls dressed in plain clothes.[9]

On the following day forces from the centre, state and the greyhounds of Andhra Pradesh launched a combined massive combing operation in the state on the Maoists in the districts of Nayagarh, Ganjam, Kandhmal and Gajapati. Around five security teams comprising large number of personnel were engaged in the exchange of fire with the Maoists at Go-sana jungle, Gallery and Tarasingi, Tikabali, Kalinga ghati and Adava area. A warlike situation prevailed in an area spreading several hundreds of squire kilometers, causing panic among the villagers. While the police killed twenty rebels, three security personnel including an assistant commandant of Special Operation Group were killed in the encounter.[10] The security forces recovered 115 rifles and huge ammunitions looted by the Maoists on the previous day. The significance of the Nayagarh incident lies in the fact that it clearly points to a new trend in the movement of the rebels. The incident took place close to the capital city and gave rise to a pandemonium in the State Assembly.

In view of the threat from the terrorists the Chief Minister of Orissa sought more aid from the centre at a meeting on internal security chaired by the Prime Minister. He demanded sanction of five more Indian Reserve Battalions (IRB), the deployment of two more battalions of central paramilitary forces in the state and special grant of 30 crores of rupees for the training resource centre of special operation group coming up in the state. The state government is developing, at present, a permanent training unit for counterterrorism, jungle warfare and anti-extremist operation.[10]

Andhra Pradesh is also one of the worst hit states by the terrorists. They killed a former state interior minister A. Madhab Reddy in 2000. They were also responsible for an attempt on the life of A.Chandrababu Naidu, former Chief Minister, in 2003. In July, 2006 the police killed eight rebels which included one top leader and five women Maoists. The clash broke out when the police raided a meeting of 80 Maoists in Prakasham district. The state police claim to have killed 80 rebels in 2006. By August 2007 as many as 650 more Maoists are added to the hit list of the state police. They are at present more active in the rural areas of Visakhapatnam bordering the state of Orissa[11]. Maoist terror has spread to Karnataka very recently where the terrorists set a government bus alight. Five of them were killed by the police in the Chikmagalur district.

The Terrorists' League

The instances of violence cited here are illustrative rather than exhaustive. The terrorists are in league with Naxalites, Maoist Communist Centre, People's War Group and other radical extremists. The Naxalbari movement started in West Bengal by the militants of the Marxist and Leninist groups in the sixties against the landlords and their movements spread to the neighbouring areas of Bihar, Orissa, Madhya Pradesh and Andhra Pradesh where radical left parties under different banners carried on their extremist activities. After the formation of the new states of Jharkhand and Chhatisgarh, the Maoists have built their powerful support bases in both the states. They have close links with the Maoists of Nepal who played a significant role in the Loktantra Andolan (Movement for democracy). In January 2007, the Maoists won 83 seats in a 330-member Parliament. In April, five of them were sworn in as ministers and one more as junior Minister in Nepal. There are talks about a revolutionary corridor extending from Nepal to Andhra Pradesh across six Indian states including Bihar, Chhatisgarh, Jharkhand, Andhra Pradesh, Orissa and Madhya Pradesh. It is being planned by them to convert the region into a compact revolutionary zone. Their slogan is` from Pashupati to Tirupati'. They are also in alliance with other terrorist groups active in South Asia. The rise of the Maoists in Nepal and their methods of revolutionary violence have very much influenced the rebels in India.

A statement attributed to the rebels reads:

> "The Indian monopoly capitalism ruling class, the successor of British imperialism, has been pursuing the expansionist policy, pressure, intervention and sabotage against the national aspirations of the people and neighbouring countries. It has been endeavouring to quell, with guns and state terror, the aspirations of the people of Kashmir and the North-Eastern States and the new democratic movement in Andhra and Bihar and intensifying the pressure, sabotage and proactive activities under the strategy of making Nepal, Bhutan, Bangladesh and Sri Lanka as new Sikkim. With an intention to isolate Pakistan after the end of the cold war and fulfill its desire for regional hegemony, the Indian ruling class has knelt down before the US imperialism and has opened the doors for them for the merciless exploitation of the people of this region under the pretext of liberalization."[12]

The rural youths as terrorists:

> Most of the rebels are young and in their teens and twenties. The recruits are school and college dropouts of the rural areas. They have a children's division-the Balmandal where the rebels provide the children military training to prepare them for any situation. The rebel leaders, however, have denied the report of the eye-witness of using the children in the armed conflict, According to them children are engaged as messengers and informers. The terrorists are dressed with military fatigues, some wear military boots, others flip-flops and some are barefoot. Young women have also joined the cadres.

Dipti, a young woman terrorist, who surrendered herself voluntarily to the police on November 25, 2007 at Sambalpur hails from a remote place near Naktideol. She comes from a poor family consisting of 6 members. She gave up her schooling when she was in VIII standard in a rural school. She was lured to the cadre on the promise of a job. She was trained by the Maoists and was involved in a number of violent incidents including burning of a truck. She has made it clear in her statement that women in the cadre are not only tortured by the Maoists but they are also sexually exploited. Rasmita Nayak, another woman Maoist, has a similar story to tell. She was educated up to IV standard in the village school of Deogarh district. A man and a woman persuaded her to join the cadre on the promise of giving her money. She was given training in the camps to use rifle and was engaged in their operations later. She also in her statement to the police admitted the charges of torture and sexual exploitation. Solostica who is 24 years old also voluntarily surrendered herself to the police. She has education up to matriculation. She along with her three other sisters used to work as daily labourers in a village in Deogarh district. She joined in the cadre in 2005 and after completion of training in various camps assumed the command of a women's' group. She was also assured of a job and regular payment of monthly salary in return of her services to the poor and needy, fight for removing injustice from the society and efforts for bridging the gap between the rich and the poor. In her statement to the police, she narrated the various forms of torture meted out to the women cadres. According to her the women Maoists are required to dance and sing in their parties to entertain the men folk. They were also sexually exploited in their parties in the forest. Solostica was highly disillusioned at sight of the carnage of poor and innocent people and extortion of heavy amount of cash which was alleged to have been appropriated by two leaders of their gang. The lavish life style of the leaders was a sore point for all.[13]

It is learnt from the statement of a Maoist leader to the police that the terrorists of Orissa contribute a sum of rupees 25 lakh per month to the central organization and spend one lakh of rupees for their state organization. It is the industrialists, contractors, cannabis traders, big businessmen and landlords from whom they collect donation furtively to finance their organization. Incidentally, it may be pointed out here that in the interior forest areas of western Orissa cannabis is illegally cultivated in large patches of forest land which has been seized by the police recently. The way they built their organization in Orissa five years back, is also clear from the statement of Dama Deo, an illiterate man of 35 years old from the state of Jharkhand who was associated with the terrorists for 18 years and worked as the secretary of the state committee of Orissa. He changed his name several times and picked up the local dialect and was instrumental in spreading the organization in western districts of Deogarh, Sambalpur, Sundargarh, Subarnapur, Bargarh and Angul, operating from his head office in Cuttack. He claimed to have inducted 6 young women to the organization and arranged their marriages with other terrorists as no girl prefers to marry a Maoist. Deo has two wives residing in Jharkhand. Further, it is revealed by him that young men and women after recruitment are imparted training in the use of arms in Paresshnath jungle in Girdih district of Jharkhand before they are engaged in their operations in Orissa. According to him the terrorists have become more powerful after the merger of the Maoists with the People's War Group in 2004.

Ideological Considerations

They champion the cause of the poor peasants and the rights of landless workers at the bottom rung of India's caste and class hierarchy. They claim to distribute sacks of rice and pulses to the masses, collect funds to run schools and organize mass weddings for the poor people. They also target corrupt officials, big landholders and bank employees who advance loans to the agriculturists. According to them people are hungry because` there is no food to eat and no job for them. They don't have clothes and successive government does not bother for their development'. They claim to lead people to a new democratic revolution. According to them people who create trouble for the poor should be dealt with. They claim: "We are not terrorists. We are fighting a people's war. We want the proletariat to rule, not the imperialistic governments."[14] Their proclaimed long term plan is to capture the cities and overthrow the Indian State. They are sustained in their hideouts in the forest with the help of leaders who run underground front organizations in cities and urban areas. In December, 2007, a Maoist leader called James was arrested by the police in a thickly populated locality of Sambalpur. The police claim that James was involved in killing more than 100 persons which included 47 police personnel. He was a trainer and second in command of the Sambalpur-Deogarh zonal committee of the Maoist organization.

Their ideological stand is supported by a few poor people in certain parts of the country but majority of them obey the terrorists out of fear of retaliation. Lack of transparency in the work of the lower echelon of revenue bureaucracy such as the land surveyor, amin, revenue inspector and Tahasildar etc who directly come in contact with the farmers and exploit them is one of the most important reasons for the villagers' support to the terrorists. The system of issuing photo-identity cards to the farmers for sale of paddy produced by them in their own land has resulted in harassment of almost all the farmers. The small and marginal farmers are hard hit by this measure introduced by the government of Orissa in recent years. Every farmer has to bribe and waste a lot of working days in obtaining the card from the revenue inspector who turns up for work casually. Further, poor people living near the forest who live on selling firewood and collection of forest produce come into clashes with the forest officials. People's grievances relating to land and forest give the Maoists an upper hand to garner support of the villagers. Mass poverty and their rising expectations compel the disgruntled rural youths exposed to school and college education to take to arms with the rebels.

The Maoists claim to run parallel government in a large part of 165 affected districts of the country. The Jharkhand High Court has expressed concern over the fact that more and more people approach the Maoists to settle their disputes with other villagers.[15] Government courts takes years to dispense justice and the justice is too costly for the poor villagers. On the other hand, the rebels, on approach, administer justice swiftly, most often from the barrel of a gun. This is particularly true in matters of land dispute mostly arising out of acts of omission and commission of the revenue officials.

The Villagers' Woes

It seems the villagers are stuck in the middle-between the Maoists and the state. The incident that took place in a village in Sambalpur district of Orissa illustrates the point clearly. A group of Maoists camping in the forest near Dakara village of Maneswar Block used to terrorize the villagers to give them food and shelter. The police and security personnel, on the other hand, hounded them to gather intelligence about the terrorists and accused them of abetting terrorism through their help to the Maoists.[16] A similar incident of harassment by the police has taken place in some villages of Jujumura Block.

For which the villagers have sought the intervention of the district administration. They are facing the problem for the last four years.[17]

The foregoing accounts leave no scope for doubt about the fact that the efforts made so far to overcome the Maoist menace have failed. Terrorism is growing fast. Large parts of the country have come under the spectre of terrorism. A survey indicates that about 17 crores of people of India are affected by the problem. The areas hit by the menace are the tribal inhabited backward parts of the country where the pace of development is very slow and social change is imperceptible. Extreme poverty coupled with malnutrition, diseases and infant mortality rule the roost in all these areas. Special emphasis is needed to accelerate the pace of development and removal of mass poverty. Funds allocated for this purpose by the Union Government, claimed to be insufficient, are not fully utilized in time. Last year a substantial amount of central grant as much as six thousand seven hundred crores of rupees could not be utilized by the government of the afflicted states. On the other hand, the state leaders clamour for more central grants and hold the rebels responsible for obstructing the developmental process. It is corruption on the part of key functionaries at the district and at the rural local levels that block the trickle down effect of developmental efforts at a cost of huge investment. An example from tribal district of Koraput on the relationship between the sarpanches(elected heads of village level local bodies) and the district administration aptly reflects the functioning of developmental projects in rural areas of the district. It is reported that feeling neglected by the district administration in matters of implementation of development projects, the elected village heads have formed a union to protect their legislative rights. Out of 226,126 of them have formed the Koraput Zilla Sarpanch Mahasangha to voice protest against the district administration as they are not involved in various works carried out by the government in their panchayat areas. The Mahasangha is intended to work as a platform to fight for their rights. It has been pointed out by them that there are several instances of unconstitutional work on the part of the administration by arbitrarily removing sarpanches. They also complained against mismanagement of funds meant for the National Rural Employment Guarantee Act (NREGA). They alleged that a bulk of the funds remained unutilized since they were not released on time and that the administration does not work as per the action plans prepared in the villages.[18]

What is still worse is that corruption thrives on political patronage of which the rebels too are the beneficiaries. Making efforts for putting down insurgency by the police on the one hand and extending political patronage to the rebels on the other can never stamp the rebellion out. The net outcome has been tragic deaths of the unfortunate civilians, policemen and the terrorists, young men and women dreaming for a brighter future.

The State versus the Terrorists

The state police invariably face the problem of deficit in resources, training, technology, and infrastructure and manpower profiles. Corrupt practices followed in recruitment, transfer and posting of police personnel very often speak of the low morale of the force. It is estimated that there is one policeman for every 700 Indians and the strength of police force is getting reduced day by day since the state government fail to make recruitment of adequate police personnel on time due to fund constraints. In India there are 143 police personnel for every one lakh of people while the UN norm for the same is 222. In western countries there are 250 to 500 police personnel for every lakh of population.[19] The colonial legacy still continues to guide the Indian police organisation which, to a great extent, is regulated by the Indian Police Act of 1861.The police in India is yet to maintain a friendly image in the eyes of the weaker sections of the people. The poor people look upon the police as an instrument of their exploitation. Far from approaching them for help, people in general fight shy of them and this attitude of the people towards the police is easily exploited by the Maoists for their purpose. It is the people-Maoists nexus that keeps the rebels fueling for more and more violent expeditions.

While the police forces need to be well equipped to face the Maoist challenge, special attention is urgently required for development of the backward and underdeveloped parts of the states. At the political level special initiatives need to be taken to start dialogues with the rebels to bring them to the mainstream of the society. It needs to be followed up as a mission in a dedicated way, making the rebels convinced of their misdeeds. Mass media focusing on assassinations and destruction of public property in large scale by the Maoists may have some impact on the terrorists.

The police have to play a proactive role to win the support

of the villagers. In this context, the public relations campaign started by the police in the Naxal-hit Rayagada district needs special mention. The police are organizing rural sports and games, tribal functions, entertainment programmes, magic shows and free medical camps in the rural areas in order to build confidence of the masses in the police force and to shed their image as exploiters as viewed by the backward masses. As reported in a local daily, this programme has brought to light the mystery surrounding a gruesome murder of a person named Mukund Madhi who was killed by a gang called Papulur Dalam, an outfit of Maoists' organization of Malkangiri district. It is reported that the rebels killed Madhi in the presence of the villagers as they suspected him as a police informer and also allegedly ate his flesh. The villagers who kept their mouth shut out of fear to the rebels revealed the truth to police when they came in close contact with them.[20]

The arrest of the dreaded Maoist leader Bir Narasingh Lu alias Anna Reddy in February, 2008 has brought to light the active involvement of the radicals in the Kalingnagar agitation against establishment of steel plant. Reddy who hails from Nalgonda district of Andhra Pradesh was sent by his party to strengthen the Kalinganagar movement. He along with his 35 aides was active in the mineral-rich region of Keonjhar, Jajpur and Dhenkanal districts of Orissa. He was also active in the anti-displacement movement of Puri for the proposed Vedanta University. Charges of multiple murders, extortion, abduction, looting and arson have been levelled against him. Women rebels earlier have complained against him for sexual exploitation.[21]

The statements of the Maoist ideologue Varavara Rao made in course of celebration of the 150 years of the First War of Independence of India in Bhubaneswar are significant in this context. Rao in the past participated in a series of talk with the government of Andhra Pradesh on behalf of the rebels. In his speech on the occasion he clearly ruled out the possibility of holding any kind of negotiation with the government of Orissa in future in view of their past experience in 2004 when the state government agreed to fulfill a series of their demands but ended in putting a ban on seven organizations without fulfilling any one of their demands. He commented, "The government is nothing but an agent of the imperialist and feudal forces." He asserted that government must ensure "fair and equitable distribution of land to improve the lot of the poor and deprived." Further, he declared that their movement in Orissa would soon gather further pace and momentum.

He said, "The Adivasis(tribals) are facing violence, oppression and fake encounters so they will fight whenever their rights are violated....The war will continue until the central and state governments do not stop toeing the World Bank's line and things improve for the poor in our country."

He denied the charges of extortion, cannibalism and sexual exploitation against the Maoists women rebels as "false" and "fictitious." He complained that the voices of intellectuals working against SEZ and supporting people's movements are stifled and several supporters of the Maoists are locked in jails. He claimed, "Maoists are the voices of countless voiceless and faceless people." "The war is still on and will continue until just MNC exists in this country," he said.[22]

Social Bases of Terrorism

The Maoist violence has greatly stirred up the deep-rooted inequities prevailing in Indian society since long. To quell up the growing menace of violence through counterterrorism by the police also involves violation of human rights of the innocent rural folk who are poor and illiterate. Political freedom has no meaning for those who wallow in abject poverty in accessible interior parts of the country. An attitudinal change on the part of policy makers is imperative. The problem is getting more complicated in view of the involvement of the Maoists in the people's movements against displacement and land acquisition at the wake of industrialization[23] in West Bengal, Orissa, Jharkhand and Chhatisgarh. They are alleged to have induced violence to all these movements.

The situation in all the afflicted areas which has been sending out shock waves to the law and order authorities during the past few years calls for an analysis. The menace persists in a large part of central India which is geographically contiguous and predominantly inhabited by tribal population. As pointed out earlier, the activities of the rebels are centered in a compact area in the states of Jharkhand, Chhatisgarh, Orissa and Andhra Pradesh. The villages in undeveloped forest and hilly areas are considered by the rebels an ideal location for making preparations for their violent programmes of action and spreading them to the towns and cities. The people in these areas are not only poor and illiterate; they are also victims of many diseases and superstitions. Poor health care facilities result in high rate of infant mortality and death of pregnant women and young mothers soon after child-birth. Men and women have to undertake hard unskilled labour for a living and their level of awareness is extremely low. Killing people mostly women for practicing witchcraft is a recurring phenomenon in the tribal areas. Dropout rates in schools and colleges are very high and the rebels tap this source for recruiting their cadres.

As mentioned earlier, the genesis of extremist politics in the sixties leading to violence out side formal institutions of parliamentary politics may be traced to the Sino-Soviet split. The militancy of the peasants' organization was manifested in the Naxalbari movement which was hailed as the "front paw of the revolutionary armed struggle launched by the Indian people under the guidance of Mao Tse Tung's teachings." The leaders who organized the peasants were Charu Majumdar,Kanu Sanyal and Jangal Santhal who were then leaders of CPI(M). Jangal Santhal was leader of the tribal peasants' organization of the party who hailed from the Darjeeling district of West Bengal. "From 15,000 to 20,000 peasants were enrolled as whole time activists. Peasants' committees were formed in every village and they were transformed into armed guards. They soon occupied land in the name of the peasants' committees, burnt all land records `which had been used to cheat them of their dues', cancelled all debts, passed death sentences on oppressive landlords, formed armed bands by looting guns from the landlords, armed themselves with conventional weapons like bows, arrows and spears, and set up parallel administration to look after their villages."[24] Lack of knowledge in military science was considered by the cadres as one of the most important reasons for failure of the movement. They also learnt from their failure the necessity of formation of small groups and taking recourse to guerrilla warfare.

The Naxalbari movement was echoed in Srikakulam in Andhra Pradesh where it gave rise to a guerrilla struggle by the rebels. Guerrilla squads were formed in the plains and also in Agency hills of Srikakulam " with the ultimate object of capturing power by overthrowing the existing government and establishing a people's democratic dictatorship led by the proletariat." The movement started on 24 November 1968 by forcible cutting of crops from the land of a rich land lord at Garudabhadra. On the next day about 250 tribesmen of several villages armed with bows, arrows and spears raided the house of a landlord-cum-moneylender and took possession of his hoarded paddy, rice, other food grains and property worth about Rs 20,000. They also seized documents, promissory notes and other records that had bound the tribal peasants all these years to the landlord through loans.[25] The movement gathered momentum, killing several police personnel and terrorizing on the landlords for a few years.

Following independence of the country from the colonial rule, mass participation in politics in a big diverse country like India has imparted a growing sense of assertiveness to the primordial sections of the Indian society. Promises of freedom and planned economic development have, no doubt, raised their expectations but in course of time they have been left disillusioned. Their feeling of neglect and frustration have been articulated in a number social and political movements launched by the tribal people in the post-independence period. Tribal movements in the north-east region resulted in reorganization of states over and over again. The state of Jharkhand owes its origin to the demands made by the tribes such as the Munda, the Santal, the Ho, the Kisan, the Bhuyan, the Kharia, the Oraon and the Birhor of Chhotanagpur plateau in south Bihar. The tribes of the adjacent tribal areas of Madhya Pradesh and Orissa also supported them.

They had a long and protracted movement since 1950 with the formation of the Jharkhand party. The movement articulated a number of issues in course of the peoples' struggle for a homeland. At the initial stage, it was a conflict between the tribals and outsiders who in the tribal language were called `Diku'. The meaning of the word has changed its meaning from time to time. Originally it meant the zamindars (landlords) and his employees who were non-tribals of upper castes. Later it meant the people of north Bihar, the other side of the Ganga and "those who earn their living here and send their earnings out to their homes in Bihar." The "dikus" stood for exploitation and the tribals aimed at driving them out of the proposed state. At that stage it was a conflict between the original settlers and the migrants.[26]

Political and economic development following the independence of the country also made the tribals restive. Large scale alienation of tribal land to outsiders added to their discontent. The causes of land alienation were: *(i)* growth of urbanization, leading to increased demand for land and appreciation of land value in money terms, *(ii)* industrial development, *(iii)* large scale migration in the wake of industrialization and *(iv)* lack of proper and adequate credit facilities for the tribal cultivators. At the initial stage the leadership of the movement was with the Mundas which later shifted to the Santal tribesmen. The Santal leadership was more militant and the Jharkhand Mukti Morcha (Jharkhand Liberation Front) organized a number of peasant movements in the seventies. During the period from 1972 to 1975 the Morcha launched a programme of forcible harvesting over the land that formerly belonged to tribes.

The developmental efforts made by the state and central government following the introduction of planned economy through five-year-plans also added to the increase of miseries and deprivation of the tribals. While certain parts of the region were heavily industrialized, other parts were predominantly rural and in both the parts of the region developmental efforts caused sufferings of the tribal population. Industrialization and urbanization have robbed the local tribes of their traditional means of livelihood without providing adequate scope for their absorption and rehabilitation. In the rural parts of the tribal belt construction of big dams has submerged large tract of lands and villages forcing them to face the problem of rehabilitation. Tribal reaction to this problem is evident in their slogan "they have made us refugees in our own home." With the participation of Dhanbad based A.K. Roy's Marxist Coordination Committee in the Jharkhand movement, the fight of the tribes for a homeland acquired a new militancy and increasingly they resorted to the politics of extremism. The Jharkhand state was formed on November 15, 2000 which left a legacy of violent struggle for the uplift of the tribal people.

The state of Chhatisgarh which was carved out of Madhya Pradesh on November 1, 2000, owes its origin to the long standing demand of the people. People's demands were voiced by almost all the major national parties as well as regional political formations. Unlike the Jharkhand movement, people's demand for a separate Chhatisgarh state was least characterized by violent methods. The state is the home of a number of primitive tribes and 45% of its total area is covered by forest. The Gonds, Murias, Bhumyas, Baigas, Kamars, Kawars and Halbas are the major tribes of the state. It is bounded by Andhra Pradesh in the south and Jharkhand and Orissa on the east which facilitate movement of the rebels between Andhra Pradesh and Jharkhand. The tribes in the past have persistently resisted interference of the outsiders and rulers in their way of life and to assert their traditional inalienable right on the local resources, land and forest. Further, they have protested against the commercial exploitation of forest resources by contractors. Growth of mega industries in steel, aluminum and cement has affected their traditional life style in recent time.

In Andhra Pradesh the outlawed People's War Group is active since 1980. It was formed by a school teacher Kondapally Seetharamaiah who left his job at a school and turned in to a radical activist. He recruited followers for his group who believed in the Maoist dictum of bringing about a "revolution from the barrel of a gun." They organized armed peasant movement and advocated for revolution in the countryside. "The group then projected itself as the voice of the poor and landless and fought oppressive landlords." The group in course of time spread its activities to Chhatisgarh, Orissa and Jharkhand and developed links with other Maoist rebel groups of Bihar and Nepal. The merger of various extremist groups and their concentration in certain areas where there is little economic development with a vast mass of poor people is a new phase of development in the terrorist movement of the country.

As far as the state of Orissa is concerned,the tribal population comes under two distinct tribal regions of the country viz., (i) the Chhotanagpur plateau and its extension, and (ii) the Eastern Ghat ranges, Dandakaranya and Chhatisgarh region. While the Santal, Kolha, Munda, Bhuinya, Kisan and Oraon are the major tribes of the former tribal region comprising the districts of Sundargarh,Keonjhar and Mayurbhanj in northern parts of the state, the major tribes of southern Orissa in the latter tribal region are the Khonds, the Gonds, the Saoras, the Parojas, the Koyas and the Gadabas inhabiting the districts of Baud–Khondmal, Kalahandi, Koraput, Malkangiri and Gajapati. The tribes of north Orissa adjacent to south Bihar were exposed to Christianity, industrialization and urbanization from a long time before independence and developed an affiliation to the tribes of Chhotanagpur, giving rise to an inter tribal solidarity. The southern tribes on the other hand were mostly localized and passed through the influences of the neighbouring people of Orissa and Andhra Pradesh. Some of them like the Gdabas are most primitive tribes. In recent past some of them have also been exposed to mining activities and industrialization in Koraput, following establishment of the National Aluminum Company (NALCO), a public sector undertaking of the Government of India. Mining and industrialization has led to growth of urbanization and development of communication facilities which has helped the tribes to build up inter- tribal unity among their numerous tribal groups. The tribes of Orissa of both the tribal regions had never been united at the political level.[27] The statewide growth of tribal identity is a very recent political phenomenon which was markedly in evidence in the Kalinganagr agitation in 2006 directed against industrialization and displacement in which the tribal people of the whole state as well as tribals from the neighboring states were involved. It is alleged that the agitation turned violent in view of the involvement of the Maoists.

It is clear from the foregoing accounts that the poor people in tribal and rural areas of central India have been facing certain pressing problems at the wake of liberalization, privatization and globalization. Mining and industrialization leads to land alienation. The process also leads to repletion of water resources and deforestation. The rivers are polluted because of industrialization and discharge of industrial waste water, causing sufferings to many. The habitat and livelihood of the people are seriously affected which results in growing discontentment.[28] Their experience has proved it beyond doubt that the income generated by the government from industries and mines are never utilized in the welfare activities of the affected people. Most of them face a host of new problems in their new surroundings. Any drive for industrialization by the government very much gives them the message that their land, forest and water, the means of their livelihood and sustenance are at stake. During the period from 1950 to 1980 five million hectares of forest land has been used for non-agricultural purposes like setting up of industries and construction of roads. The wealth that is generated in this process follows the general prevailing trend of making the rich, richer and the poor, poorer.

The Maoists capitalize on this situation and spread terror among the government and the people. They strive for rousing the peasants and sponsor peasant insurrections, totally rejecting the politics of parliamentary democracy. They aim at acquiring political power through protracted armed struggle based on guerrilla warfare which they call "New Democratic Revolution." Their strategy entails building up of bases in rural and remote areas, transforming them first to guerilla zones and then to liberated zones, besides area-wise seizure and encircling of cities with the ultimate objective of people's government through people's war.

The Maoist menace, thus, may be viewed as a revolutionary movement which mobilizes its supporters from the exploited classes who are away from the orbit of political power. It focuses attention on the relationship between the state and the peasantry. The peasantry is protesting against the denial of subsistence rights worked out in state policy. Judged by the trend that the movement has followed over the past few years, it is clear that it has been passing through a critical phase of violence. Violent methods did characterize the earlier movements of the downtrodden sections of the people of India in ameliorating their grievances. What distinguishes the present movement from the earlier ones is its large-scale violence. Participation of women in the movement in large number is widening its social base. Recurrent incidents of violence without the knowledge of the intelligence agencies negate the state claim that the Maoist terror is under control.

REFERENCES AND FOOTNOTES

1. Statement of the Prime Minister in the meeting on internal security. As many as 19 meetings have been convened till the end of December, 2007.
2. Sitaram Yechuri, CPI (M) "Maoist Violence: Revolutionary or Anarchist," December 1, 2005
3. *Yahoo News,* December 22, 2007.
4. *The Times of India,* (Bhubaneswar-national), 17 July, 2006.
5. *The Times of India,* (Bhubaneswar-national), 20 December, 2007.
6. *The Times of India,* January 31, 2008.
7. *The Times of India,* January 2, 2008.
8. *The Times of India,* January 4, 2008.
9. *The Times of India,* February17, 2008.
10. *The Times of India,* February 18, 2008.
11. Indiatimes.com, August 13, 2007.
12. Quoted in B. Raman, South Asia Analysis Group, Paper No 446, April 18, 2002.
13. See the statements of the rebels circulated in the *Sambad* in Oriya, 26 November, 2007.
14. *The Christian Science Monitor,* "Maoist rebels spread across rural India" from the August 22, 2006 edition.
15. *Ibid.*
16. Information gathered by the authors from the villagers and others government agencies.
17. *The Samaj,* (Sambalpur edition in Oriya) January 20, 2008A.
18. Sunday *Times of India,* (Bhubaneswar-National), January 20, 2008.
19. See K.P.S. Gill, *Pioneer,* April 28, 2007.

20. *Sambad,* (Sambalpur edition in Oriya), January 14, 2008.
21. *The Times of India,* (Bhubaneswar-National), February 1, 2008.
22. *The Times of India,* (Bhubaneswar-National), February 4, 2008.
23. For an account of the protest movements see R.N. Mishra and A. Mitra "Industrialisation and Protest Movements in Orissa" www.Boloji.com., Analysis, January 14, 2007.
24. Sumanta Benerjee, "Naxalbari and the Left Movement" in Ghanashyam Shah (ed) *Social Movement and the State,* (New Delhi), Sage Publications, 2002, pp. 128-135.
25. *Ibid.,* pp. 146-150.
26. See *Tribal Heritage of India,* Vol. I, (New Delhi: Vikas Publishing House, Pvt. Ltd, 1977) p. 1. Also see V. Venkat Rao, *A Century of Tribal Politics in North-East India (1874-1974),* (New Delhi: S. Chand & Co. 1976 and Surajit Sinha, "Tribal Solidarity Movement: A Review" in K. Suresh Singh (ed.) *Tribal Situation in India,* (Simla: India Institute of Advanced Studies, 1972), pp. 410-22.
27. R.N. Mishra, "Tribal Politics in Orissa", *Teaching Politics,* Vol. VIII, 3 & 4, 1 (University of Delhi), 1982, pp. 21-36.
28. Michel M. Cernea "Understanding and Preventing Impoverishment from Displacement: Reflection on the State of Knowledge", *Social Action,* (Delhi) July-September, 1995, Vol. 45, No. 3, pp. 261-275.

7

Human Rights of Accused to Legal Defence under Indian Criminal Justice Administration

RANJAN KUMAR MISHRA*

A person who is accused of a crime is morally and mentally a shattered man and in most cases is unable to defend himself against the resourceful state machinery for lack of legal knowledge and pecuniary resources. The right of the accused to be represented by a counsel in India has been recognized and practiced from ancient times. A study of the administration of Criminal Justice as prevailing under the ancient Hindu Legal System and Muslim Legal System unfold many cases wherein a person accused of a crime had his honover and dignity protested and defended by Pandits and Maulvis well versed in scriptures, literatures and God's revealations.[1]

In America, if a person is arrested he must be afforded opportunity to consult lawyer of his own choice and if he is unable to employ a counsel it is the duty of the court to employ a lawyer for him.[2] In India, before Article 22(1), which envisagesthe accused's rights to consult and engage a lawyer was incorporated in the Constitution of India, the right to

* Assistant Professor, Tripura Govt. Law College, Agartala, Tripura.

legal defence was protected by section 303 of the criminal procedure code, 1973 [section 340 (1) in the 1898 (code)]. The said section embodied a statutory ritght which could be invoked by any person accused of an offence for the protection of his rights. By the insertion of Article 2291) in our Constitution this statutory right of an accused to be represented by a lawyer of his choice has been elevated to the status of a fundamental right. The language used under Article 22(1) thus says that "No person who is arrested—shall be denied the aright to consult, and to be defended by a legal practitioner of his choice." The rationale of such aright has been appropriately summed up by Medgavker J. of Bombay High Court[3] as follows:

"If the ends of justice and the spirit of justice is fairness, then each side should have equal opportunity to prepare its own case, and to its evidence fully, freely and fairly before the court. This necessarily involves preparation. Such preparation is far more effective from the point of view of justice, if it is made with the aid of skilled advice—advice so valuable that in the gravest of criminal trials when life or death hangs in the balance, the very state which undertakes the prosecution of the prisoner also provides him, if poor, with such legal assistance". Under the Indian Code of Criminal Procedure, 1898, section340 (1) (Section 303 of the Cr. P. C.) only extended opportunities to the accused for being defended by a legal practitioner of his choice. Though the section provided that any person accused of an offence before a criminal court or against whom criminal proceedings were instituted under the Code, as of right, be defended by a pleader, it in no way cast a duty upon state to provide the accused with free legal aid. On the other hand, the rules of court procedure framed by various High Courts for the guidance of subordinate courts provide that when a person who is charged with capital offfences punishable with death is unable to defend himself by a lawyer because of poverty or other reasons, the State Government should provide him with a lawyer[4]. This rule which is now contained in section 304 of the Criminal Procedure Code was applied by the High Courts and Courts of Session only when the accused was charged with murder or in cases of other capital offences punishable with death penalty. Thus, an analysis of Article 22(1) of the Indian Constitution reaffirms the fact that apart from making the statutory right, enshrined in section 340(1) of 1898 code, a fundamental Constitutional guarantee inviolable by ordinary legislation, the Article has in no way modified or improved the provisions of the section 340(1) of the 1998 Code. But with induction of Article 39 A into the Constitution of India the desideratum of the basic right to legal defence has been transformed into an inalienable fundamental right of the indigent accused to be provided with free legal aid.

When does the Right to Defence begin?

According to Article 22(1) of the Constitution of India a person is entitled to consult a legal practitioner of his choice as soon as he is taken into police custody following a commission of a criminal offence. In Motibai v. State[5] it was held that Article 22 "gives to a person arrested a right to consult a legal adviser of his own choice and to be defended by him from the moment of his arrest and also to have an effective interview with the lawyer, out of hearing of the police officers though it may be within their presence". In Nandini Satpathy v. P. L. Dani[6] the court held that the right to consult an advocate of one's choice does not mean that the persons who are under arrest or custody can be denied this right. While explaining the true spirit of Article 22(1), the court said that "it is fundamental to the rule of law that the services of a lawyer shall be available for consultation to any accused person under circumstance of near custodial interrogation".[7]

In Nandini Satpathy's case the court, following the American Miranda case[8] enlarged the scope of the right to counsel during custodial interrogation. It held that, the right to consult a lawyer at the near custodial interrogation stage would promote the observance of the right against self-incrimination and obviate its over reaching by the police. It said further that on account of imbalance between the policemen and the accused who is poor, illiterate and ignorant, the latter loses the advantage of adversary process. He cannot also make a choice between speech and silence during interrogation. Even others who had prior legal advice might overcome easily by secret interrogation process. So, the presence of a lawyer during interrogation minimizes coercion, ensures accurate recording of statements of the accused and facilitates their faithful transmission to the trial court. It pointed out that the right against self-incrimination in Article 20(3) and the right to counsel in Article 22(1) may be telescoped to permit the presence of the advocate of the accused during interrogation. The court also, in the instant case, laid down certain guidelines in the context of accused's right to consult a lawyer during interrogation. First, the court held that if the accused expresses a desire to have his lawyer by his said when the police interrogate him, then the same should not denied to him. At the same time, if the accused's advocate does not appear without a reasonable time then the police is free to carry out the interrogation secondly in the absence of a lawyer of his choice and after being examined, the accused must be taken to a magistrate, doctor or other willing and responsible non-partisan officer or non-official before whom he may unburden the suffering that he had undergone without any inhibition and beyond the hearing of the police. After this, accused must be taken to judicial or some other custody making him inaccessible to the police. The Collector should then record the relevant conversation and commutate it to the nearest magistrate.

The question whether the guidelines laid down in Nandini Satpathy case were in the nature of binding directions was raised before the Delhi High Court, in Ram Lalwani v. State.9 After considering the observations in Nandini and Miranda, the High Court felt that subject to a few exceptions Section 162 of Cr. P. C.,1973, and Sections 24 to 30 of Indian Evidence Act, 1872, do take care of the constitutional rights by excluding evidence of all self-incriminatory statements whether involuntary or otherwise and, therefore, there was no need to give any directions. The High Court observed that the main objective of the Supreme Court in Nandini case was to make the police more sensitive to humanity and to respect the however and dignity of an individual. Thus, if at any time the accused wishes to have the services of this lawyer during interrogation in order to be free from the fear of being subjected to physical or psychic torture, then the police must make it a policy to allow the accused a lawyer of this choice. The high Court held that the Supreme Court was not laying down a binding direction but only a precedent policy for the police to follow:

The claim for permitting an accused's counsel to be present during interrogation came up for consideration in Abdul Rajak Haji Mohammed v. Union of India.[10] On reading of Article 20(3) and 22(1) of the constitution, an accused person is entitled to the presence of an advocate during interrogation by a police officer. In Rajak Haji Mohammad case, petitioner approached the Sessions Court for anticipatory bail because he apprehended arrest for offences under Foreign Exchange. Regulation Act, 1973. The court rejected his prayer and advised him to attend the Enforcement directorate and to surrender his passport. He then prayed for taking a lawyer with him during interrogation, which was rejected by the court. Thereupon he approached the High Court, which after examining the provisions of the Act and the case law laid down, by the Supreme Court reasoned as under:

"On a reading of Article 20(3) and Article (22) 1 of the Constitution, it appears clear that an accused person is entitled to the presence of an Advocate during his interrogation by a police officer. That position has been assented without reservation in Nandini Satapthy's case—If an accused person during interrogation by a police officer be permitted, the right to the presence of his advocate; there is no reason why an accused person or a persons suspected of an offence, should not be afforded the same right when he is being interrogated by an officer of the Enforcement Directorate. There does not appear to be anything in the Foreign Exchange Regulation Act, which forbids the presence of an advocate during interrogation. Quite contrary the provisions of the FERA permit such a right to a person summoned under the section.[11]

The Court concluded that it was only in cases where the accused or the suspect made a written application to the Enforcement Officers to his advocate's presence during interrogation that the accused or suspect must be permitted to do so.[12]

In K.T. Advani v. State,[13] the Delhi High Court held that

if a suspect is entitled to the presence of a counsel in an investigation governed by the Code of Criminal Procedure, there is nothing in the provisions of the Foreign Exchange Regulation Act which purport explicitly or implicitly must such right. If the right to the presence of counsel were fundamental to the rule of law it makes little difference if investigation is one under Code of Criminal Procedure or independently of it in view of the provisions of Article 22(1) of the Constitution. The divergent procedure which has the effect of divesting a suspect of certain right, privileges and safeguards which are available in a corresponding investigation under the Code of Criminal Procedure would itself provide further justification for the right of the presence of counsel, to deny such a suspect the right to consult counsel and to the presence of counsel at the state of investigation, where the investigatory procedure makes a departure from the normal procedure and deprives such suspect of a member of rights, privileges and safeguards would open such procedure to justifiable criticism of being unjust, unfair and unreasonable. The Delhi High Court further held that to deny such right of suspect to consult counsel and the presence of counsel at the time of interrogation would be antithesis of just, fair and reasonable procedure contemplated by Article 21 of the Constitution.[14]

The Supreme Court in Delhi Judicial Service Association, in Tis Hazari Courts, Delhi v. State of Gujrat,[15] held that arrested judicial officer should be permitted to have legal consultation and his medical examination has to be conducted in the presence of his lawyer. These decisions are thus an offshoot of Nandini Satpathy. The attempt to reason out this right from the reasoning in Nandini Satpathy case seems to encouraging.16

In order to make the right to consult a lawyer more meaningful, care should be taken that the interviews take place out of the hearing of the police though within their presence. It is important. It is important that there should be a free interaction between the lawyer and the accused without the fear of interruption by the police officer. The consultation with the lawyer may be in the presence of the police officer but not within the hearing.[17] At the time of consultation the accused should have free and unfettered consultation not only with his lawyer but also with his friends and relations out of hearings of the police officer. This right of free access to an interview between the accused and the lawyer extends to communications between the accused and his relatives as well. Any unreasonable survilliance and restirictions kept during his interview with them is a transgression of his right of communication.18 of course, this right should not be unfettered and must be made subject to reasonable restrictions like the taking into consideration, the time and convenience of both the police authorities as well as the party seeking an interview.

In United States the police are required to inform the accused of his right to get legal aid immediately on arrest. It is pity that in spite of the weighty words, constitutional and legal provisions, the police in this country almost always refuse to allow when lawyer to interviews their clients in custody unless covered by umbrella of a court order. It would improve the image of the police tremendously if the police on their own permit the accused to consult his lawyer immediately on his arrest as suggested by Krishna Iyer, J. at the time of interrogation. The fear of losing a confession due to lawyer's presence should not inhibit the police from giving effect to legal and constitutional provisions. It the accused is really repentant, he will make a confession even in the presence of a Lawyer.

In its pertinent part Article 22(1) says that a person arrested shall not be denied " that right to consult and be defended by a legal practitioner by choice." Defence of a person arrested by a police and consultation of a lawyer by a person arrested is two distinct and different rights. The occasion for the exercise of these rights are also different. A person arrested needs badly the assistance of lawyer during interrogation, as he may not incriminate him. Consultation with a lawyer during interrogation will enable the person arrested to decide when he may exercise his right to silence. The spirit of the right to consult a lawyer is that custodial interrogation should not be incommunicado. Now that Nandini Satpathy has recognized that the right to counsel makes the right against self-incrimination effective, the supreme court in D.K. Basu case has transformed these rights into a bulwark against custodial violence by permitting a lawyer during interrogation. Counsel could advise the accused of proper statements to make, should the accused wish to make a statement; see to it that the police does not use brutal means to obtain a confession; and assure that the police does not trap the defendant in to a making a statement coercive atmosphere of the invisible police process.[19]

Right to Legal Aid

The Constitution of India under Article 39-A has provided that the opportunities for securing justice are not denied to any citizen by reason of economic or any other disabilities. A comprehensive report on legal aid was submitted in may 1973, by the Krishna Iyer committee appointed by the Government of India by an order dated 27/101972. As a consequence of the Report of the Committee a new Article 39 A was added in the Directive Principles of State Policy of the Constitution by the 42nd constitutional Amendment Act,1976, making a provision for free legal aid to ensure that opportunities for securing justice should not be denied to any citizen by reason of economic or other disabilities." However, no concrete steps were taken in this regard for providing various schemes of legal aid and, therefore, a second committee was appointed by the Government of India, headed by Mr. Justice Bhagwati and both Krishna Iyer were members. The committee submitted a comprehensive report containing various recommendations on the basis of which the Central Govt. of India and the State Govts. made several schemes for providing legal aid and advise to the poor. One of the important aims objects of these schemes was to achieve social justice and to reduce social disparity by providing free legal aid to the weaker sections of the society and by encouraging and promoting settlement by conciliation in legal proceedings. For the effective implementation of these schemes a new legislation, namely, Legal Services Authorities Act, 1987 was enacted but which was delayed for ten years for implementation. The Act was implemented in the year 1997 and various Legal Services Authorities were established at National, State and District level throughout India to implement the schemes of Legal Aid and Lok Adalat.

Further more, as it has been held by the Supreme Court, the State is under a Constitutional Mandate (implicit in Article 21) to provide free legal aid to an indigent accused person, and this constitutional obligation to provide legal aid does not arise only when the trial commences but also attaches when the accused is for the first time produced before the Magistrate, as also when he remained from time to time.[20] The Rajasthan High Court accorded the right to legal assistance to a poor woman.[21] In the instant case, the petitioner was denied an interview with a legal counsel after being arrested and detained, in police custody. The court held that a denial of this right was a clear violation of the right to consult a legal counsel of one's choice guaranteed by Article 22(1) of the constitution and also section 303 of Code of Criminal Procedure.

Access to justice is an integral part of social justice enshrined in the Preamble of the Constitution. On this basis the Supreme Court, held in case of Hussainara Khatoon v. home Secretary, State of Bihar,[22] that "in view of our Indian society of which poor and weaker section constitute larger part of it, free legal service is inalienably relevant or reasonable, fair and just procedure for without it person suffering from economic or other disabilities would be denied of justice." Legal Aid is really voting else but equal justice in action and in fact is delivery system of social justice – intended to reach justice to common man. This is a constitutional right of every accused person who is unable to engage a lawyer.[23] The State is under a mandate to provide a lawyer to an accused person if the circumstances of the case and the needs of justice so required, provided of course the accused person does not object to the provision of such a lawyer. The State's obligation starts when the accused was produced first time before the court of Magistrate. That is the stage at which an accused needs competent legal services. The Magistrate or Session Judge, before whom the accused appears, is under an obligation to inform the accused that, "if he is unable to engage the services of a lawyer on account of poverty or indigence, he is entitled to obtain free legal aid at the cost of State."[24]

In M.H. Hoskot v. State of Maharashtra[25] regarding the right to free legal aid, Justice Krishna Iyer declared, "This is state's duty and not Government's charity." If a prisoner is unable to exercise his constitutional and statutory right of appeal including special leave to appeal for want of legal assistance, there is implicit in the Court under Article 142, read with Articles 21 and 39 A of the Constitution, the power to assign counsel to the prisoner provided he does not object to the lawyer named by the court. Equally, is the implication that the state which sets the law in motion must pay the lawyer an amount fixed by the court.

In state of Maharastra v. Manubhai Pragaji Vashi[26] the court has considerably widened the scope of the right to free legal aid. The court held that in order to provide "the free legal aid" it is necessary to have welltrained lawyers in the country. This is only possible if there were adequate number of law colleges with sufficient number of well-trained or properly equipped law graduates in all branches necessary infrastructure, good teachers and staff. Since the Government is unable to establish adequate number of law colleges, it is the duty of the Government to permit establishments of duly recognized private law colleges and afford them grants in-aid on similar lines on which it is given to Government recognized law colleges. This would facilitate these colleges to function effectively and in a meaningful manner and turn out year after year. This will in turn enable the state and other authorities to provide free legal aid and ensure that opportunities for securing justice are not denied to any citizen on account of any disability.

In Suk Das v. Union Territory of Arunachal Pradesh,[27] the court has held that failure to provide free legal aid to an accused at the state cost, unless refused by the accused, would vitiate the trial. He need not apply for the same. Free legal aid at the State cost is a fundamental right of a person accused of an offence and this right is implicit in the requirement of reasonable, fair and just procedure prescribed by Article 21. This right cannot be denied to him on the ground that he has failed to apply for it. The Magistrate is under an obligation to inform the accused of this right and inquire that he wishes to be represented on the state's cost, unless he refused to take advantage of it. In the instant case, the appellant was tried and sentenced to two years imprisonment under section 506 read with section 34, IPC. He was not represented at the trial by any lawyer by reason of his inability to afford legal representation. The High Court held that the trial was not vitiated since no application was made by him. On appeal the Supreme Court set aside the conviction on the ground that he was not provided legal aid at the trial which was volatile of Article 21 of the Constitution.

In Sheela Barse v. State of Maharashtra[28] the Apex Court held that "it is a sine qua non of justice and where it is not provided, injustice is likely to result." In this case Bhagwati J. observed that the court had occasion to point out in numerous decisions that "Legal assistance to the poor and indigent who is arrested and put in jeopardy of his life or personal liberty as a constitutional imperative is mandated not only by Article 39 A but also by Articles 14 and 21.[29] Although the court has not specifically said that custodial interrogation should take place in the presence of the counsel for the female suspect, the comprehensive direction given by the court on legal aid might enable the District legal Aid Committee to provide the suspect with a lawyer during custodial interrogation on her request.

Thus it may be summed up that "right to legal aid" to the poor and down trodden has been accepted by the judiciary as the backbone of the "human right to fair trial and the approach of the Indian judiciary towards the implementation of this human right has been realistic and praiseworthy. It is now well settled that the duty of the Magistrate and Session Judge, before whom an accused is presented to provide the services of a lawyer at the expense of the state is not dependent on the demand to be made by the accused and any trial would be vitiated if the accused remains unrepresentative by a lawyer. The only exception to this rule is when the accused himself refuses to accept the services of a lawyer provided to him at the cost of the state.

References

1. Chaturbedi A. N., *Right of Accused under Indian Constitution,* 1984, Deep and Deep Publication, New Delhi, p. 231.
2. Powell V Albama. 247 U. S. 45.
3. In re. Uewlyn Evans, AIR 1926, Bom 551.
4. Section 304, Criminal Procedure Code, 1973.
5. Matibai v. State, 1954, Cr. L. J. 1951 (Raj).
6. AIR 1978 Sc 1025, 1978, Cr. L. J. 968, 976.
7. Reiterated by V.R. Krishna Iyer, J. in Nandini Satpathy.
8. Minranda v. Arizona, 384 US 430 (1966).
9. 1981 Cr. L. J. 97 (Del).
10. 1986 Cr. L. J. 2018 (Bom)
11. Ibid., at 2020 (per Justice V. N. Mehta)
12. Ibid.
13. 1985 Cr. L.J. 1325 (Delhi) (per Anand J.)
14. *Ibid.,* at 1327
15. AIR 1991 SC 2197 at 2213.
16. K. N. Chandrasekharan Pollai, *Criminal Procedure,* Vol. XXII A. S. I. L., 208 at 249 (1988)
17. Surinder Singh V. Emperor AIR 1930 Lah. 945;
18. Francis Coralie v. U. T. of Delhi, 1981 Cr. L. J. 306 (S.C), AIR 1981 S. C. 738.
19. Khatri (II) v. State of Bihar, 1981, SCC (G) 228.
20. Moti Bai v. State, 1954 G. L. J. 1951 Raj.
21. Surinder Singh V. Emperor AIR 1930 Lah. 945;
22. Francis Coralie v. U. T. of Delhi, 1981 Cr. L. J. 306 (S.C), AIR 1981 S. C. 738.
23. AIR 1979 SC 1369.
24. AIR 1979 SC 1369, 1374.
25. Khatri and others v. state of Bihar, AIR 1981 SC 928,
26. 76. AIR 1978 SC 1548.
27. (1995) 5 SCC 739.
28. (1986) 25 SCC 401.
29. Swaran Singh V. State of Punjab, AIR 1957 SC 637.

8

Rights of Children Affected by Terrorism (With special Reference to State of Tripura)

B.N. BEHERA*

Children are the greatest gift to the humanity. Mankind has best hold of itself. The children signify eternal optimism in the human being and always provide the potential for human development. If the children are better equipped with a broader human output, the society will feel happy with them. Neglecting the children means loss to the society as a whole. If children are deprived of their childhood—society, economically, physically and mentally—the nation gets deprived of the potential human resources for social progress, economic empowerment and social stability.

Due to poverty, children are subjected to many visible and invisible sufferings and disabilities, in particular, health, intellectual, social degradation and deprivation, poor economic conditions and contrary social circumstances force the children to work as boot polish, milk selling, newspaper selling, rickshaw pulling, begging and daily wages earner. Even children are also victim of poverty and hungriness by terrorism in India. When they became grown-up, they are

* Lecturer, Tripura Govt. Law College, Agartala, Tripura.

so weakened with hunger and illness so they become problem before country as because they are unable for self-sufficiency. Our Nobel loureate Rabindranth Tagore once express "We are miserably bankrupt in social, educational, spiritual and universal cognition."

Tripura is one of the border states of NorthEast India and it is almost surrounded by Bangladesh except the north-eastern part which is bounded by Assam and Mizoram. It is an area of 10,492 sqkm with a population of 31,91,168 (2005). Nearly 60 per cent of the total land of Tripura is hilly, while the remaining 40 per cent constitute plain lands. Tripura was ruled by the Maharajas for about 1,300 years before its accession to the Republic of India on October 15, 1949. Tripura made a Union Territory and then it was declared a state of India on 21st January 1972.

As per 2001 census the total population of Tripura was 31,91,168. The original inhabitants of Tripura were the tribal. The demographic scenario of this state has been completely changes due to partition of the country. The influx of Bengali Hindus from the then East Pakistan to Tripura outnumbered the original inhabitants. These migrants have taken over increasing charge of the administration, trade and commerce and cultural life of Tripura. The native Tripura tribal with their traditional economy and archaic ways of living have had a subordinate place through out in their won homeland.

The population complex of Tripura is different from that of any tribal state within the North Eastern region. Because the tribal of Tripura are outnumbered by the Bengal Hindu immigrants from the neighbouring Bangladesh. So, Tripura was not listed as tribal state in the constitution of India, although its original inhabitants are the Tripura and other tribal. Bengali and Kokborak language is the official language of the state.

Due to maladministration, political dominance and hippocratic attitude of leadership are the main cause of terrorism. Needless to say that that Tripura rebels are getting training and logistic help from Bangladesh, Pakistan and Hong Kong. Thereby, "All Tripura Tiger Force" and "National Liberation Front of Tripura" hard core banned terrorist organisation are continuing their activities in Tripura.

Due to terrorism the peoples of Tripura are migrated from one place to another place. Murder, kidnap and abduction are the prime activities for the collection of ransom. Peace living society are disrupted due to activities of several terrorist organisation. According to above aspect the children are vulnerable section of the society in Tripura.

Human society has witnessed substantial changes in the passage of time through democratic process. After the passing of 60 years of India independence innocent children are not protected by legislative, executive as well as judiciary interference. According to preliminary investigation on child's rights are not protected due to terrorist activities. They live in the house without any security and very often they are victimise due to attack of rebels group. Life, liberty, equality, fraternity and justice are the dead letters for the children who are living in the state of Tripura. However government of Tripura rehabilitated and affords entire expense to 42 number of children who are victims by terrorism.

Children are our greatest hope and asset. In India there are over 350 million children. They constitute 35 per cent of the total population. They are our most vital national resource. Right of the child, child care, and child development problems have been attracting the attention world over. Article 18 of the U.N. convention of the Rights of the child, 1989 recognises the right of the child to be protected by any meance. U.N. was declared, 1979 is International Year of the Child .

Article 25(2) of the Universal Declaration of Human Rights express "Childhood are entitled to special care and assistance."

Indian Government has drawn up a National Program of Action (NPA) taking into account the development of goals for the 1990's enunciated at the World Summit for children held on New York in September, 1990.

The founding father of the Constitution, Dr. B.R. Ambedkar, was for ahead in his wisdom projected in the Directive Principles including the children as beneficiaries. Their deprivation has deleterious effect on the efficacy of the democracy and the rule of law. The principle of substantive legitimate expectation i.e. exception of minimum opportunity, standards of living, good or positive mind-set should be applied from welfare state like India.

Children are the future of the country and they need special protection because of their age, physical and mental faculties. The constitution of India has conferred enabling powers on the Government to make special provision for children in pursuance of Article 15 (3) of the Constitution. Every child is nation's wealth. Under Article 39(7) of the Constitution provided that children are given opportunities and facilities to develop in a healthy manner and youth are protected against exploitation and against moral and material abandonment.

The Hon'ble Supreme Court in Sheela Barse and other V. Union of India has expressed that a child is a national assets. In Indian scenario a child requires proper care, love, affection and nourishment but experience shows that the children are subjected to maltreatment in some situation. A child is treated with cruelty when his parents are victimised by terrorism. Every child has a right to love and be loved and to grow-up in an atmosphere of love and affection, moral and material security and this is possible only if the child is brought up in a family and congenial environment.

Lastly, children are "Supremely important national asset" and the future well being of the nation depends on how its children grow and develop. The great poet Milton put it admirably when he said,

"Child shows the man as morning shows the day."

REFERENCES

1. The Constitution of India Article –14,15(2), 21,21(A), 23,24,39(F), 86th amendment and others related provisions.
2. "Quality of Life" – Fakhrudin
3. *Human Rights* – Dr. Umesh Chandra
4. *Human Rights and Social Work* – A. S. Kohli.
5. *Law of the Child in India* – S. P. Shaw.
6. *Law Relating to Women and Children,* Dr. S.C. Tripathi.
7. *North East India: A Systematic Geography* – N. N. Bhattacharjee
8. The Child Labour (Prohibition and Regulation) Act, 1986.
9. The Children Act, 2003.
10. Some Basic Statistics of Tripura – 2006 by Planning (Statistics) Department, Govt. of Tripura.

9

Customary Laws in the Social Structure of the Jamatias of Tripura

K.B. JAMATIA*

Law consists of a set of princiles which permit the use of force to maintain political and social organization in a particular society. When an individual's mode of verbal and non- verbal behaviour is all his own, it is termed as typical and idiosyncrasy. When some people of the society in contact with him share this, it becomes a usage. When a time dimension is added to initial spatial extension, i.e. when the behaviour of the junior generation is affected and influenced by an individual's one time idiosyncrasy, we have a custom. When organized force steps in as a sanction and drive behind a custom, it becomes a law, an institution. But in tribal society, it is difficult to pinpoint as to when and how exactly this transformation takes place.

It is also difficult, unlike the modern law or jurisprudence, to differentiate between a usage and a custom in the tribal society. Usage is in fact the early stage of custom. By usage we generally mean those habits which are often repeated by the people of a given society. "A custom begins", as Prof. Starke succinctly put, "where the usage ends. Usage represents

* Registrar (Officiating), Tripura University, Agartala, Tripura.

the twilight stage of custom and is a habit of action that has not yet received the legal attestation." Usages may be inconsistent and contradictory but this can never be the case with the custom. Thus usage, in order to become custom, has to receive the general acceptance of recognition by the people of the society. It is not necessary that usages should always precede a custom. It is also not a necessary corollary that a usage must always become a custom. A usage, however, has to have the ingredients like long duration, uniformity and consistency, generality of practice, etc to become a custom.

If the above given definition is taken too literally, it may be difficult to locate law in the institutions of the tribal society. It is mainly so because the tribal society is devoid of policemen or magistrates to fit into the role of somebody. There is no legislation in the sense we know in the modern civil society. When laws come into existence, it is not a selected group of individuals, like the legislature, who are responsible for it, but the society as a whole. The tribal laws are identical with ethical norms and public opinion, and it does not distinguish between crimes and torts i.e. between public and private wrongs as is done in modern jurisprudence.

In tribal society, public opinion is considered as one of the most powerful influences in the life of its individual members. The number of people constituting a tribal society being generally small, the total picture we have is that of a well-organized homogeneous group of people, where each is known to each other. The social institutions of any society are 'those patterned sets of positions, relations and activities involved in biological reproduction, socialization and enculturation, production and distribution of goods and services, and the maintenance of order. The total network of all the social institutions and the connections among them constitutes the core social structure or social organization of the society'. The social structure is that important system of elements which lasts and which everyone takes account of. The tribals have their own social structure, which are closely-knit and self-contained units. As they form a community of their own in a particular territory, their relations are direct and intimate. This is, perhaps, why Andre Beteille, a renowned sociologists, said, 'the tribal communities are small, isolated self-sufficient and autonomous'. Social structure indicates an ordered arrangement of parts, which can be treated as transposable, being relatively invariant, while the parts themselves are variable. It has been noticed that laws often coincide with ethical norms and thus a collective opinion is found to be very vigilant in the tribal society and the most striking feature of their society is the preponderance of the law of torts over the law of crimes.

Nature and Characteristics of Customary Laws

Intention: In the tribal society intention is not taken into cognizance while determining the legality or illegality of a person's action. On other hand, modern civil society recognizes intention as one of the important determinants of the legality or illegality of an action. Even the provocation is accepted as a partial excuse for the commission of a crime. According to the customary laws of the tribals, the result of an action is important rather than an enquiry into the motive or presence of provocation.

Collective responsibility: Laws in the tribal society are based on kinship principle. Justice is administered through kin groups. Village councils consisting of the representatives from different kin groups conglomerate for judgment over the breaches of the tribal norms. Where there are chiefs, the cases are decided by them, rarely without consulting family heads or village headmen e.g. the Jamatia Akra in the case of the Jamatias of Tripura. The Hoda Akra is the supreme guardian and the interpreter of customs in the Jamatia society. Whatever decision is taken, the whole Jamatia society bears the responsibility. Divorce can be obtained among the Jamatias, on the adjudication by the Hoda Akra. Insanity, cruelty, impotence, infidelity, barrenness, adultery are the grounds on which divorce can be sought in the Hoda.

Evidence: In the administration of justice importance is stressed on establishment of the guilt which we generally call the evidence. But in the tribal society, an ordeal is decided upon. The accused may be asked, in the Jamatia society, by the Hoda Akra to go though some ordeals like putting his hands in boiling water or cutting of his hair and so on. If the accused escapes without injury, he is acquitted, otherwise he is guilty.

Wergild: Fine which is appropriated by the state in modern society as a sort of punishment is conspicuous by its absence in the tribal society. Instead fines are charged in their society which is generally paid as compensation or wergild to the aggrieved party. In paying wergild in compensation for the wrong done, there is again a gradation which determines how much is to be paid for a particular offence or felony, by whom and to whom. In case of divorce in the Jamatia society, the Akra decides how much to be paid by the husband to his wife as alimony and vice versa.

Punishment: From no where in the tribal society, barring in Uganda, do we have any evidence of imprisonment as a form of punishment. In the olden days, in deciding the punishment, there was often a gradation of crimes. Even the same crime may not be treated alike. In Jamatia society, the punishment may even be the death depending upon the nature and significance of the crime or felony. In 1985, a group of five anti-socials and thieves were buried alive after being found that they embezzled the golden-made head of Garia (Garia is the traditional God of the tribes of Tripura)

Conclusion

There has, of late, been a tendency to codify the customary laws of the tribes. There are obvious advantages to be gained from codification of the customary laws. The rules, if codified, are likely to become more precise and more accessible. The people would seem to be more willing to accept those rules which they themselves practised from the time of antiquity. But in view of the divergences between the practices of different tribes, codification might often mean compromise. The association, of which law is the institutional activity, is government. And it is the government to define the limit of compromise.

The functioning of the chieftainships of some tribes, wherever it still exists, seemed to have, in some cases, collided with the functioning of the modern democratic institutions like Panchayati system. With the dawn of independence the introduction of Statutory Panchayati System throughout India, urbanization and other arrangements of modern welfare state have adopted almost all the functions of the traditional tribal council and chieftainship. The traditional political organization of the tribal community in India, permitted to function during the pre-British and even during the British times, is now, since independence, threatened by the increasing pressures of the administrative control of the modern government. Some recent studies on the tribal socio-political formations have objectively demonstrated the fact that tribal societies have not been static ones and having potential for change they have kept on changing due to forces working from within and without.

With the emergence of the new institutions, some of the traditional leaders of tribes tried to swim with the new current, as there was fear of being drowned in the oblivion of the village masses The tribal councils which used to be powerful in directing the behaviour of its tribes are now soon weakening, for the administration has abrogated the right of the Council to sit in judgment for criminal cases. All these changes marred the age-old traditional institution of the tribes of Tripura also. Some tribes could withstand these changes, and some could not. As an outcome of this ineluctable process of change, the traditional Chieftainships of Reangs, Noatias, Tripuris almost became defunct. On the other hand, the Hoda system of the Jamatias appears to have established important links between 'old and new' ideas, values and institutions and operated both in traditional and modern constitutions. The socio-political set-up of the Jamatias thus, since independence, reflects a paradoxical situation in which traditional age-old Hoda system and modern democracy co-exist.

The Jamatia Hoda exists, and functions in its own genius. It does for the vitality of their culture that it has not disappeared altogether. The Jamatia Hoda is confronted with the problem of the preservation of their social existence and the transformation in the form of system of values. Modernity, in the form of education, hinduisation, westernization and also urbanization, has entered into their society but it has done so through assimilation and not through replacement. In the interaction between tradition and modernity, not all traditional values, ideas and attitudes are discarded. Rather they seemed to have been transferred to the new objects. This exemplifies the historical trend of continuity and change in society of the Jamatias of Tripura. This phenomenon can be called "modernity of tradition" in the society of the Jamatias.

NOTES AND REFERENCES

1. Tumin, Melvin M., *Social Stratification,* New Delhi, 1987.
2. Beteille, Andre, *Studies in Agrarian Social Structure,* Delhi, 1974.
3. Nadel, S.F., *The Theory of Social Structure,* London, 1965.
4. Vidyarthi, L.P. and Rai, B.K., *The Tribal Culture in India,* New Delhi, 1985.
5. Singh, Yogendra, *Modernization of Indian Tradition,* Jaipur, 1986.

10

An Inquiry in to the Process of Urbanisation in Tripura

INDRANEEL BHOWMIK*

Kingsley Davis (1962) considers urbanisation as a long-term process of transfer of human population from a spread out nature to that of a concentrated one, which all nations and states experience in its way of progress. Basically, urbanisation can be considered as an index of transformation of the traditional agrarian economy to a modern industrial country (Datta, 2006) and its history is traced back to the initiation of the industrial revolution and the consequent economic development. Presently developed countries are branded with high level of urbanisation and some of them are even experiencing slowing down of the process due to host of factors (Brockerhoff, 1999; Brockerhoff and Brennam 1998). India however, is typical of the developing countries and falls in the accelerating stage as per the three-fold classification of urbanisation[1].

The process of urbanisation in India has begun well in the late 18th century itself, but the real focus began only after the process of Census started. In India both civic status as well as demographic aspect is taken as criteria for declaring

* Assistant Professor in Economics, Women's College, Agartala, Tripura.

a settlement as urban[2]. The recent census of India (RGI, 2001) defined the urban places on the basis of the following criteria:

i) All places with a municipality, corporation, cantonment board or notified town area committee etc.

ii) All other places which satisfy the following criteria:
   a) Minimum population of 5000
   b) At least 75 % of male working population engaged in non-agricultural pursuits and
   c) A density of population of at least 400 persons per square Km.

The number of urban agglomeration / town in India has, over the last one-hundred years, grown from 1827 in 1901 to 5161 in 2001 and the number of urbanites during the same period increased from 2.58 crores (10.84 percent) in 1901 to 28.53 crores (27.78 percent) in2001. The extent of urbanisation in the north-eastern region of the country is further low and 15.4 percent of the population were urban dwellers in 2001 which however shows marked increase from the levels of 1981 and 1991, 11.8 percent & 13.8 percent respectively. Mizoram with 49.5 percent and Sikkim with 11.1 percent exhibits the highest and the least extent of urbanisation in the region. Manipur, Arunachal Pradesh, Nagaland and Meghalaya occupies the second, third, fourth and fifth place, while Tripura precedes Assam with 17 percent urbanites at the sixth place.

Objective, Scope & Methodology of the Study

The present study attempts to trace the process of urbanisation in Tripura. Starting with the extent of urbanisation in Tripura, the paper studies the trends and volume of urbanisation in the state. It further analyses the urban morphology and emphasizes on the present scenario. Moreover, the paper will map out the features of urbanisation and finally conclude with some policy suggestions. The study depends entirely on secondary data and Census publications are the major source. The standard mathematical estimations have been applied as and when required in the course of the study.

Extent of Urbanisation in Tripura

Table 1: District–wise Urban Population, Urban Proportion & Number of Urban Areas (UAs) in Tripura (2001)

District	*Total Population*	*Urban Population*	*Urban: Rural Ratio*	*No. of Urban Areas*
West Tripura	1532982	410067	27:73	13
South Tripura	767440	54167	7:93	4
Dhalai	307868	18867	6:94	3
North Tripura	590913	62669	11:89	3
Total	3199203	545750	17:83	23

Source: RGI (2001).

The Census 2001 figures show that the urban population of Tripura is comprised of 545750 persons living in 23 urban areas and the domain of urban Tripura is dominated by the West Tripura district. This district leads in terms of all the parameters considered in Table 1. Dhalai district is the most backward district of the state and it is in the nadir of urban characteristics in the state. Interestingly, even though the number of urban areas in the South Tripura is more, the extent of urbanisation is greater in the North Tripura district.

Fig 1. District wise break-up of Urban Population in Tripura

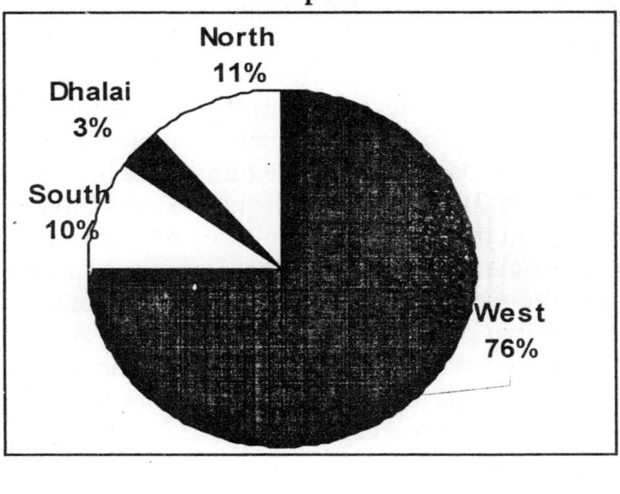

Fig. 1 further shows that 76 percent of the urbanites in Tripura live in the West Tripura district while the South Tripura and the North Tripura district is residence to 10 percent and 11 percent of the urban population and only 3 percent of the urban populace are dwellers of the Dhalai district.

Table 2: Number of Urban Areas in Tripura During 1901-2001

Year	*Class I*	*Class II*	*Class III*	*Class IV*	*Class V*	*Class VI*	*Total*
1901	-	-	-	-	1	-	1
1911	-	-	-	-	1	-	1
1921	-	-	-	-	1	-	1
1931	-	-	-	-	1	-	1
1941	-	-	-	1	-	-	1
1951	-	-	1	-	-	-	1
1961	-	1	-	1	4	-	6
1971	1	-	-	4	1	-	6
1981	1	-	1	4	2	2	10
1991	1	-	4	7	4	2	18
2001	1	-	6	9	7	-	23

Source: Various Census Reports.

The spread of urban population as shown in Table 2 suggest that though presently, there are 23 urban areas in the state, till 1951, the number of such areas was only 1 (one), Agartala, the capital city which continued being a Class V town till 1931. In course of the following four censuses till 1971, Agartala graduated to the next higher level and has continued being a Class I town since 1971. The first thrust to extension of urban areas came in 1961 as the total number of towns increased to 6 with the new inclusion of 4 Class V towns and one Class IV town. The number of towns did not change in the 1971 census though three towns have moved a step higher in the hierarchy. However, ever since the 1981 census, the total number of towns has increased successively. Currently, the extent of urban governance is extended to 1(one) municipal council and 12 (twelve) Nagar Panchayats. The census classification however in addition to these 13 urban areas considered another 10 Census towns for its classification of urban areas.

Volume & Trend of Urbanisation

Table 3 shows that over the past 100 hundred years, total population of Tripura has increased by more than 17 times whereas the rise in the urban population was more than 84 times. The growth of urban population over the years has been for various factors like natural growth of population, in-migration from rural areas, immigration and inclusion of new areas under the urban classification fold. Interestingly, the share of the urbanites in the total population had declined successively from 3.70 percent in 1901 to 2.50 percent in 1931 but has since then been increasing consecutively as expected till 2001.

Table 3: Population of Tripura by Residence, 1901-2001

Year	*Population*		*Urban Share*	*Decadal Change (%)*	
	Total	*Urban*		*Total*	*Urban*
1901	173325	6415	3.70	-	-
1911	229613	6831	2.98	32.48	6.48
1921	304437	7743	2.54	32.59	13.35
1931	382450	9580	2.50	25.63	23.72
1941	513010	17693	3.45	34.14	84.69
1951	645707	42595	6.60	25.87	140.74
1961	1142505	102997	9.02	76.94	141.81
1971	1556342	162360	10.43	36.22	57.64
1981	2053058	225568	10.99	31.92	38.93
1991	2757205	421721	15.30	34.30	86.96
2001	3199203	545750	17.05	16.03	29.41

Source: Various Census Reports.

Fig. 2. Urban & Total Population of Tripura

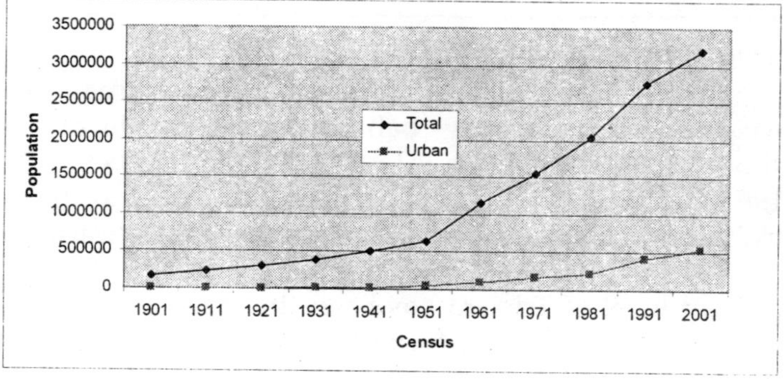

The decadal change of the urban population has been highest during the period 1951-61 and it was least during the period 1901-1911. The partition of India and associated migration have been a possible reason for the increase in urban population, however the influx of the refugees had been maximum post 1951. People from the erstwhile East Pakistan came in large numbers and had a large role in the alteration of the demographic profile of the state and associated social fabric. Since 1971 Census onwards, the increase in the number of urban areas have also been a significant contributor to the increased urban population. Moreover, the insurgent activities have also been responsible for migration of rural people towards Agartala and its adjoining areas particularly from1981 to 1991.

Table 4: Degree/Index of Urbanisation (Urban –Rural Ratio)

Year	*India*	*Tripura*
1901	12.16	3.84
1911	11.47	3.07
1921	12.58	2.61
1931	13.63	2.57
1941	16.08	3.57
1951	20.91	7.06
1961	21.91	9.91
1971	22.31	11.65
1981	30.44	12.34
1991	34.63	18.06
2001	38.47	20.57

Source: Various Census Reports.

However, if we consider the 'degree of urbanisation'3 we find that Tripura lags behind the national level. Table 4 shows that the urban- rural ratio of India had been 12.16 in 1901 and it is 38.47 in 2001 whereas for Tripura it was 3.84 in 1901 and 20.57 in 2001. It is observed that Tripura's level of 1981 is at par with the national level of 1901 while the present level of Tripura has been the stage attained by the national level in 1951. Moreover it should be noted that the degree of urbanisation in Tripura had reached double digit only after the 1971 census. Thus, though both India and Tripura belongs to accelerating stage of urbanisation the degree is certainly much lower for the state in the context of the nation.

Table 5: Annual Growth Rate (AGR) of Population in Tripura

Year	*AGR (%) of Urban Population (rgup)*	*AGR (%) of Rural Population (rgrp)*	*Urban- Rural Differential[4] (urd)*
1901-1911	0.63	2.89	-2.26
1911-1921	1.25	2.87	-1.62
1921-1931	2.13	2.29	-0.16
1931-1941	6.13	2.84	3.29
1941-1951	8.79	1.97	6.82
1951-1961	8.83	5.44	3.39
1961-1971	4.55	2.93	1.62
1971-1981	3.29	2.71	0.58
1981-1991	6.26	2.45	3.81
1991-2001	2.58	1.28	1.3

Source: Computed Various Census Reports.

Notes: rgup-growth rate of urban population & rgrp- growth rate of rural population, urd- rgup-rgrp.

Table 5 shows that the pace of urban population growth was fastest during the decade of 1951-1961 and was marginally higher than the rates prevailing in 1941-1951. Incidentally, the AGR for rural population was also at its zenith during 1951-1961. Such a scenario is in sharp contrast with that of India because the lowest rate of growth in urban population for the whole country had been during 1951-1961 (Datta, 2006). However, it is observed that the annual growth rates in the state have been fluctuating as the rates dropped for two successive decades and then increased during 1981-1991 again to drop down for the period 1991-2001.

Fig 3: Annual Growth rates of Urban & Rural Population of Tripura and the urban-rural differential

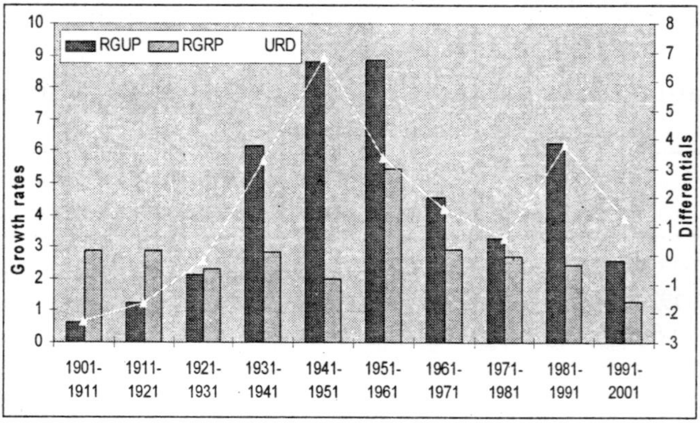

The urban-rural differential in the annual population growth rate in Tripura had been negative till 1931 and has turned positive since then indicating the start of the process of urbanisation of Tripura. In other words, it is expected that rgup > rgrp (Table 5), and in case of Tripura, such an observation is evident only from 1931. The differential was also at its peak during the period 1941-1951 and has since then decreased successively only to rise between 1981 & 1991 and again fall in the consequent period.

Urban Morphology of Tripura

From Table 6, we find that the process of urbanisation in the state began with Agartala as a Class V urban area and continued being the only urban area till 1951. With the emergence of other urban areas over the years, we find that the share of the lone Class I town in the total urban composition declining. It was only in the 1991 census that the contribution of Class I towns came below 50 percent. In the Indian context however we find that the percentage contribution of the Class I cities among the urban population increasing over the years (Datta, 1996).

Table 6: Urban Population and the Number of Urban Areas in Tripura According to Size Class During 1901-2001

Year	*I*	*II*	*III*	*IV*	*V*	*VI*	*Total*
1901	-	-	-	-	6415	-	6415
					(100)		(100)
1911	-	-	-	-	6831	-	6831
					(100)		(100)
1921	-	-	-	-	7743	-	7743
					(100)		(100)
1931	-	-	-	-	9580	-	9580
					(100)		(100)
1941	-	-	-	17693	-	-	17693
				(100)			(100)
1951	-	-	42595	-	-	-	42595
			(100)				(100)
1961	-	54878	-	13240	34879	-	102997
		(53.28)		(12.85)	(33.86)		(100)
1971	100264	-	-	52758	9338	-	162360
	(61.25)			(32.49)	(5.75)		(100)
1981	132186	-	20806	52018	13530	7028	225568
	(58.60)		(9.22)	(23.06)	(6.00)	(3.12)	(100)
1991	157358	-	116131	105782	33384	9066	421721
	(37.31)		(27.54)	(25.08)	(7.92)	(2.15)	(100)
2001	189998	-	182234	125061	48457	-	545750
	(34.81)		(33.39)	(22.92)	(8.88)		(100)

Source: Various Census Reports.

Notes: Figure in parentheses indicate the percent share of total.

The 1961 census figures show the emergence of five new urban areas, all sub-divisional headquarters, in the state. Among these, Dharmanagar was the largest and the other four were almost of the same size and it remained as the secand largest urban area in the state as per census specifications till 1981. Interestingly, the 10 urban centres of Tripura were the 10 sub-divisional headquarters of the state. Thus urbanisation was mostly due to the necessity of public administration.

However, since 1991, we find new areas being classified as urban areas and among the eight newly inducted areas, four were the suburbs of Agartala and has presently (in 2005) engulfed in the Greater Agartala city. It should be noted here

Table 7: Urban Centres of Tripura Along With their Population

	1901	*1911*	*1921*	*1931*	*1941*	*1951*	*1961*	*1971*	*1981*	*1991*	*2001*
Agartala	6415	6831	7743	9580	17693	42595	54878	100264	132186	157358	189998
Dharmanagar	-	-	-	-	-	-	13240	16858	20806	25897	30790
Udaipur	-	-	-	-	-	-	8778	13924	16304	18223	21758
Kailasahar	-	-	-	-	-	-	8575	10602	12938	16166	20286
Belonia	-	-	-	-	-	-	8744	11374	12054	13274	15760
Khowai	-	-	-	-	-	-	8782	9338	10722	12552	17689
Amarpur	-	-	-	-	-	-	-	-	7150	8550	10861
Sonamura	-	-	-	-	-	-	-	-	6380	8136	10074
Kamalpur	-	-	-	-	-	-	-	-	3688	4300	5143
Sabroom	-	-	-	-	-	-	-	-	3340	4766	5768
Badharghat	-	-	-	-	-	-	-	-	-	35576	47713
Teliamura	-	-	-	-	-	-	-	-	-	27668	19605
Jogendranagar	-	-	-	-	-	-	-	-	-	26990	34850
Kumarghat	-	-	-	-	-	-	-	-	-	14641	11593
Pratapgarh	-	-	-	-	-	-	-	-	-	13972	26837
Barjala*	-	-	-	-	-	-	-	-	-	16954	
Gandhigram	-	-	-	-	-	-	-	-	-	7538	10669
Singarbil*	-	-	-	-	-	-	-	-	-	9160	

Indranagar(part)	-	-	-	-	-	-	-	-	-	-	17807
Ranirbazar	-	-	-	-	-	-	-	-	-	-	11003
Gokulnagar	-	-	-	-	-	-	-	-	-	-	9659
Kanchanpur	-	-	-	-	-	-	-	-	-	-	7679
Kunjaban(part)	-	-	-	-	-	-	-	-	-	-	7343
Narsingarh	-	-	-	-	-	-	-	-	-	-	6820
Ambassa	-	-	-	-	-	-	-	-	-	-	6045

Source: Various Census Reports.

Notes: * - abolished/reclassified with different name.

Table 8
Annual Growth Rates of Population in Urban Areas of Tripura

	1901-1911	*1911-1921*	*1921-1931*	*1931-1941*	*1941-1951*	*1951-1961*	*1961-1971*	*1971-1981*	*1981-1991*	*1991-2001*
Agartala	0.63	1.25	2.13	6.13	8.79	2.53	6.03	2.76	1.74	1.88
Dharmanagar	-	-	-	-	-	-	2.42	2.10	2.19	1.73
Udaipur	-	-	-	-	-	-	4.61	1.58	1.11	1.77
Kailasahar	-	-	-	-	-	-	2.12	1.99	2.23	2.27
Belonia	-	-	-	-	-	-	2.63	0.58	0.96	1.72
Khowai	-	-	-	-	-	-	0.61	1.38	1.58	3.43
Amarpur	-	-	-	-	-	-	-	-	1.79	2.39
Sonamura	-	-	-	-	-	-	-	-	2.43	2.14
Kamalpur	-	-	-	-	-	-	-	-	1.54	1.79
Sabroom	-	-	-	-	-	-	-	-	3.56	1.91
Badharghat	-	-	-	-	-	-	-	-	-	2.94
Teliamura	-	-	-	-	-	-	-	-	-	-3.44
Jogendranagar	-	-	-	-	-	-	-	-	-	2.56
Kumarghat	-	-	-	-	-	-	-	-	-	-2.33
Pratapgarh	-	-	-	-	-	-	-	-	-	6.53
Gandhigram	-	-	-	-	-	-	-	-	-	3.47
Urban Tripura	0.63	1.25	2.13	6.13	8.79	8.83	4.55	3.29	6.26	2.58

Source: Computed from Various Census Reports

that among the six Class III towns of the state, three have been incorporated into Agartala city leaving only two in the North Tripura and one in South Tripura district. The low extent of urbanisation in Dhalai district is attested by the fact that all the three urban areas of the district are Class VI town and even though Kamalpur has been an urban area since 1981, its population was the lowest among all the urban areas of the state in 2001.

The annual growth rates of population as shown in Table 8 suggest that the growth of urban population in Tripura has been mostly due to growth areal reclassification. Migration and Natural growth rates have been of lesser impact. The high growth rate of urban population during 1981 to 1991 is not attested in the growth rates of the existing urban areas, rather it was the inclusion of the new areas that caused this huge rate for the state. over the years, the annual growth rates have been highest in Agartala during the period 1941-51 and excluding Agartala, the maximum growth rate visible is for Pratapgarh for the period 1991-2001.

Among other district towns, we find that in Udaipur, headquarter of the South Tripura district, the annual growth rate was high during the period 1961-71 but has slowed down since thwn. On the otherhand, the headquarters of the North Tripura district, Kailasahar exhibits a stable growth rate in the vicinity of 2 percent per annum all over. In this context, it should be also noted though very erratic, two of the urban centres of Tripura- Teliamura and Kumarghat exhibited negative growth during the period 1991-2001.

The Present Scenario

Table 9: Area, Population and Density of Urban bodies of Tripura

Urban Bodies	*Area*	*Population*	*Proportion*		*Density*
			Area	*Population*	
Agartala MC	58.84	367822	47.67	64.91	6251.22
Dharmanagar NP	7.77	30785	6.30	5.43	3962.03
Kailashahar NP	6.19	20279	5.02	3.58	3276.09
Kumarghat NP	3.5	11591	2.84	2.05	3311.71
Kamalpur NP	10.16	10633	8.23	1.88	1046.56

Khowai NP	5.82	20435	4.72	3.61	3511.17
Teliamura NP	3.75	19606	3.04	3.46	5228.27
Ranirbazar NP	1.95	11878	1.58	2.10	6091.28
Sonamura NP	4.13	10335	3.35	1.82	2502.42
Udaipur NP	6.1	31023	4.94	5.47	5085.74
Amarpur NP	8.55	10863	6.93	1.92	1270.53
Sabroom NP	2.53	5766	2.05	1.02	2279.05
Belonia NP	4.13	15687	3.35	2.77	3798.31
Urban Tripura	123.42	566703	100	100	4591.66

Source: Economic Review of Tripura, 2004-05.

Notes: MC- Municipal Council, NP- Nagar Panchayat.

The Economic Review of Tripura (GOT, 2005) identifies the urban structure of the state to be comprising of one (1) Municipal Council and 12 Nagar Panchayats covering 123.42 sq.kms and a population of 566703. These 13 urban areas are scattered in 11 sub-divisions indicating the absence of any urban bodies in six subdivisions namely- Kanchanpur, Ambassa, Longtarai Valley, Gandacherra, Bishalgarh and Santirbazar. Table 9 attests the dominance of Agartala in the process of urbanisation of Tripura. The capital city leads all others in terms of all other parameters by miles.

Fig. 4. Density, Proportional Area & Proportional Population of Urban Bodies of Tripura

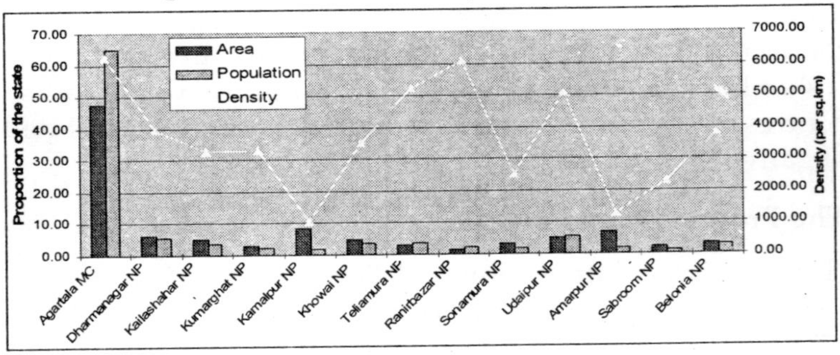

Leaving aside Agartala, it is seen that among the other towns, Udaipur NP has the highest population and Sabroom NP has the lowest population. On the other hand, in terms of area it is seen that Kamalpur NP occupies the top slot and Ranirbazar NP stands at the bottom. These two NPs interchange their position when density is considered as the parameter.

Features of Urbanisation in Tripura

The three factors (Bhagat, 1992) responsible for urbanisation or growth in urban population are- a) Natural increase, b) Net migration and c) Areal reclassification. In Tripura however, we find that natural growth rate of population for urban areas is less than that of the rural areas (THDR, 2006), therefore it is unlikely that natural increase will be the most important factor for urban growth. However, the partition of India has altered the demographic profile and social fabric of the state and there had been huge migration of refugees (Bhowmik, 2007) from the erstwhile East Pakistan. Moreover distress migration and internal displacement due to insurgency has also led to growth in the urban population particularly after 1980. Yet one can definitely say that industrialisation induced migration in Tripura has not occurred therefore growth in urban population due to urban pull is limited. Areal reclassification has occurred as is evident in the various census reports but surprisingly, only 27. 72 percent of the additional urban population in 2001 came from the newly inducted areas while the bulk, 72.28 percent are attributed by older towns. Moreover, it should be noted here that the areas classified as Census Towns (CTs) are mostly in the fringes of Agartala and have now been incorporated in the Agartala Municipal Council area in 2004.

Thus it becomes imperative to suggest that there are no definite patterns of urbanisation in the state in accordance with the major theories of economics. Most of the towns in Tripura are over grown villages; trading centres with some rural development administrative outfits which became urban settlements often to meet the need of the administrative machinery. It should be noted that almost all the urban units leaving aside those on the suburb of Agartala are administrative headquarters and thus have benefited and progressed to being an urban centre but do not enjoy modern sanitation facilities, portable and safer water supply.

Thus, the important features of the process of urbanisation are as follows:-

- Lopsided urbanisation with growth in the capital city and its suburbs- the real estate prices in Agartala are at par with that of any metropolis and as a result there has been fragmentation of the older residences and emergence of tiny plots

- Urbanisation occurring without industrialisation and formation of strong economic base because of the absence of large-scale public/ private sector enterprises
- Public administration led urbanisation occurring in erstwhile villages which are not capable of providing urban lifestyle and facilities. For their growth as vibrating life centres, Tripura's economy must be expanded with agricultural surplus to sustain urban development
- Distress migration and internal displacement resulted in uneven growth of urban centres

Conclusion

It is true that the degree of urbanisation in the state is much lower to that of the national level but the growth rates have been encouraging. The state government has initiated its developmental programme 'Nagaradoy' in all the 13 urban administrative units with the rationale of decentralised planning to fulfil its objective to provide better civic amenities and economic opportunities to the urban dwellers.

Nevertheless the process of urbanisation in the state would receive great fillip if –

a] there is a redirection of investment to develop a strong economic base for the medium and smaller urban areas in particular

b] there could be greater integration of the rural and urban economy with emphasis on plantation and horti-based industries,

c] comprehensive use of the high levels of education and literacy are made to explore the potentials of the BPO and call centre units

d] the coverage of the Integrated Development of Small and Medium Towns (IDSMT) is extended with transparency and fairness, e] initiation of Urban Development Authorities with more executive powers is undertaken,

f] scientific and hygienic garbage disposal and waste management systems are adopted with the introduction of the underground sewerage system and covering of the open drains,

Notes

1. Davis (1965) has mentioned three stages in the process of urbanization. Stage one is the initial stage characterized by rural traditional society with predominance in agriculture and dispersed pattern of settlements. Stage two refers to acceleration stage where basic restructuring of the economy and investments in social overhead capitals including transportation, communication take place. Proportion of urban population gradually increases from 25% to 40%, 50%, 60% and so on. Dependence on primary sector gradually dwindles. Third stage is known as terminal stage where urban population exceeds 70% or more.

2. The population Census in India classifies urban settlement into six size classes as per the limits indicated below:-

Population Size	*Category*
100,000 and more	Class I
50,000 to 100,000	Class II
20,000 to 50,000	Class III
10,000 to 20,000	Class IV
5,000 to 10,000	Class V
Less than 5000	Class VI

3. Urban-rural ratio [(U/R)*100] is the most commonly used for measuring degree of urbanization. The ratio U/P has lower limit 0 and upper limit 1ie. 0< U/P <1. The index is 0 for total population equal to rural population. When whole population is urban, this index is one. When 50 percent of the population is rural, it means that there is one urbanite for each rural person. The urban-rural ratio has a lower limit of zero and upper limit 8 i.e 0<U/R<8. Theoretically upper limit will be infinite when there is no rural population (R=0) but this is impossible.

4. The difference in the annual growth rates of the urban population and the rural population is considered as the urban-rural differential.

REFERENCES

Bhagat, R.B. (1992) Components of Urban Growth in India with Reference to Haryana : Findings from Recent Censuses, *Nagarlok,* Vol. 25, No. 3.

Bhagat, R.B., (2002) *Urbanisation in India: A Demographic Appraisal.*

Bhowmik, I. (2007); Migration Profile of Tripura, Presentation at the Census Data Dissemination Workshop, MBB College, Agartala

Brockerhoff, M. (1999) Urban Growth in Developing Countries: A review of Projections and Predictions, *Population and development Review,* Vol 25. No. 4.

Brockerhoff, M. and Brennam, E. (1998) The poverty of cities in Developing Regions, *Populations and Development Review,* Vol. 24, No. 1.

Datta, P. (2006): Urbanisation in India, Regional and Sub-Regional Population Dynamic Population Process in Urban Areas European Population Conference.

Davis Kingsley and Golden, H.H. (1954): "Urbanisation and development in pre-Industrial Areas", *Economic Development and Cultural Change,* Vol. 3, No. 1.

Davis Kingsley (1962): "Urbanisation in India – Past and Future", in Turner, R. (ed.) *India's Urban Future,* University of California Press, Berkley.

Davis, K. (1965). The urbanization of the human population; *Scientific American,* 213(3)

Govt. of Tripura (2006): Tripura Human Development Report.

Govt. of Tripura (undated), Tripura State Development Report (Draft).

Registrar General (1991) Census of India, General Population Tables Tripura, Series 24 Part II-A.

Registrar General (2001) Census of India, 2001.

Tripura Darpan (2007) Tathyapanji-O-Nirdeshika.

www.planningtripura.gov.in

11

Ethnicity and Human Rights in the Northeast: Forms of Discrimination against Marginalised Tribes#

RUPAK DEBNATH*

Abstract

In Northeast India, the human rights situation is not cheerful. Specifically, within tribal communities, the marginalised suffers from discrimination. Externally, alien socio-political structures perpetuate endemic bias against them; internally, ethnic contentions and subculture denying mechanisms keep them distraught, their cultures and traditional institutions jeopardised. Dominant groups that control the administrative machinery systematically exclude them from full and normal participation in social life, political activities and economic development. To preserve their indigenous culture and

Paper presented at NHRC, New Delhi, sponsored National Seminar on 'Human Rights in North-East India: Issues and Challenges' organised by the Department of Political Science, Tripura University, at the Central Library Hall on November 11, 2008.

* Rupak Debnath is Assistant Director in the Directorate of Distance Education, Tripura University.

languages, these groups sometimes endorse the consensus mechanisms for ethnic alliances but the denial of subculture aspirations by the dominant tribes creates schismogenesis within those alliances. Ethnic rivalry and armed violence for territorial domination is not new to the Northeast. Often, the small groups are caught in the crossfire of rival outfits and suffer great losses of life and property. Development projects causing displacement of tribal habitats are not always followed up by adequate rehabilitation schemes, which has in recent years adversely affected housing conditions, healthcare and education in many parts of Northeast India.

The social and cultural conditions and practical needs of marginalised tribes of the Northeast are matters of deep concern. Concerted efforts must be made by both the government and the ethnic peoples to create productive synergies in the region, dismantling all discriminatory structures and creating an environment where not even the smallest ethnic group will need to fear violation of the right to preserve its traditional culture and language.

Key terms: ethnicity, human rights, Tibeto-Burman, domination, discrimination, valley-dweller, highlander, marginalised tribe, PVTGs, swidden farming, culture, subculture, ethnos, schismogenesis, empowerment, ethnic cleansing, synergy.

1. Introduction

Ethnically and linguistically, Northeast India is one of the most diversified zones of the world, home of numerous Tibeto-Burman groups besides small populations of Siamese-Chinese and Austric-speaking peoples. Until the mid-20th century, very few 'non-tribal' Bengalis were familiar with this region. Within the indigenous population, no two ethnic groups speak the same language nor have identical customs or dress. Officially, 'tribal' is now a cover term, the equivalent of Indo-Aryan 'upajati'; in political rhetoric though, mainstream legislators will avoid 'upajati' for the more fetish 'adivasi' and speak of indiscriminate uplift of the indigenous peoples and their inclusion in mainstream socio-political structures. Paradoxically, the notion of indiscrimination itself has over the years frogspawned discriminations within tribal societies, affecting especially the rights of the marginalised tribes to preserve their distinct cultures and languages.

2. Ethnic Situation in the Northeast: Historical Summary

At the core of Indian civilisation lies what may be called 'Aryan-bias' with attempts to civilise other races (Dravidians, Austrics, Tibeto-Burmans, etc.) perceived as 'wild' or 'primitive.' In ancient Indian literature, the term 'Kirata' was applied pejoratively to the Tibeto-Burman hill dwellers of eastern Nepal (Chatterji 1974: 30-31); an expansion of its meaning in subsequent periods led to the inclusion of all Tibet-Burman peoples of the central and the eastern Himalayas within the *kirata*-kind. Indian epic-heroes are eulogised for having achieved victories over *Kirata* chieftains and for generating Hindu transforms in indigenous cultures. In Manipur, the Meithei established their hegemony in the 15th century CE but Aryanisation did not perpetrate into the Imphal Valley until the early 18th century. (It was then a militant form of Brahminisation, which asphyxiated old customs, literatures and religious practices, even pre-dated ethno-history to epic times by imposing Arjuna-Babruvahana ancestry on the native). A 19th century British account (Dunn 1885: 13) shows six-fold caste-taxonomy in the Meithei society with Brahmins at the hierarchy-apex and Methers at the base. In addition to that, there was the 'Loi' class formed by flocking a subjugated race of early Tibeto-Burmans (the Chakpa who enjoyed political ascendancy in Upper Burma in the 8th-14th century CE) with the social degenerates of Meithei. Between the 16th and the 18th century, the ruling houses of Tai-Ahom, Tippera, Jayantiya and Kachar were brought into the Hindu fold.

Interestingly, the groups that absorbed the mainstream system India were primarily valley-dwellers and wet-rice cultivators who considered the highland tribes or swidden-practising groups as uncouth and barbaric. When the Tai-Ahoms formed their civilising polity in the Brahmaputra valley, they sought to induce the subjugated 'Kha' people (the 'inferior' Tibeto-Burmans, mainly sections of Nagas, Morans and Karbis) systematically into wet-rice cultivation, and create, in the 16th-17th century, a Hindu-based feudalistic society with distinct *sevya-sevak* (master-slave) classes. As already said, social hierarchy existed in pre-colonial Meithei, where the dominated or the marginalised could not access natural resources without reference to their social masters; they were also denied the right to persist with their traditional cultures and religious practices.

Prior to the British rule, little is known about the remote tribes of Northeast India. Not until the growth of anthropological interest on indigenous peoples and cultures has the ethnic diversity of the region emerged. The highland cultures and languages did not quite fit into the mainstream structures; they also lived in remote hamlets and there was little attempt to reach them or to bring them into the Aryan fold. (Linguistically, many of those groups are included under the so-called 'Old Kukis'; ethnographically, they constitute the least studied communities of the region.) Far from the civilising influence of Aryanised valley-dwellers, they lived in small groups enjoying precarious independence along the eastern frontiers of India until stronger tribes from the east dispersed them from their old habitats or forced them into subjugation. In the 16th-18th century, there was much feud and struggle for economic supremacy in Chin societies of upper Burma, especially in the Chindwin valley, and many groups of early Chins migrated into the northern parts of the Lushai Hills (now Mizoram). Those settlements extended from Champhai to Tipaimukh (the tri-junction of Mizoram, Manipur and Cachar). Later, around the close of the 18th century, the Lushai clans entered Mizoram, and in their attempt to extend control over the extensive ridges for swidden farming, they subjugated some Old Kuki groups and expelled the others from that area.

The socio-political structures of the mainstream did not affect these highlanders but several phases of domination and displacement within highland societies created new supra-structures among the Bawm and the Lakher (Shendu) who institutionalised social inequality in terms of access to vital resources. Pre-Christian Lushai society was not as strictly stratified as that of Bawm or Lakher but some social distinction was perpetrated and clientele status enforced on old vanquished groups like the Ralte. Socially, the Raltes were outcastes, assigned to live in a separate portion of the Lushai village; economically, they were a means to secure surplus for their Lushai masters. Systematic attempts at 'civilising' the highlanders of the region came with the British, mainly with Christian missionary activities, which promoted individual rights above birth-ascribed or ethnicity-based restrictions on social intermixing or intermarrying. Consequently, some dominant tribal groups got social impetus but a sense of alienness to the Indian ethos also developed in them. When the British left India in 1947, the Mizo and the Naga tribes were opposed to their inclusion in the Union of India; within a decade of the Northeast merger, these groups took to armed revolt, demanding independent statehood.

After Independence, the indigenous groups of Northeast India were flocked under the Scheduled Tribes (ST) category, but the valley-dwelling Meitheis and Assamese (who had already adapted their socio-political structures to that of mainstream India) preferred exclusion from that category. Few like the Chakpas (the so-called 'Lois') opted for a Scheduled Caste (SC) status. Perceptually, these social taxonomies were generated for the uplift of backward sections of the Indian population but discrimination against tribals, especially the marginalised communities of the Northeast, continues. To make matters worse, a steady influx of Bengalis from East Pakistan (afterwards Bangladesh) to Assam and Tripura between 1947 and 1971 has multiplied threats to the indigenous systems, and older settlers seeing a tightening of their natural access to the exploitable resources of the region have persistently sought extradition of the 'outsiders' from 'tribal land.' Another problem in the region, including the states where the population is predominantly Tibeto-Burman, is the systemic exclusion of ethnic minorities by the dominant groups from full and normal participation in social life and political activities.

This paper focuses on the marginalised tribal groups of the Northeast, particularly the forms of discrimination they encounter in everyday life.

3. Identifying the Marginalised Groups

The term 'marginalised groups' is used for those tribal

ethnoses that either suffer the domination of the major ethnic groups or remain socially, economically and politically excluded. Under this category would come several Kuki tribes of Manipur, the Hmars of North Cachar Hills, the Halam subgroups of Tripura, the Tanchangyas of Tripura and Mizoram, the Khamtis and the Wanchos of Arunachal Pradesh, etc. In some states, the dominant groups are also known to carry out armed violence against the smaller groups. Many communities have either skeletal or no representation at the government level.

Small groups like Dap, Langkai, Bongcher and Karbong (all micro-entities within the Halam ethnos) of Tripura, Madahi of Assam, Chirr of Nagaland, as well as many Kuki-Naga subgroups of Manipur that could be identified as PVTGs (Particularly Vulnerable Tribal Groups) are also included in the marginalised category. Their distinct cultures or subcultures, as well as languages are threatened with extinction. The likes of the Karbong of Tripura (total 27 families having 109 individuals) barely know the priorities that could improve individual lives and sustain their traditional beliefs and social institutions.

Displaced ethnic groups like the Chakmas and the Haijongs of Arunachal Pradesh are denied the right to vote; on the other hand, the Mizoram government refuses to give an autonomous council to the Bru. In violation of the International Convention (Article 7) on Indigenous and Tribal Peoples in Independent Countries, the dominant ethnic groups now controlling administration agencies violate the right of smaller communities to participate in formulating, implementing and evaluating such plans and programmes for national and regional development as would affect them directly.

4. Forms of Discrimination against Marginalised Tribes

Despite affirmative policies of the Indian Government to promote the uplift of all tribal peoples, the present situation of the marginalised tribes of Northeast India is not encouraging; the future would be dismal if attempts are not genuinely made to eliminate old discriminations as well as bridge new ethnic schisms. Most marginalised groups are subjected to discrimination, externally from the imposition of alien socio-political structures to a systemic perpetuation of endemic bias against them and internally from ethnic contentions and other subculture denying mechanisms that have emerged with the new adjustment structures in the region.

This will become evident in the following sections.

(a). Denial of the right to life. To consolidate hegemonies, dominant groups have always tried to absorb the minority tribes. If this process succeeded, the assimilated group became culturally and linguistically indistinguishable from the group disseminating the transforms. At other times, the assimilatory process persisted briefly or until subculture incompatibility with group norms compelled schismogenesis within culturally allied subgroups. In the latter case, the numerically weaker section suffered reprisal action by the dominant group. When the Paites of Manipur decided to abandon the nomenclature 'Kuki' in favour of 'Zomi' identity, the major Kuki groups took exception to it. In June 1997, ethnic clashes broke out and hundreds of men, women and children were killed. Scores of houses were set ablaze and many families abandoned their old villages.

In addition to these clashes, the minority Kuki and Naga villages in the hilly parts of Manipur suffer reprisal action carried out by the two strongest outfits in the region, the KNA and the NSCN, simply because of their ethnic affiliatedness to one or the other of the contending outfits. A Kuki would most likely be killed if he went to a Naga village; the same would happen to a Naga if he entered the Kuki belt. During ethnic clashes, these groups cannot leave their native villages, because there is no place for them to go. (The Mizoram government is not keen on receiving displaced Kukis; on the other hand, an exodus of Nagas from Manipur would thwart the NSCN dream of Greater Nagaland.) The Meitheis of the Imphal valley, and, covertly the government of Manipur, give some support to the Kuki outfit because they are opposed to the NSCN demand. To make the picture bleak, state backed security forces have, on the plea of tracking down NSCN militants, harassed innocent tribals, restricted their natural activities, killed many in fake encounters, even violated the rights against rape and custodial death.

Several generations of children from these minority groups have grown up in this conflictful environment; many of them have been compelled by circumstances to enrol themselves in ethnic 'armies' at a very tender age.

(b). Denial of right to access natural resources. Most state governments of the Northeast lack in the most essential insight into the symbiotic relatedness between tribal communities and their rainforest habitats. Traditionally, the rainforest has provided them with sustenance. Except for the dominant valley-dwelling groups of Assam, Manipur and Tripura, the other groups subsisted by swiddening. Their right to access forest resources was first denied by the British. The subsequent government of India has persisted with the colonial attitude, arguing that swidden farming was detrimental to ecological balance. Yet, neither colonial nor post-colonial governments hesitated to exploit natural resources for cash-earning timber and tea industry, rubber plantation and for development purposes. Theoretically, nothing is amiss with development programmes. But is it not imperative to safeguard the rights of the indigenous people to land and natural resources?

There is little concern for indigenous minorities whose lands have been taken over for development purposes. Rehabilitation measures remain inadequately implemented and displaced families are denied proper ration, housing and health facilities. In the 1970s, the Soil Conservation Department of Government of Assam found the Mikir Hills conducive to rubber plantation. Many swidden-practising Karbi families were then relocated in model villages in the plains of that District but there was no follow-up programme to ensure that those families did not lack in the basic amenities of living. When some of them returned to the hills, they faced official restrictions on swiddening. Conversely, the other Karbi families resettled in the plains of Majuli have to cope with yearly floods, poverty and diseases. The government has done little to improve their living conditions. A section is now disgruntled, and it might not be long before a new Karbi outfit is added to the list of militant groups operating in Assam.

(c). Denial of citizenship rights. The majority of Chakma and Haijong settlers of Arunachal Pradesh are excluded from electoral rolls, owing primarily to a policy of discrimination followed against them by the state government. They had come to India as refugees from the Chittagong Hill Tracts following displacement during the construction of the Kaptai Dam. In 1964, many of them were settled in Arunachal. By the provisions of the Indira-Mujib pact of 1972, Chakmas and Haijongs became naturalised citizens of India; yet, after four decades of legalised settlement, they are denied citizenship rights. Sections of the Arunachalese tribals also clamour for their deportation.

(d). Educational disparity. Educational policies have failed to provide equal facilities to all underprivileged sections. In each state, schools foster an atmosphere familiar to that of the dominant ethnic group. This pattern has persisted despite the fact that different tribes 'are at varying stages of economic development' and that there is 'much difference in the skills they have attained and the technologies they use' (REC 1966). Special provisions (cf. Articles 15-19, 25, 39, etc.) for their uplift have been envisioned in the Constitution of India. Yet, state governments tend to favour dominant groups or sections living within accessible limits of capitals and district headquarters; the remote and the marginalised remain unreached, neglected. A 2007 Report to the UN CERD Committee by NNHRTMI highlights the condition of the Bru refugees of North Tripura: 'The state government of Tripura deprived educational facilities to the children in the Bru internally displaced persons' camps under Kanchanpur sub-division. Effectively, over 5,000 children have been denied the right to education and an entire generation of the Brus has been kept illiterate in the last eight years.'

Most marginal tribal groups of Northeast India live in remote areas where there are few or no schools. In some villages, primary schools exist with skeletal staff and a near-zero infrastructure. To make the picture even bleaker, in the insurgency affected areas of Tripura and Manipur, existing schools building are used to camp security forces. In the interiors of Meghalaya, Mizoram, Nagaland and Tripura, Christian missionaries have done commendable work. Yet, not all places have missionary schools, while in states like Arunachal Pradesh, Christian missionary activities are disallowed. Christian missionaries have consistently favoured a mother-tongue based primary instruction, but government schools, on the other hand, either make a mainstream language (as in Assam and Tripura) or the language of a dominant ethnic group (as in Nagaland, Mizoram, Meghalaya) the medium of instruction. Students from marginalised ethnic groups are confronted with an atmosphere of unfamiliarity in these educational institutions; it discourages natural talent and retards the development of traditional skills. In Tripura, Halam children who learn their own language at home find it difficult to cope with Bengali, which is the mode of instruction in schools. Similarly, in Mizoram, Pawi and Lakher (Mara) speak their mother tongues at home but in schools, they use Mizo (or Duhlien, the language of the Lushai).

The percentage of literacy in Northeast India may satisfy local politicians and state governments as indicators of achievements in their respective states but it does not show the actual educational situation. A case may be made of the Tanchangyas of South Tripura. With a population around 2500 individuals, they constitute a small group of the state (unreturned in Census Reports; unmentioned in pamphlets released by the Tripura Tribal Autonomous District). Only 30% attends or has attended schools (Debnath 2008b: 235). Another marginalised group, the Molsom is also educationally backward but with a section presently attending Christian missionary schools, they are slightly better off than the Buddhist Tanchangya.

(e). Denial of the right to empowerment. Regional ethno-politics perpetrated by politically dominant groups in Assam and Arunachal Pradesh has led to the exclusion of the Khamtis from empowerment programmes. There is now a high percentage of uneducated as well as school dropouts among them; consequently, very few of them have government jobs. In the early the 19th century, they were known 'as far more civilised than most of the other Shan tribes of Assam' (Grierson 1967: 63); they had also enjoyed political ascendancy in upper Assam, dominating sections of Assamese and other

races of that region. But after their subjugation by the British, the tribe was divided to prevent future uprising; today, they live as a divided people in the north-eastern parts of Assam and in the south-eastern villages of Arunachal Pradesh. After independence, the dominant groups of Assam and Arunachal Pradesh marginalised them, steadily pushing them into areas where there is little scope for educational attainments and almost no other means to earn livelihood than to pursue agriculture. Religiously, they are Buddhists, not responsive the idea of conversion as the Wanchos are, and that diminishes the chances of Khamti children leaving their homes to attend missionary schools and colleges in Meghalaya.

Similar denial of education and empowerment is faced by the Deori-Chutiya tribe of Assam, the Chakma and Haijong settlers of Arunachal Pradesh, the Brus refugees from Mizoram, as also several Kuki subgroups of Manipur. Systemic repression of the socio-political aspirations of the Wanchos of Tirap (Arunachal Pradesh) and their exclusion from empowerment have forced them to the path of insurgency. In recent years, a section of their people has joined hands with the NSCN. Sadly, in almost all Northeast states, a quiet but systemic exclusion of minority tribes from empowerment is at work. In one paper (Debnath 2008a), I had indicated that by virtue of increased representation that dominant ethnic groups have in state government offices and by the group domination they perpetrate at state-level politics, they tend to obstruct the minority tribal groups from carrying out necessary strategies that would allow them to overcome constraints, internal and external, on the acquisition of essential life skills.

(e). Threats to minority cultures, languages, etc. Marginalised tribal groups, their culture and language are often threatened by alien institutions and customs imposed upon them by dominant entities enjoying demographic majority and wielding state power. In the past, the assimilatory process had created regional identities and homogenous groups with the absorption of weaker or numerically smaller, even culturally heterogeneous groups into larger ones. This has already been noted in an earlier paragraph. Historically,

several other groups of Northeast were also assimilated into dominant tribal entities. Some of them like the Bru who now have a sizeable population can afford to denounce the process of diachronic fusion with the Tippera who once dominated and transformed their language and culture.

A few groups wielding political power over small areas had tried to foster consensus mechanism to preserve indigenous cultures and languages; they had allied with the larger groups to discover a common ground. Briefly, the thing worked but when smaller entities within those ethnic blocks realized that their own subculture identities were being swept away under the consensus mechanism, they sought to distance themselves from the dominant member of the block. The KNA (Kuki National Assembly), which was formed in 1947, largely catered to the political aspirations of the Thado, marginalising smaller groups like the Paite and the Vaiphai, who then generated schismogenesis within the 'Kuki' fraternity. The Paites have also denounced the first Kuki Bible as Thado Bible and published a separate Bible in their own dialect.

While the Paite is now capable of asserting the right to preserve its traditional culture and language, several smaller ethnic entities like the Karbong remain vulnerable, facing what seems certain extinction.

(f). Campaigns of ethnic cleansing. In some parts of Northeast India, one finds tendencies to force ethnic minorities out of the places where they have been living for sometime. Cleansing campaigns are palpably carried out to demarcate areas for culturally homogenous groups and to enjoy new autonomies unhindered. One compelling issue is that of the Hmar cleansing now being carried out in Cachar and North Cachar Hills by the Dimaraji Revival Demand Committee (DRDC) to create a future Dimasa (Karbi) state. Hmar and Karbi differ culturally and linguistically from one another; even in former times, they were not quite peaceful neighbours but open hostilities between them broke out when the Hmar began agitating for separate statehood. The Assam government then played a devious role; instead of encouraging 'integrationist multiracial organizations and

movements and other means of eliminating barriers' (ICEAFRD, Article 2) between the two contending groups, it fuelled their traditional rivalry, often allowed the Karbi to use the state law enforcement machinery to repress the fundamental rights of the Hmar.

5. Recommendations and Conclusions

The human rights situation in Northeast India is grave, and it is imperative that immediate cognisance is taken of discriminations against marginalised tribes. To ensure administrative reforms in consonance with the ethnic diversity of the region and to promote cultures and languages of ethnic minorities, the following recommendations are made to the Government of India:

(a) All tribal identities, indigenous cultures and subcultures should be officially recognised; besides, specific stages of socio-economic development in which different tribes are presently poised must also be taken into consideration. In doing so, instituted commissions or inquiry agencies should not take for granted the statistics/ information supplied solely by state governments; instead arrangements must be made to interact directly with community members, insurgent outfits or discontent groups to assess the situation impartially. This will help identify the marginalised groups within the states, as also the PVTGs, and to discover what precise forms of violations they now suffer.

(b) In formulating policies, priority should go to preserving the cultures and languages of marginalised groups. Mere inclusion of these groups within the Scheduled Tribes category may not necessarily ensure their uplift; therefore, adequate arrangements should be made to see to it that the rights to education, housing, healthcare, employment and public representation are not denied to target communities. In the recent past, state government sponsored discrimination of minority tribal groups has marred many social uplift programmes. Policy monitoring committees should also be instituted to regulate the activities of implementing agencies/ state governments.

(c) Policies for uplift of marginalised tribes of the Northeast should address core issues pertaining to –

(i) *their right to life*. Agencies found guilty of violating this human right should be punished. Victims of inter-ethnic violence and state-sponsored atrocities must be adequately compensated, and, if necessary, their families relocated at places where they shall not face threats to life and property. In places vulnerable to insurgency operations and reprisal actions, proper security arrangements must be made to protect innocent lives.

(ii) *the right to land and natural resources*. Tribal institutions are the least threatened in their natural rainforest habitats. Therefore, the informed consent of communities must be taken before initiating development projects in tribal land or in demarcating areas for cash-crop plantation programmes. Should relocation of habitats become necessary, the government or the developing agency must ensure that rehabilitated communities do not lack in basic amenities (fooding, housing and healthcare) and that avenues to alternative sources of income exist in the neighbourhood.

(iii) *their citizenship rights*. Small displaced peoples recognised as legal citizens of India enjoy as much right to enfranchisement as native dwellers or autochthons. If any tribal community is denied voting right by the State Government, the Central Government should take up the matter, bring the contending parties to the table and initiate dialogues to find amicable solution to the problem.

(iv) *right to education and empowerment*. The Government of India should summarily dismantle such discriminatory structures as tend to block marginalised tribes from availing of the benefits of Scheduled Tribes (ST) reservation in educational and occupational spheres. To begin with, primary education should be imparted through the mother tongue. At a later stage, English or a State language can be taken up. Also, provisions must be made for coaching and training individuals from marginalised communities so that they become capable of competing with individuals from the advanced tribal communities. Encouragement must also be given to minority graduates to sit for central and state public service commissions examinations, which would give access to the administrative machinery.

(v) *right to preserve indigenous culture and language*. The Government of India acknowledges the tribals' right to maintain their cultures and institutions; hence, financial support must be extended to marginalised groups and precise policies drafted to promote their same. Invariably, PVTGs should get maximum priority.

(d) With respect to law enforcement groups, the Government of India should see to it that security agencies abide by the international convention against torture and other forms of degrading punishments. They should also act neutrally, not be partisan to either state government or any dominant group fostered discrimination. Juvenile insurgents must be treated in accordance with the Juvenile Justice Act 2001.

(e) Specifically in Northeast India, all forms of discontent in tribal communities should be directly addressed by the Government of India, not through the State Governments whose past policies have only fuelled discrimination. In many states, the Convention concerning Indigenous and Tribal Peoples in Independent Countries has been violated following non-implementation of special measures to safeguarding the persons, institutions, property, labour, cultures and environment of the tribal peoples (Article 4). Disgruntled ethnoses and insurgent groups should be invited to the table so that they may negotiate peacefully with the government. In a region where peace is purchasable by granting of regional, district or sub-district level autonomies to dissident groups, the price cannot be high for the government.

The following proposals are made for the ethnic peoples of Northeast India.

(f) To respect the cultures and languages of others. All ethnic groups must transcend the limitations of specific group demands, dismantle their discriminating structures and sympathise with the problems of the other groups living in the region. This will help create productive synergies within specific states, even across the states.

(g) Micro-entities within some ethnoses face threats of extinction or absorption. The violations of the past cannot be adequately redressed but present acknowledgement of the basic rights of the small and marginalised groups to preserve their culture and language would add to the enrichment of the culturally most diversified region of the world. To allow a minority group to enjoy autonomy is to acknowledge its right to preserve its own traditional institution and customary laws.

(h) Displaced or relocated sections of other ethnic groups have already suffered exclusion from their familiar structures and faced gross violations of human rights. Their plight should be considered from a humane point of view and the ground so prepared that their children can share equal socio-economic and political rights with the children of the original dwellers.

(i) Conflicting groups must learn to respect territorial jurisdictions and to refer disputes over territories or areas of control to peaceful dialogues, not armed attacks and reprisals. In crossfire, the innocent highlander suffers. In some places, generations of children have grown up in an environment of terror, denied the right to life, education, healthcare and such amenities as children in other parts of the country enjoy. The ethnic peoples of Northeast India must decide if they will allow another generation of children to grow up in the same environment.

By following a policy of discrimination against demographically small and culturally threatened tribal minorities, the dominant tribes may temporarily secure some economic and political gains for themselves. But in the long run, it will only backfire on them, creating new areas of instability within already unstable territories and amid increasing concerns over human rights violation. As far as marginalised tribes are concerned, it is possible that some of them, the PVTGs in particular, will become extinct unless attempts are made to preserve their cultures and languages. Therefore, a concerted effort should be made by the Government of India, as well as by the ethnic peoples of the region to make the Northeast a better place to live in.

REFERENCES

Barpujari, H. K. (1981). *Problems of the Hill Tribes: North-East Frontier*. Guwahati: Spectrum Publications.

Chakma, S. (2007). India: Stakeholders' Report under the UPR. New Delhi: Asian Centre for Human Rights.

Chatterji, S.K. (1974) (2nd edn.). *Kirata-Jana-Krti* (*The Indo-Mongoloids: Their contribution to the History and Culture of India*). Calcutta: Asiatic Society.

Chaube, S.K. (1999). *Hill Politics in North-East*. New Delhi: Orient Longman Ltd.

Danda, A. K. (1973). *Tribal Economics and their Transformation*, New Delhi: Indian Council of Social Science Research.

Davis, A.W. (1891). Naga Tribes. *Assam Census Report* 1891, I, 237-51.

Debnath, R. (2008a). A Policy for Inclusion in Northeast India? Quality HE and Constraints on Tribals' Participation. (Paper presented at UGC sponsored seminar of 'Quality in Higher Education,' BBM College, Agartala, March 25-26, 2008).

_____ (2008b). *Ethnographic Study of Tanchangya of CHT, CADC, Sittwe and South Tripura*. Kolkata: Kreativmind.

Elles, E.R. *Military Report of the Chin-Lushai Country*. Simla: Government Printing Press.

Grierson, G.A. (1967) (Reprint). *Linguistic Survey of India*, 2. Delhi: Motilal Banarsidass.

Dunn, E.W. (1885). *Gazetteer of Manipur*. Calcutta: Superintendent, Government Printing.

Furer-Haimendorf, C. von. (1982). *Highlanders of Arunachal Pradesh*. New Delhi: Vikas Publishing House.

ICEAFRD. (1969). International Convention on the Elimination of All Forms of Racial Discrimination. Adopted and opened for signature and ratification by General Assembly resolution 2106 (XX) of 21 December 1965 (*entry into force* 4 January 1969, in accordance with Article 19).

ICESCR. (1976). International Covenant on Economic, Social and Cultural Rights Adopted and opened for signature, ratification and accession by General Assembly resolution 2200A (XXI) of 16 December 1966 (*entry into force* 3 January 1976, in accordance with article 27).

ILO. (1991). Convention (No. 169) concerning Indigenous and Tribal Peoples in Independent Countries. Adopted on 27 June 1989 by the General Conference of the International Labour Organisation at its seventy-sixth session (*entry into force* 5 September 1991).

IWGIA and AITPN. (2006). India: No Democracy for those living on the margins. (A joint submission for examination of India's human rights obligations and commitments under the UPR of the Human Rights Council). Copenhagen and New Delhi: IWGIA and AITPN.

Mackenzie, A. (1884). *History of the Relations of the Government with the Hill Tribes of the N.E. Frontier of Bengal*. Calcutta: Home Department Press.

McCall, A.G. (1949). *Lushai Chrysalis*. London: Luzac & Co.

Mey, W. (ed.) (1984). *Genocide in the Chittagong Hill Tracts, Bangladesh*. Copenhagen: IWGIA.

NNHRTMI. (2007). *Dimensions of Discrimination in India*. A shadow report to 15th to 19th periodic reports (CERD/C/IND/19) of India to UN CERD Committee. New Delhi: ACHR.

Parry, N.E. (1932). *The Lakhers*. London: Macmillan.

REC. (1966). *Report of the Education Commission*. New Delhi: Ministry of Education, Govt. of India.

Risley, H.H. (1891). *Tribes and Castes of Bengal*. Calcutta: Bengal Secretariat Press.

Shakespeare, J. (1900). *The Lushei Kuki Clans*. London: Macmillan.

Sinha, S. (ed.). (1987). *Tribal Polities and State Systems in Pre-colonial Eastern and North Eastern India*. Calcutta: K. P. Bagchi.

12

Jamatia Hada Okra; the Traditional Institution of Jamatia: Change and Continuity

CHANDRIKA BASU MAJUMDER*

In Tripura since long past people of various communities have been peacefully co-existing and upholding their own social rules of administration.Tripura was once a Princely State ruled by the Kings and it was merged with the Union of India in 1949. There are nineteen Tribes in Tripura having their separate entity with diversity. The Jamatia Community holds the third position in respect of numerical strength among the nineteen tribes of Tripura. According to *Sri Rajmala* written by Kaliprasanna Sen, the Jamatias were the most important fighting tribes of Tripura during the reign of early kings. The army constituted by them was called 'jamat' and from word 'Jamat' they later on came to be known as Jamatias. Tripura District Gazetteer records, 'the term 'Jamatia' has originated from the term 'Jamayet' which means gathering or mobilization. According to another popular belief, the word 'Jamatia' is derived from the word 'Jama' and 'Twia' 'Jama' means 'Tax' and 'Twia' means not to bear the burden of.Thus the word Jamatia means a person who does not bear the

*Reader, Deptt. of Political Science, Tripura University.

burden of taxes. The Jamatia Community has their own culture and characteristics. Since very ancient time they are controlling their social life in a democratic way. The process continued and was maintained by unwritten Hada Structure.

One of the main objectives of Jamatia Hada is to eradicate superstition and ignorance after protecting the social unity and own characteristics and to develop the cultural activities. A total development of society and recognizing the status of woman in society is deemed to be a pure objective of this institution.So the Jamatia Hada was established with special aim to:

1. render self sacrifice and hard labour in the educational and social development of the Jamatiya Society
2. encourage all types of development in industry and health
3. to strenghthen social fighting unitedly in perspective of time and situation. The name of the highest organization of the Jamatia Community is Hada. Hada means Society. It is limited within the JamatiaSociety only. So it is termed as Jamatia Hada. The Jamatia Hoda is a firm and independent social institution free from party politics It was formed with a view to heightening the social character as well as protecting the Indian democratic rights.

The aim of the paper is to focus on the changing aspects of the traditional institution of Jamatia Hada. One of the main objectives of this institution is to eradicate superstition and ignorance with a view to protect social unity and to develop the cultural activities. A total development of society and recognizing the status of women in society is seemed to be a pure objective of this institution. The traditional structure of the Jamatia Society is formed in three stages— Hada, Mayal and Luku. Hada is the highest organization of the society. It directs and decides the social rules and practices of entire Jamatia Society. Previously un-written Hada Structure maintained the identity of their culture and characteristics. But in this changing era of advent of more complex issues in society the need for written constitution for Hada Institution was felt. As such a written Hada Structure was accepted for the first time in pursuance of the decisions adopted in the

Annual Conference of Jamatia Hada held in in Koaimura Para on 25th, 26th Agrahayan, 1382 Tripurabda.

It has been observed that all the social norms and regulations essential for guiding the activities and attitudes of the society did not come under the purview of the first written constitution of the Hada Structure. Some additions and alterations became essential. So in the successive annual conference of Hada some important regulations were adopted. In the recent past some militant organization has been posing threat to the traditional religious beliefs of tribal people They are being warned for practicing 'Hinduism' and are being asked to avoid idol worship. April, 1998 witnessed the Jamatia rebelling against the militant organization when they were given instruction not to participate in their most popular festival Garia Puja. Since then Jamatia Hada has been relentlessly organizing community activities against militants to save their traditional culture and religion from their onslaught. A peep into the working system of Jamatia Hada System reveals the fact that the community is trying to maintain its customary system of unity and religious faith of oneness. Time and again it has appealed to the Tribal Customary Law Committee, TTAADC for codification of their customary law but yet to get any response from the appropriate Authority on this important issue.

Observations

1. With the advent of time and increased activities of the leaders of the society it was felt that a Committee should be formed to assist the Hada Okra to perform their daily responsibilities. Accordingly a progressive and strong Advisory Committee was formed in the Annual General Meeting in1377 Tripurabda in the Kaiseng Bulai Bari for directing Hada and perform developmental works. This Committee is formed unanimously for a period of five years in the annual meeting of Hada.The member of the Committee shall be at least seven to nine. The prime duty of the Committee is to help and give suggestions to the Okras for making the working policies of Hada popular and effective and heightening the standard of living as well.

2. There is provision for amendment of the Hada Institution.To amend the constitution at least two third members of the Hada Advisory Committee should give their consent. Moreover, Proposal regarding amendment should be discussed in full session and can be accepted only when approved by the Hada Okra.
3. A brief study of the Constitution of Jamatia Hada System reveals that there is system of Checks and Balances on the power of Hada Okra. The Advisory Council acts as a check on the dictatorial tendencies of the Okras. The Okras can also be terminated before their tenure on ground of dishonesty, corruption and moral degradation.
4. The women section of the society is generally honored and torture on the women is considered as a serious crime. The accused on this respect face severe punishment in comparison with other crime. This proves that the society as a whole stands for the dignity of women. In respect of widow marriage there is liberal attitude of the society as we find in article 246 of section 26.Another point to be noticed is that with the change of time the Jamatia Society is giving more importance to women's participation in Hada activities. Earlier also women were members of Hada Working Committee. But a resolution has been passed confirming that one third participation of women representatives in the Working Committee must be ensured.
5. Recently Jamatia Hada Institution is fighting against the religious threat to its religious beliefs posed by Insurgent Groups April 1988 witnessed the Jamatia rebelling against the NLFT for the first time when the latter instructed the community noi to participate in their most important festival ,Garia Puja but to worship Jesus. That year Garia Puja was held at Pitra, South Tripura District with the largest ever congregation. This was an avert defiance against militants to save their traditional culture and religion from their onslaught.
6. A peep into the working system of 'amatia Hada System reveals that the community is trying to maintain

its customary system of unity and religious faith of oneness. Time and again it has applied to the Tribal Customary Law Committee, TTAADC for codification of their customary Law but yet to get any response from the appropriate authority on this important issue. Their grievance has been expressed in the memorandum submitted to the Chief Minister and Prime Minister respectively.

7. During the regime of Manikya Rulers the tribes enjoyed their traditional freedom based on the concept of self administration and the relation between the king and the subject tribes was maintained through the tribal chiefs or community Spokesman.These ancient self governing institutions differed from tribe to tribe. The Tripuris,Lushai and the Chakmas have a one tier system of self-governing system, but the Jamatias and the Reangs have a three tier system of self- governing . These hierarchical systems of administration demonstrate a very developed system of social administration. Before giving the verdict the Village Headman consulted other members on the basis of the complaints made by the disputants and witnesses. Violation of this verdict was seldom found. Although the leaders of the council were not elected, they were acceptable to all.
8. The system of traditional social institutions of Jamatia Community of Tripura again proves the statement of Dr. Radha Kumud Mookherji made long years ago that 'the culture of the ancient Indian races was conserved and promoted through the indigenous machinery of appropriate institutions handed down from time immemorial, which embraced the manifold spheres of national life, economic and educational, social and religious. Thus the genius of the races was never in danger of being chocked and stiffed for as it was never in want of the adequate means of its self expression.' Like all other tribal communities the Jamatias are also in transitional phase and exposed to the influences of modern and new social forces. But it is to be noticed that with the advent of time the self

governing institutions of the community has laid down some necessary modifications. For example, minimum marriage time of boys and girls being 21 years and 18 years respectively has been specifically mentioned. In respect of widow marriage there is liberal attitude of the society as we find in article 246 of section 26 (present Hoda Constitution). Another praiseworthy feature is that with the change of time the Jamatia Society is giving more importance to women participation in Hada activities. Long back also women were members of Hoda Working Committee. The Working Committee passed a resolution that one third participation of women representatives in the Working Committee must be ensured. The introduction of delegate fee has been a recent phenomenon. The system has been accepted to overcome financial crisis in the festival of Garia which is the major festival in the Jamatia Society.

In spite of some weakness the traditional tribal self governing institutions can be termed 'democratic' in the sense that even in much earlier times the decisions on any issue used to be taken in an open meeting of the community and not surreptiously. This was unlikely in feudal system of other society where the so-called feudal lords took autocratic decision neglecting the common voice.

REFERENCES

1. Radhakumud Mookherjee, *Local Government in Ancient India*, Edn,1958
2. P.N. Bhattacharya, *The Jamatias of Tripura*, Directorate of Research, 1983.
3. Pratap Choudhury, Local Self Governing Institutions of Tripura, an article presented in the Seminar on 'Local Self Government of Tripura, organized by Government Women's College, Agartala, NOV, 1991.
4. Hada Constitution, adopted on Tripurabda, 1404.
5. Leaflet of the proposed legislation adopted in the annual conference 11th December, 1993.
6. Dr. Chandrika Basu Majumder, Democratic Heritage of Tribes of Tripura, Tribal Research Institute, Government of Tripura, 2002.

13

Terrorism and Mass-Media: A Symbiotic Relationship—An Overview

ANJANA GHOSH*

Terrorism in the 21st century has taken the form of a transnational non-state warfare , as the terrorist groups are no longer operating within the territory of a particular state and nor do these groups require a conventional army to attack or resist the enemy or to inflict maximum damage on the adversary. They are identified as 'terrorists without state'. Infact, modern means of communication has given global terrorism a new dimension, where terrorism and media have virtually developed a symbiotic relationship. Today, media brings before the terrorist groups wide opportunities to go beyond the direct victims and to reach out to a larger population, with the aim of waging a psychological warfare through violence and intimidation. Bruce Hoffman observes that "the contemporary terrorists, motivated by a religious imperative are engaged in more indiscriminate acts of violence against a far wider category of targets, encompassing not merely their declared enemies but anyone who does not share their religious faith and even persons who are of the same faith but who do not share the terrorists' extreme political

* Selection Grade Lecturer in Political Science, Mrinalini Datta Mahavidyapith, Kolkata 51.

views and theological constructs[1]". Brian Michael Jenkins says that, terrorism is a theatre and the terrorists do not want a lot of people dead, rather they want a lot of people watching and listening. This watching and listening has ranged from a few villagers who stood by, while terrorists act to live television coverage, piped into millions of homes[2]. Terrorism therefore should not be seen merely as an act of violence, deliberately performed to attract attention, but should be viewed as an act to communicate a message to a target population[3]. According to Frederick Hacker, "Terrorists play to and for a audience and solicit audience participation[4]." Infact, terrorist attacks are often carefully choreographed to attract the attention of media, because media helps to bring the aims, ideas, demands of the terror outfit before the Government as well as the ordinary people. For example Al- Zajeera, a Qatar-based television channel is widely used by the terrorist groups specially Al-Qaeda, for showing the video clippings of the beheading of the captives abducted by them. A video tape of the captured American journalist Daniel Pearl was shown on several terrorist websites after his abduction and brutal murder in 2002. It is relevant to mention here that, the murder of Pakistani journalist Moosa Khankhel (in February 2009) ,who was reporting from the volatile Swat Valley near the Pak-Afghan border certainly conveyed a message to other journalists working there[5]. It was no doubt a 'threat' to them, so that they leave the Taliban-controlled Valley.

Gabriel Weimann observes in this context that, terrorist acts sometimes becomes "media events", hence a terror unit consists of atleast four members : the perpetrator, a cameraman, a soundman and a producer[6]. Infact all important terrorist groups today have their own media and publicity wings, like radio and television channel, magazines, video and audio cassettes and even own websites. Al-Qaeda's television channel 'Voice of Caliphate' played an important role in publicizing its own extremist ideas[7]. Weirnann further says that the terrorist websites target different types of audience such as—potential supporters, international public opinion and the enemy public[8]. For the potential supporters these websites use slogans and even offer items for sale, such as flags , badges, T-shirts , video tapes and audio cassettes. For attracting international public opinion, terrorist websites welcome people to interact with them[9]. One of Hezbollah's sites specifically address journalists and invites them to interact with the organization's press office via e-mail[10]. The pro-LTTE website Tamil Net is continuously providing news on the genocidal attacks, carried on by the Sri Lankan army against the innocent Tamil civilians, trapped in the war-zone. The main aim of such campaign is not only to create sympathy in favour of the Tamil cause, but also to mould international public opinion against the Mahindra Rajapakse Government. So far as the enemy public is concerned, these terrorist websites try to initiate a public debate within the enemy state to change public opinion and subsequently to weaken public support for the Government or the ruling elite[11].

However, the use of Internet by the terrorist groups have largely increased their communication capabilities. Gabriel Weimann says that in 2006 there were almost four thousand eight hundred online forums, chat rooms and websites to serve the interests of different terrorist groups[12]. Infact, terrorism in the internet has become a dynamic phenomenon because these websites suddenly emerge, change the online address, often modify their format and even swiftly disappear[13]. Terrorist websites not only provide the history and activities of the organization but also give information regarding its political and ideological aims and carry on a vociferous criticism of their enemies. These websites also carry threat messages. For example , following the terrorist attack in Mumbai on November 26, 2008, when an aggressive diplomatic row was going on between New Delhi and Islamabad, an Al-Qaeda leader, Mustafa Abu Al Yazid , organizations' military commander in Afghanistan conveyed a threat message to the Government of India through a video tape[14]. The message was that, if India attacks Pakistan, it will have to be prepared for more 26/11. However this Al-Qaeda leader has taken responsibility for Benazir Bhutto's assassination[15]. In February 2009, Osama bin Laden has issued an audio statement which called for a jihad against Israeli aggression in Gaza and to restore Jerusalem and Palestine[16].

However, the main reasons behind the increasing use of Internet by the terrorist groups are[17]:

a) Internet access is easy due to the mushrooming of the cybercafés.
b) The identity of the communicator remains anonymous.
c) Flow of information is very fast.
d) It reaches out to vast population spreading across the world.
e) Use of internet is relatively cost friendly.
f) Internet is not subject to Government control and censorship.
g) Internet serves as an interactive medium between the communicator and the receiver or the target population.
h) It gives an opportunity to the users to see, read and download photo, films, and books and other propaganda materials supplied by the terror websites.

Terrorist groups not only use Internet as their propaganda machine , but also raise fund, recruit members, provide training and incite violence through it[18]. Infact, as terrorism is becoming more and more techno friendly it is attracting more and more educated persons towards its ideology, specially the engineers and even doctors. Terrorist groups use internet for planning, networking and coordinating attacks through it. Bruce Hoffman observes that internet has helped Al-Qaeda to communicate with its fighters , followers, supporters and sympathizers, spread all over the world[19]. However, propaganda through Internet has come to be known as 'e-jihad'[20]. It is not an exaggeration to say that, Internet has played an important role behind Al-Qaeda's transformation from a transnational terror group to an ideology and a movement thereafter and Osama bin Laden's glorious image of a messiah of the oppressed and exploited in the Islamic world.

Terrorist groups at present use Internet for conducting both intra-group and inter-group ideological debates. For example, an ideological conflict between different Saudi Jihadi groups led to the online publication of a book named, 'Osama bin Laden : The Reformer of Our Times and Defeater of the Americans', by a Saudi scholar, to impress the minds of a targeted audience[21]. Hamas, the Palestinian militant organization, now in control of Gaza, has been using Internet extensively for its propaganda purpose. In January 2004, Hamas posted the photo of its first woman suicide bomber, Reeim Raiyshi, on its webside, holding a rifle and her two children[22]. Actually Hamas was justifying the sending of women suicide bombers for attacking Israeli targets. Hamas wanted to project that Israel's torture and oppression even motivates an woman to be a suicide bomber, inspite of her attachment to her children, as some Palestinian groups had opposed such action[23].

Internet is also providing an ideal medium of communication to the numerous small and semi independent terrorist cells spread over the territory of different states. These small cells may not be directly connected with a big and much known terrorist organization. These are known as sleeper cells, consisting of local operatives, providing logistical support for an attack. These sleeper cells often become active and then go to hibernation and hence it becomes very difficult for the security forces to locate and crush such cells. In case of the terrorist attacks in different cities in India such sleeper cells were involved in carrying out the operation.

Jessica Stern observes that, the presence of terrorist groups in the cyber space has facilitated a new type of 'leaderless resistance[24]'. At present an individual does not necessarily require the membership of a particular terror outfit to inflict damage on the enemy or the adversary, as the jihadi websites now offer training in the production of explosives and their uses. In an online article, titled "Culture of Jihad", a Saudi Islamist once argued that, he does not need to take permission from Osama bin Laden to carry out an operation and it is not also important to know whether Laden is dead or alive[25]. What is important is that, Al Qaeda's sympathizers and supporters should not abandon the way, which Laden has shown. In fact, Jihadi websites target tortured and aggrieved persons through their campaign to turn them into supporters. Such campaign can also make an individual a radical perpetrator. Thus, Internet has become the primary medium for promoting radical Islam[26]. Now it has become easy only for a few indoctrinated persons to carry on an attack in a shopping mall, market place, cinema hall, tourist bus or railway station by detonating explosive devices as these places are soft targets and remain less secure, though crowdy. But such attacks create trauma in the minds of a large population. Terror experts also think that 'suicide bombing' is more an individual act than a collective action, because online stories, speeches of the leaders, photos etc. can incite a potential supporter to become a heroic martyr[27]. Gabriel Weimann has identified these terrorists, who are not only media oriented but prefer to use modern technology like internet , for propaganda, recruitment and operation within a decentralized and loosely knit network, as 'post-modern' terrorists[28].

Terrorism and Internet are related to each other in another way also. Terror groups can attack and destroy the computer network and thereby paralyse the command, communication and control chain of the defence forces, as military logistics today are largely dependent on computer system. The aim of such attack is to disrupt, deny, degrade, destroy or deceive an adversary's information system. In fact, the US air force is actively seeking 'cyberspace attack scenarios' at present, as it thinks that cyberspace has emerged as a war-fighting zone like land, sea and air. However, Gabriel Weimann observes that currently terrorist groups are more inclined towards utilizing the internet for achieving their goals rather than going for a cyber warfare[29].

Finally it may be said that modern communication technology has brought a fundamental change in the traditional concepts of 'threat' and 'security'. Today, media-based terrorism is throwing a new challenge to the state. As transnational terror outfits are operating increasingly through Internet for extensive propaganda and indoctrination, these are in an advantageous position to wage a war of ideas against their adversary, even after the liquidation of their operational base. Brian Michael Jenkins observed as early as in 1978, that, in future, highly destructive warfare may be waged without the necessity for armies and Government, by people or gangs with little to lose[30]. Global war on terror, based on military method is gradually becoming invalid in this situation. It has been found that the US drone attacks in volatile Pak-Afghan region have practically strengthened Pakistani Taliban forces. Infact, the grave situation in Pakistan, accompanied by the rise and spread of Taliban, frequent suicide bombing in different parts of the country, virtual statelessness status of the tribal areas adjoining Pak-Afghan border, introduction of Shariah laws in Swat Valley is an indication to this reality. However, this is completely a new type of power conflict between the state and the non state actors in the post-cold war international politics.

REFERENCES

1. Bruce Hoffman , 'A Form of Psychological Warfare', *E-Journal USA, Foreign Policy Agenda,* Volume 12, No. 5, May 2007, p. 9.
2. *Ibid,* p. 10.
3. *Ibid.,* p. 9.
4. *Ibid.*
5. *Ananda Bazar Patrika,* February 19, 2009.
6. Gabriel Weimann, Mass-Media Theater, *E-Journal USA, Foreign Policy Agenda,* Volume 12, No. 5, May 2007, p. 30.
7. Ibid.
8. Gabriel Weimann, www.terror.net. How Modern Terrorism Uses The Internet www.usip.org/pubs/special reports/ sr116.html-68k-
9. *Ibid.*
10. *Ibid.*
11. *Ibid.*
12. Gabriel Weimann, Virtual Disputes : The Use of Internet for Terrorist Debates, *Studies in Conflict and Terrorism,*Vol. 29, 2006, p. 624.
13. Gabriel Weimann ,www.terror.net. How Modern Terrorism Uses The Internet www.usip.org/pubs/special reports/ sr116.html-68k-
14. *Ananda Bazar Patrika,* February 11, 2009.

15. *Ibid.*
16. *The Statesman,* January 15 2009.
17. Gabriel Weimann,Virtual Disputes :The Use of Internet for Terrorist Debates, *Studies in Conflict and Terrorism,*Vol. 29, 2006, p. 624.
18. Editors of Discover, The Future of Terrorism, *Discover,* Vol 27, No. 7, July 2006, p. 35.
19. Bruce Hoffman, 'A Form of Psychological Warfare', *E-Journal USA, Foreign Policy Agenda,* Volume 12, No. 5, May 2007, p. 11.
20. Editors of Discover, The Future of Terrorism, *Discover,* Vol 27, No. 7, July 2006, p. 32.
21. Gabriel Weimann,Virtual Disputes :The Use of Internet for Terrorist Debates, *Studies in Conflict and Terrorism,*Vol. 29, 2006, p. 625.
22. *Ibid,* p. 627.
23. *Ibid.*
24. Jessica Stern, The Protean Enemy, *Foreign Affairs,* Vol. 82, No. 4, 2003, pp. 34-35.
25. *Ibid,* p. 33.
26. *The Statesman,* January 3, 2009.
27. Mohemmed M. Hafez, A Case Study: The Mythology of Martyrdom in Iraq, *E-Journal USA, Foreign Policy Agenda,* Volume 12, No. 5, May 2007, p. 33.
28. Gabriel Weimann ,Virtual Disputes: The Use of Internet for Terrorist Debates, *Studies in Conflict and Terrorism,*Vol. 29, 2006, p. 636.
29. Gabriel Weimann, Mass-Media Theater ,E-Journal USA, *Foreign Policy Agenda,* Volume 12, No. 5, May 2007, p. 30.
30. James Fallows , Success Without Victory, *The Atlantic Monthly,* January/February, 2005, p. 80.

14

A Comparative Analysis of the Role of Managers in the Small and Medium Enterprises in India

PRALLAD DEBNATH*

Abstract

This paper attempts to make an in depth study of the role of managers as well as the policies pertaining to management of small ad medium enterprises in India. To this purpose, it presents the theory of management and policy thereby based on principles. This is followed by an analysis of major management functions for SMEs which create more jobs in different directions than large firms in some total and have a distinctive role to play in innovation from sector to sector. The study has been focused on the careful analysis of the role of managers in managing the SMEs through the specific categories of managerial issues in the context of Indian environment. In this regard, the Small and Medium Enterprises have been playing a pivotal role during the last three decades in shaping the industrial economy of the country. The needs of successful management of Small and Medium Enterprises required changes capability of the

* HOD, Commerce, Tripura University.

managers. As it is an on going process which should always be ready for leaving the door opens to innovation and opportunities in future in any exigency. The conceptual framework presented in this paper provides a foundation from which learning as well as development can be provided. The only thing is to make those enterprises into profitable enterprises is of the right role be played by the managers in the management of small and medium enterprises in India.

Key-words: Innovation, Pivotal role, Exigency, Profitable, Opportunity.

Introduction

The paper is an attempt to analyze the role of managers in the Small and Medium Enterprises in India. A dynamic manager is always pragmatic. Given the potentialities of the enterprises, he sets attainable goals, which are to be accomplished in specific timeframes. He must believe in, create, and practice "win-win" situations. A successful enterprise is a focal point behind the economic prosperity of any state as well as the country as a whole either it is in Small or Medium Scale sector. The Small and Medium Enterprises account for a considerable majority of industrial units and highest proportion of employment of most developing as well as developed countries. They produce about 25% of Organization for Economic Cooperation and Development (OECD) exports and 35% of Asia's exports (OECD, 1997). But in the current era of globalization, those SMEs that are internationally competitive are able to grow as well as survive better in the domestic markets. For that, the SMEs must be market oriented and offer product and services of international quality too. Small producers face a variety of challenges- some related to markets and others related to capabilities. Inability to develop technological capabilities has often restricted small as well as medium enterprises from growing large. Though the Small and Medium Enterprises have been playing a pivotal role during the last three decades in shaping the industrial economy of the country. However, there is as yet no proper or complete census of the number, product range, output and financial results of enterprises that are classified under the umbrella of small scale industry. But the industrial policy Statement of 1980 stressed on the balanced and harmonious development of all sectors of business enterprises in the states as well as in the district level, especially in the industrially backward areas to generate as many ancillary and small and cottage units as possible. Now it is redefined to include all those manufacturing and repairing units. The upper limit on investment to facilitate modernization and speedy growth, the upper ceiling on investment, plant and machinery, has been raised in respect of small scale units from Rs.20 lakhs to Rs.35 lakhs and in the case of ancillary units from Rs.25 lakhs to Rs.45 lakhs. It is true that often the fruit of entrepreneurial activity is the founding of a small business. After the entrepreneur has determined what business has to be in and has developed a strategic plan of entry he or, she is otherwise stated, must focus on the operational aspect of running a small or medium business enterprise. All the activities of Industrial Finance Corporation of India (IFCI) are developmental and promotional in character since the beginning. But they were confined to medium and large scale industrial concerns operating in corporate and cooperative sectors. Thereafter it was decided in the Silver Jubilee Year of IFCI to make necessary amendment in IFCI Act, 1948 so as to encourage the promotion of small and medium scale enterprises in consonance with Industrial and planning policies of India. Thus the BRF and IDFs were originated in pursuance of amendment to IFCI Act, 1948 in December 1972. Benevolent Reserve Fund (BRF) is financed out of profits earned by the IFCI. Likewise, Interest Differential Funds (IDFs) is financed out of money received from India. As such the funds of both the resources are creatively utilized for the purpose of the promotion of Small and Medium Enterprises in India. As such, the details of running the business are important and the entrepreneur must be a generalist, doing a little of everything. So the management of Small and Medium Enterprises (SMEs) is very important where in entrepreneurship rests mostly with the owner or the owner-manager. It has been observed that the small and medium enterprises have been playing a pivotal role for the development of urban as well as rural areas. As such this has to propose distinctive determinants of a collaborative model for engaging SMEs in technological innovation over a period of time. It was found that almost 49% of the 2006 enterprises were engaged in technological innovations mostly informally. These innovations are primarily incremental in nature and product oriented. Self-efforts are the major source of innovation and the role of external agencies, particularly Government agencies, was found to be minimum. External factors, particularly competition and customer needs, were the major motivating factors for small and medium enterprises to engage in motivations to achieve the objectives of enhancement of competitiveness through quality improvement, cost reduction and meeting market needs. However, there is hardly any management literature, which comparatively analyzed the innovations of enterprises with references to any particular industry in India as well as abroad. The role of government promoted institutions was not significantly visible as well as responding, this is only supplementary, to say the least. In this globally competitive environment, there will be greater pressure on large enterprises to improve there competitiveness through quality improvement and cost reduction. This is in turn, will pressurize small enterprises who are vendors to large enterprises, to innovate for quality improvement and cost reduction, on their own or with customer support. Given this, it is likely to more small and medium enterprises will become or will continue to remain in India. What is important to the managers in the SMEs are: focus of the enterprise, interactive producers, processing and product manufacturing, innovation investment, markets, market makers and regulatory support.

In view of the afore –mentioned observation, the present study aims –

1. To ascertain the scenario of various managerial issues for Small and Medium Enterprises in India;
2. To ascertain the causes of basic problems in Small and Medium Enterprises in India;
3. To make an in-depth study of the efforts made in the direction of various managerial issues for Small

and Medium Enterprises in India and what lacunae have crept therein;

4. To ascertain the future prospect of Small and Medium Enterprises in India.
5. What suggestions can be offered to make India a developed industrial country in Small and Medium Enterprises?

Resume of Related Literature

A Number of publications germane to managerial issues and its various facets have appeared during recent years. Propose to discuss here very briefly, some of the very useful and significant publications and their main points as follows:

The illustrious writers, Andrew P. and Richard W. have very calculative in presenting the scenario world-wide of SMEs as "International evidence from OECD countries also points to the major impact of the growth in small businesses." They also narrated that "it is noticeable that the more successful organizations have been much more self – critical of their planning."

One distinguished author, Chandra, Prasanna has very nicely presented that "the production plan is geared to meet the requirements of sales. Goods flow from the production line largely in conformity with the needs of sales. There may however, be significance divergence between the pattern of sales and the pattern of production. This happens under two conditions :(i) there is a pronounced seasonal variation in sales where as production is planned in a stable manner;(ii) production necessarily has to be carried out during a certain period of the year, where as sales occurs round the year though there may be some seasonal variations".

In the case of Small and Medium Enterprises the steps involved in preparing the production budget as "1.assess the productive capacity of the firm, 2.specify the finished goods inventory policy of the firm. 3. Estimate the total quantity of each product to be manufactured during the budget period on the basis of sales forecast and finished goods inventory policy. 4. Schedule the production during the budget period, taking into account the pattern of sales, the finished goods inventory policy, and the productive capacity".

In an outstanding article, Chandra and Sastry have beautifully illustrated capabilities building of the entrepreneurs in India.

The definition of small business in India has frequently changed over the years. A retrospective picture of this changing definition is as follows:

Small and Medium Enterprises in India, employments and earnings, examined some long term treads in output, earnings in manufacturing. It documents and explains the building of capabilities and integration with global markets of small scale firms.

One illustrious writer, Charanthimath has beautifully discussed the various issues in Small Business Enterprises in India and their development as well in removing bottlenecks as "India has an extraordinary talent pool with virtually limitless potential for entrepreneurship. India must, however, commit to creating the right environment to develop successful business builders: To do this, India must focus on four areas: Create the right environment for success, Ensure that entrepreneur have access to the right skill: Ensure that entrepreneurs have access to "smart" capital: Enable networking and exchange."

Dollinger Marc J. has rightly observed that "Qualitative objectives are more concerned with the effectiveness of the new venture. Effectiveness is the extent to which the firm is able to maintain and expand its position in the competitive environment".

Halt, David H. has judiciously observed as "Borrowers also must have appropriate collateral as security; the Small Business Administration does not accept unsecured applications. Collateral includes assets normally considered as security by lenders, including real estate, machinery, inventory, equipment, personal property, and receivables."

An outstanding author on the management of finance, Pandey, I M has advocated very eloquently that "Banks are the main institutional sources of working capital finance in India. After trade credit, bank credit is the most important sources of financing working capital requirements.......sales and production plans and the desirable levels of current assets in determining its working capital requirements"

So far the frequent changed definitions of small business over the years were witnessed in India; a survey was made in this regard taking into account the merits of changing definitions of Small Business in India.

Various scholarly editors have also merited attention regarding the different levels of management in Small and Medium Enterprises in India.

Noted Scholars, Mitra, R, & Pingali, V. of the time have categorically narrated Small and Medium Enterprises in India as "Small and medium-sized enterprises (SMEs) play a key role in generating employment, promoting innovation, en Small and Medium Enterprises in India gendering competition, and creating economic wealth (Sengenberger, Loveman, and Priore 1990)". They also very logically presented the need for re-thinking SMEs in India. As pointed "the long tradition of promoting small-scale enterprise in India is being re-examined in light of its success in creating a sector with the potential of performing all the above roles".

Peter F. Drucker, in his valuable contribution in management has said as "Many middle- sized and small businesses will have to become active in the world economy. To maintain leadership in one developed market, a company increasingly has to have a strong presence in such markets world wide."

In a study of the pre-1990s period, Sandesara (1988) concludes that "small firms experienced a decline relative to large-scale industries in terms of five important parameters - number of factories, fixed capital, and number of employees, output, and value added. In the post-liberalization era, this issue has assumed renewed importance".

Again they narrated that the small and medium scale sectors in India have now been identified by the government as "one that can assist in generating additional employment, indigenizing technology, and leveraging cheap labor and flexibility of operations to create competitive advantage for Indian industry".

As a result, the government recently raised the asset size

limit used to define small firms for government aid eligibility to include what had been defined as the medium-size sector. Thus small firms can now openly pursue a growth objective without running the risk of losing their small firm status and all the accompanying promotional subsidies.

In an investigation into the reasons why some SMEs grow and others don't, Hay concludes that "over the long term it is internal rather than external barriers to growth that exerts the decisive influence upon SMEs' rate of growth".

In the Report presented by the World Association for Small and Medium Enterprises (WASME), (1980), New Delhi, India, elaborate discussions were made in regard to various facets of micro, small and medium enterprises of the 112 countries including India.

Ron Adner has beautifully proposed that "successful innovation requires tracking your partners and potential adopters as closely as you track your own development process."

David A. Garvin and Lynce C. Levesque has very nicely observed as "For large companies creating new business is the challenge of the day. After years of down sizing and cost cutting, corporations have realized that they cannot shrink their way to success. They have also found that they cannot grow rapidly by tweaking existing offerings, taking over revivals, or moving into developing countries."

Rosabeth Moss Kanter has also beautifully written that "Innovation is back at the top of the corporate agenda. Never a fad, but always in or out of fashion, innovation gets rediscovered as a growth enabler every half – dozen years (about the length of a managerial generation).

John S. Hammond, Ralph L. Keeney & Howard Raiffa have very nicely presented as "In making decisions you may be at the mercy of your mind's stranger workings. Here is how to catch thinking traps before you become judgment disaster".

The Three distinguish authority on Management, Stoner, Freeman, Gilbert, Jr., have very articulately presented the impoitance of Small and Medium Business as "Small business plays a central role in our lives because we conduct much of our own personal economic activity with people running small business. Whenever you have your bicycle repaired, get your hair cut, or visit your dentist, you are part of the small business economy."

Concepts of Small Business

Small Business has emerged as India's engine of growth in the new millennium. To run the business focused attention is required to the various functional activities of an enterprise, such as accounting and legal, personnel, finance, marketing, manufacturing and engineering (operational areas), maintenance, and security. In medium enterprise, of course, each of these functions is executed by a departmental team of managers and employees. But, in case of small business, often the entrepreneur has only a manager or two to help him coordinate the entire operation of the enterprise and sometimes, he himself is the self-styled owner-manager. Indian Government's recent definition:

Small Company - Those companies which have 1 crore as total capital in plant and machinery. Medium Company - Those companies which have 1 crore as total capital in plant and machinery.

A European definition has a complex formula considering the revenue, No of employees etc., this definition considers a company which employs about 250 people as a Medium Enterprise and 50 People as Small Enterprise.

In India, SME companies account for a 45% of Industrial employment and produce 50% of the industrial output. The definition of small business in India has frequently changed over the years. A retrospective picture of this changing definition is as follows:

Table 1: Year-Wise Changing Definitions of Small Business in India

	Year	*Defining Authority*	*Defined As*
1.	1950	Fiscal Commission	A unit operating mainly with hired labour (Usually10 to 15 hands)
2.	1955	Small Scale	A unit employing less then 50 persons

		Industries Board	if using power and with a capital investment not exceeding Rs.5 lakhs
3.	1966	Ministry of Industry	An undertaking having a capital investment in plant and machinery and not more than Rs.7.5 lakhs irrespective of the number of persons employed.
4.	1975	Government of India	An undertaking having a capital investment in plant and machinery of not more than lakhs Rs. 10 and Rs. 15 lakhs in case of ancillary units
5.	1980	Government of India.	An undertaking having an investment in plant and machinery and not more than Rs. 25 lakhs and more than Rs. 20 lakhs in case of ancillary unit
6.	1985	Government of India	An undertaking having an investment in plant and machinery of not more than Rs. 35 lakhs and not more than Rs. 45 lakhs in case of ancillary units
7.	1990	Government of India	An undertaking having an investment in plant and machinery of not more than Rs. 60 lakh and not more than Rs. 75 lakhs in case of ancillary units
8.	1996	Ministry of Industry	An industrial unit with a capital investment in plant and machinery and not more than Rs.75 lakhs irrespective of the number of persons employed
9.	2001	Government of India	An undertaking in which the investment in fixed assets, in plant and machinery, whether held ownership terms or on lease or by hire purchase, does not exceed Rs.100 lakh and in case of ancillary unit ,does not exceed Rs.1crore. as on March 31,2001

There is a frequent change in the investment ceiling that small has become big in course of time. The investment ceiling in plant and machinery was Rs.5 lakhs in the fifties, Rs. 7.5 lakhs in the sixties, Rs.15 lakhs in the seventies, and Rs.35 lakhs in considering the proposal to raise it to Rs. 3 crore thereafter. A picture in regard to changes in the investment ceiling of SSI and Ancillary Units (AU) is furnished below:

Table 2

Year	*Investment (Rs.)*	
	SSI	*AU*
1955	5 lakhs	—
1966	7.5	—
1975	10	15
1980	25	20
1985	35	45
1991	60	75
1996	75	85
2001	100 lakh	Rs.1crore

Major Management Challenges for SMEs

The producers of Small and medium enterprises, especially in emerging economies, face a challenge of becoming part of a capability driven economy. While large enterprises internalize many of the costs associated with developing capabilities to meet the requirements of the markets, small and medium producers do not possess the scale needed to drive such activities internally. Most simply, they do not have access to complementary resources needed to run their business effectively. Scarcity of working Capital also means that many investments required increasing the product quality, lead times and productivity is not available to them easily. Moreover, the overwhelming power of high channel forces these producers have to sell at razor thin margins. This may be exaggerated when the market for the products produced by SMEs is not located in the vicinity of production unit. One of the important features of modern manufacturing in India has been the dilemma of strategic positioning of SMEs. The SMEs wishes to become ancillary producers of large plants whereby they can create stable demand but where the economics of production favours a large supplier. Often managers in the SMEs need to identify areas of innovation that have commercial value than that of job shop only. Many of these challenges drive the enterprise towards survival rather then growths driven strategies and these disabling efforts take these firms away from becoming leaders in the industry in India. However, the hope for better future to lead the country is still awaited.

The key areas of management relating to SMEs for over all development are:

(a) Financial resources including liquidity and borrowing power;

(b) Personal resources, relating to numbers, depth, and quality of people, particularly at the management and staff levels;

(c) System resources, in terms of the degree of sophistication of both information and planning and control system;

(d) Business resources, including relations, market share, suppliers relations, manufacturing and distribution processes, and technology and reputation, all of which give the company in the industry and market;

(e) Managerial ability of the owner- manager and manager and willingness to delegate responsibility and to manage the activities of others;

(f) Strategic ability of the manager for looking beyond the present and aligning the strengths and weaknesses with his or her goals and so on.

In all the above cases, there are some styles of management in the Small and medium enterprises in regard to its functional areas such as finance, marketing, production, purchases, sales and human resource management. Small enterprise- small investment and medium enterprise- medium investment, but the peculiarities are not so small so far the shift in time and relationships that we have been seen through out the organizational world in its direct-activity and indirect-activity environments. There is also a changed environment in regard to financial activities, marketing activities, production activities in the day to day's operational periphery of the management of Small and Medium Enterprises. It is obvious that all these activities need a suitable managerial style to administer and manage those enterprises for the benefits, profitability, of course, of the organization in the long run to sustain in the risk- return trade-off which is the ultimate goal of an enterprise along with maximization of value too.

So a comprehensive study of the important areas of management of Small and Medium Enterprises categorically is very important to identify the special problems and challenges of this important economic sector. In this context, an emphasis has to be given on the following major management areas:

- Financial Management in small and medium enterprises
- Production Management in small and medium enterprises
- Marketing Management in small and medium enterprises
- Human Resource Management in small and medium enterprises

It is thus the study of all those managerial functions for the Small and Medium Enterprises assumes importance.

Considering the above essential areas of the management in Small and Medium Enterprises, an elaborate explanation of the enterprises is essential in regard to their positions in the respective patterns as follows:

- Financial Management in small and medium enterprises

There exists an inseparable relationship between finance on the one hand and production, marketing and other functions on the other. Almost all business activities, directly or indirectly, involve in the acquisition and use of funds. Thus, Financial management is the conscious effort to formulate long term policies with regard to major aspects of financing, investment and dividend decisions with a view to fulfilling the objectives of the firm. It is the operational activity of a business that is responsible for obtaining and effectively utilizing funds necessary for efficient operations of both small and medium enterprises. In that case, it has been observed that the entrepreneur must be the enterprise's chief financial officer(CFO) during the initial capital formation phase and often remains the CFO for the enterprise in case of small business operations. The officer, in the simplest terms, the fully responsible for managing the balance between the sources and uses of these funds. Though there is a conflict over maximization of profit and maximization of wealth, the enterprises with wealth maximization objective will ultimately sustain in the long run for earning profit on its business. The objective of the financial management of small and medium enterprises is to see that adequate cash is in hand to meet the required current and fixed expenses in such a manner so that the profit of the enterprises is magnified in all circumstances. In India, the growth of small and medium scale enterprises (SMEs) has been placed as one of the most important features in the development of industrial economy. It has recorded a significant increase in the number of small and medium scale units, value of production, value of exports, employment and investment. The small and medium scale sectors contribute about more than 50% of the manufacturing sector's gross value of output and value added in India. A brief review of the sources of financing to Small and Medium enterprises in India is as follows:

Table 3

Sources of finance	*Financing scheme*	*Form of Financial Assistance*
1. Commercial banks	Normal lending Priority sector lending Differential interest rate scheme	Working capital loans and term loans
2. Cooperative banks	Lending to SSI units organized on cooperative basis	Working capital loans
3. Regional Rural Banks	Extending lending to Tiny, SMEs	Working capital loans
4. RBI/DICGC	Credit guarantee scheme/small loans guarantee scheme	Guarantee of loans
5. IDBI	Refinance	Term loans
	Rediscounting of machinery bills	Rediscounting (loan)
	Special capital assistance for SMEs	Soft loans
	In Backward Areas	
	Seed capital	Equity / loan
	National equity fund	Equity
6. IFCI	Risk capital	Bridge loans
7. SFCs	Term lending	Term loans

	Special capital scheme	Equity and soft loans
8. SIDBI	Refinancing	Term loans
9. NSIC/SIDCs	Hire purchase facilities	Hire purchase

India has integrated structure of financial institutions known as All India Financial Intuitions (AIFIS) that provide term finance and other assistance to Small and Medium Enterprises, which have been developed since independence. These include banks and special financial institutions such as IDBI, IFCI, SFCS, SIDCS and recently constituted SIDBI. The assistance includes lending for investment of acquisition of capital- working capital and equity participation. Generally, banks are the chief suppliers of loans to the SMEs, but the percentage of share has been declined for SMEs in the credit made to the priority sector. In addition to this, there are other special financing schemes for seed capital, rediscounting bills, and so on. Until 1981, the RBI had been supporting lending to SMEs through a Credit Guarantee Scheme. A similar guarantee scheme for sanction of loans to SMEs is being operated by the Deposit Insurance and Credit Guarantee Schemes which is a fully owned subsidiary of RBI. However, for the Indian situation, what will be more appropriate is the definition of retail loan given under the February 2005 guidelines of RBI for large and medium enterprises, which also covers the small enterprises. There are four criteria in these guidelines in regard to claims that meet all the criteria may be included in a regulatory retailed portfolio and assigned a risk-weight of 75%. These are (OPGL):

1. Orientation criterion- This relates to individual person or persons or to a small business; small business is one where the total annual turn over is less than Rs. 50 crore.
2. Product criterion – The exposure takes the form of any of the following:

Line of credit- an arrangement specifying the maximum amount of unsecured credit the bank will permit to owe at any one time. Usually, credit lines are established for a one-year period and are subject to one-year renewals and other is revolving credit agreement (including credit cards and overdraft) by a bank to extend credit up to a maximum amount under a commitment. While the commitment is in force, the bank must extend credit whenever the borrower wishes to borrow, provided the total borrowings do not exceed the maximum amount specified.

3. Granularity criterion – In that case the bank must ensure that the regulatory retail portfolio is sufficiently diversified to a degree that reduces the risks in the portfolio, warranting the 75% risk weights.
4. Low value of individual exposure - This relates to the limit which the maximum agreed retail exposure to one counterpart should be the threshold limit of Rs. one crore to five crores depending on the total capital of the bank. Moreover, under the current Basel Capital Accord, loans to small business (i.e.SMEs), the strategic decisions about the different finance functions regarding small & medium enterprises are going far beyond the traditional concept of the procurement of funds and their uses. As per the RBI guideline in adopting the Basel Committee Suggestion by 31st March, 2007 banks can use standardized approach for credit risk. This may affect negatively on small and medium enterprises because loan sanction to SMEs whose credit ratings are not good, require 150% risk weight. But according to RBI regulation about retail portfolio (February 2005),banks can classify the sanction of loans to SMEs as retail loan and can assign risk weight of 75% provided a prescribed criteria is fulfilled. In regard to advanced approach to credit risk offered by Basel II also gives the concession of 25% risk weight for sanction of loans to small enterprises but not to medium enterprises. In spite of elaborate institutional system of financing for small or new entrepreneurs they have to meet a substantial part of their financial needs from their personal savings as well as support from their friends and relatives, whereas financing in medium scale enterprises must have to depend on the banks and financial institutions to a great extent.

Despite all the sources of financing to finance in Small

and Medium Enterprises in India, they are not free from drawbacks. The norms in regard to financing by the Govt. sponsored/controlled institutions act as the constraints in case of quick financing requirement to operate in the risky industries in the terrain of equity capital, risk venture, project evaluation and so on. Consequently, the traditional industrial finance in India is not of much help to SMEs specially, in case of new and emerging enterprises. So far the collateral is a concern, they are unable to offer collateral in teams of fixed assets, and rather it is contained in technical know-how and new idea. In other cases, it also can not maintain a balance between negative cash flow and positive cash flow for unavailability of financing during the entire period of operation. Also, the new enterprise would require development finance to enable them to pass from the pre start- up to start -up phase to the expansion phase. Thus, the venture capital is the financing mechanism befitting the requirements of the small and medium enterprises in India. What is necessary is to give a big push from policy makers for a sustained and large scale development of the enterprises in India as a whole.

Production Management in Small and Medium Enterprises

Management of production refers to the application of major management functions almost in all SMEs. This can be defined "as the process through which goods and services are created" Production is the combined output of the efforts of the five big agents namely, land, labour, capital, enterprise and management. Once the production schedule has been established, estimates can be made of the needs in materials, labour and additional fixed assets. As with receivables, there is a lag between the time a purchase is made and the time of actual cash payment. If suppliers give average terms of net 30, and the firm's policy is to pay its bill at the end of this period, there is approximately a one month lag between a purchase and the payment. So the Production Cycle is very carefully taken into account in this crucial period. The cycle should positively be influenced the growth of the enterprises, only when the managerial skills on the part of production manager may be restored.

The operations manager is in charge of producing items or services that the marketing department can sell to he or she must handle a vast amount of information from other department, and must plan and control the internal operations. Production planning and control is often performed by a separate functional department and serves as the nervous system for the production department. The controlling of production activities in the small enterprise assumes special significance at least in the early stages of the venture as much as almost each and every aspect of the business and its operation is new. This is simply because of inadvertent errors and limited resources, it is thus quite essential to detect and correct problems as quickly as possible for smooth function of the enterprise. In most small business ensuing that funds are in hand to pay immediate expenses is a particularly troublesome task in case of small enterprises. But this does not happen in case of medium enterprises, where the diversification of product is the order of the day. The medium enterprises manufacture not only one product but a host of product and question of immediate, therefore, is not as severe as in case of small enterprises. Production relates to the different kinds of products in the operation cycle of production. Classical studies conducted by Joan Woodward and her colleagues in a manufacturing firm in regard to small production, medium production and also mass production. Small production refers to products made in small quantities in separate stages and later assembled. Medium or mass production refers to the manufacture of large quantities of products, sometimes on an assembly line. But all those come across production cycle either in part or in toto. It is so complex in case of medium scale in comparison to small scale in the total round of the circle of the enterprises. The production cycle from material ordering to finished goods. This starts with the arrival of stock, and ends when the cash is received. The production manager affects the length of operating cycle by managing and controlling manufacturing cycle, which is a part of operating cycle and influences directly in case of medium enterprises . Longer the manufacturing cycle, longer will be the operating cycle and higher will be the enterprises' working capital requirement. To come out of this poor situation the following important points may strictly be taken care of:

1. Proper planning and coordination of all levels of the activities.
2. Proper maintenance of machinery, plant and other infrastructural facilities of the Enterprises.
3. Up-gradation of manufacturing system and technological change if requires.
4. Finding of shortest operating cycle out of the various alternatives to achieve maximum gain out of business operations.

Marketing Management in Small and Medium Enterprises

The present Indian scenario is so diverse and full of contrast and contradictions that one can sell almost anything. A progressive enterprise in the pattern of variation in marketing over the years to come through the actual marketing strategy of the enterprises running under small and medium scale is very important in the present competitive world. This strategy must be consistent with the goals of the enterprises. In case of small enterprise there're local or limited markets where as regional or the national market in case of medium enterprises. To exploit resource base of the enterprises for creating total marketing focus is essential to connect the customers for the success of the enterprise in marketing. The internet and entrepreneurship have grown together and have resulted in new concepts such as on line marketing, digital market place, and virtual organizations. To cover the fullest extent of the strategy in marketing, these focal indicators are to consider along with P-M-T as:

(i) Competitors
(ii) Product's strengths
(iii) Competitors weakness
(iv) Market research and particular segment
(v) Appeal to this segment
(vii) Image of the product and its consistency with the product
(viii) Proper packaging, branding and labeling of the product to market

(ix) Advertisement and campaigns along with promotional activities and combination of techniques and media for message to the customer,

(xi) Cost of the use of mediums and so on.

Once these were settled, the pricing strategy of the products will emerge in comparing with those of the competition. This must follow the image and value for the customers along with the profit margin either in the short run and long run operations. The credit policy of the enterprise, purchasing pattern, after sales services and on going relationship with the customers for enhancing business activities in the long run depending upon the nature of the business enterprises. The marketing manager has to apply all these strategies to achieve the ultimate goal of the enterprises.

Now, the question of distribution of the products in using the various distribution channels which is profitable to enterprises so as the product is to reach the market. Under the situations discussed here the sales forecasts will differ in case of small as well as medium enterprises. A very concept is of the buyers' location as well as the nature of purchasing decisions of the firm for the products: local, regional and national as well. But all enterprises must engage in marketing as a principle. The motto of marketing is to reach the buyers as much as possible in increasing the sales of products of the enterprises. The sales forecast on the part of enterprises is done in such a manner so that the ultimate objective is achieved. That is definitely not common in all type of enterprises. What is common in sales forecast is to earn profit over costs incurred on the products. The marketing concept is of strategic significance of any enterprise. It thus expresses the observation as "the consumer is the king". Specifically, the consumer is seen as the "fulcrum, the pivotal point on which the enterprises move in operating for the balanced best interests of all concerned". Enterprise of all seizes, small, medium or large, try to establish as the market research. Researching product is usually more difficult because inventors are unlikely to disclose the ideas until they are ready to go to the market. Excellent cooperation with expert planning systems rare understands what will take place in distant future. The typical marketing-research report will contain a summery of the key findings on which the marketing manager must look in to consider the strategy to proceed further for a successful profitable enterprise.

Human Resource Management in Small and Medium Enterprises

In the SMEs the role of HRM is important as human capital is vital for the enterprises. The challenge of human resource management of today is people - their development, their well-being and satisfaction. Management is usually a human process. It is something more than expert knowledge in systems and procedures. It is thus, the manager is oriented to solving problems with techniques, tailored to situations, must develop, a uniform framework of thought that encompasses the total and integrated aspects of the entire enterprises, small and medium. Of course, HRD manager must learn the art of management. They must learn to build organization and its people. It is rightly said that the best executive is one who has sense enough to pick good men to-do what he wants done, and self – restrain enough to keep from meddling with them while they do it. The 1980s were pivotal, for both academics and practitioners, in the coupling of the strategy concept to the human resource management function. This coupling of the concept to the functions itself very much linked to the development of the personnel function and pressures to "professionalize" and elevate the status of the personnel / human resource management department. The traditional concept was linked with the personnel management which was commonly associated with the functions such as hiring, firing, and record maintenance, while human resource management associated with more sophisticated management of human relations within and beyond the enterprises. Porter in 1985 advocated the HRM as the integral part of the value chain at firm level. The term HRM originated in the USA in the non-union companies and developed initially in the large scale industry like Texas Instrument, Hewlett Packard, and IBM and later extended to other firms which had traditional system. The commonly used definition in the UK is that set out by Guest in 1987as "comprises a set of policies designed to maximize organizational integration, employee commitment, flexibility and quality of work". He itemized four essential goals that are implicit within human resource management in regard to: (i) Integration, (ii) Employee commitment in the enterprise, (iii) Flexibility and Adaptability on the part of the rigidity, hierarchical, bureaucratic structure, and (iv) Quality in regard to maintenance of high standard in the enterprises.

To provide a comprehensive frame work and methods for the development of human resources in the small and medium enterprises for generation of systematic information about the management of human resources for the purpose of man power planning, right placement, increasing capabilities, motivating talented employees, and creating environment so that the human being in the enterprises can be utilized to the fullest extent.

The large or medium-sized enterprises require a separate HRM to assist the top management for doing a good deed of human relations. But a small scale concern can neither afford nor does it need a separate department to carry out this HRM function. However, the necessity for sound human resources policy and practices in building good employee morale is just as essential in the small enterprise as in the medium or large one. In small scale enterprise, with a smaller number of human resources, it is easier to build an intimate relationship between employees at all levels, and to make them into a good working team of the enterprise. The owner-manager in a small enterprise, often, has more men to manage than has his counterpart in medium or large enterprise, and less help from staff specialists, and therefore, has less time to devote to the individual problems of each worker. In developed countries, many small enterprises are often assisted in there human resource management problems by management experts in the lines.

Conclusions

Given the strong analytical role of managers in the small and medium enterprises is required a high degree of sophistication in all the areas wherein the success of the SMEs lies. To look in to this matter for the management of the SMEs over a period of time along with the competition and technological improvements, we must pay equal attention to all four aspects of important management functions in regard to its implementations in managing SMEs. And at the same time, the increased complexity in the links between financial management, production management, marketing management and human resource management may be avoided if issues are properly adhered to. The enterprises' efficiency mostly depend on the proper assimilation of these various management patterns along with other criteria like Performance budgeting, cost accounting, work study, consumer research, creation of employment opportunities, productivity, minimization of various costs, etc. Almost each of these factors involves technical and special expertise for the smooth and uninterrupted run of the Small and Medium Enterprises. The needs of successful management of Small and Medium Enterprises required changes capability as it is an on going process which should always be ready leaving the door open to innovation and opportunities in future in any exigency. In fine, Innovative concept is the only shield to protect from any untoward incidence in the management of Small and Medium Enterprises. It is thus; need of the hour that the sustenance of small and medium enterprises in this competitive world after L.P.G, management of those has been emerged. As the competition intensifies one may see stronger linkages between all major functions of management. It must be mentioned that enterprises have also not been pro-active in seeking out these linkages to advance their research capabilities. Increased competition in recent year seems to have led to a large number of alliances. Finally, at a broader level, these linkages in India need to be analyzed in the context of a few larger issues. SMEs 'continue to suffer from certain inherent weakness and handicaps largely because of their inability to furnish suitable security for obtaining adequate credit, inability to hire the services of skilled and technically qualified personnel for management, marketing, etc. WASME is continuously engaged in identification of such constraints and finding appropriate solutions. Till recently, the small and medium enterprises was not very research oriented partly because of lack of competitive pressures and bulk of the research was done in large industry. SMEs producers have an inherent advantage in performing innovative activities within the enterprises. Though, they also face coordination failures on account of variety of reasons. To overcome these drawbacks, enterprises need to design ways and means of coordination, especially on those issues that reasons market and capabilities failure. So a mechanism of coordination between small and medium producers should be developed so that capability and demand may restore as well. The much larger challenge, however, is to design appropriate work environment so that the SMEs can be done somewhat better than others in Indian business environment. To make those enterprises into vibrant and profitable enterprises is the management of small and medium enterprises to pick in a big way so as to cater to all requirements to make solid impact. The key to success of SMEs is the extent of trust and reliability within the members of the enterprise's network. It also reduces the market related search of cost for SMEs. Finally, this study opens doors for a broad range of research work on the part of Small and Medium Enterprises in India to make India a better India in the field of small and medium enterprises in this global competition.

REFERENCES

Books

1. Alam K., (1984) Planning in North Eastern India, Western Book Depo, India.
2. Andrew P. and Richard W. (2001) Change Management, India, Infinity Books.
3. Bernerd, B.W., (1997) Selecting the right form of business, Burr Ridge, IL: Richard D Irwin, Inc.
4. Batra G.S., Dangwal R.C., (2000) International Business, Deep & Deep Publication. India.
5. Batra G.S., Dangwal R.C., (2003), Entrepreneurship and Small Scales Industries. Deep & Deep Publication. India.
6. Bhatia, B.S and Batra, G.S.(2003) Entrepreneurship and Small Business Management, Deep and Deep. India.

7. Carter, S. and Jones-Evans. (2000), Enterprise and Small Business, Pearson Education. Harlow.
8. Charanthimath, M. Purnima. (2007), Entrepreneurship Development-Small Business Enterprises, Pearson Education, India.
9. Chandra, Prasanna, (1992), Managers Guide to Finance and Accounting, Tata McGraw- Hill publishing, India.
10. Drucker Peter, F. (1992), Managing for the Future – The 1990s and Beyond. Tata McGraw- Hill publishing, India.
11. David H. Holt .Entrepreneurship, New Venture Creation, (1992), Prantice-Hall, India.
12. Dollinger Marc J. (2004), Entrepreneurship, Strategies and Resources. Pearson Education, India.
13. Down Simon, Narratives of Enterprise,(2007) , Edward elagar Publishing, UK.
14. Haynes, W. (1999), Principles of Management and Entrepreneurship Development, Central book agency, India.
15. Jayagopal, R.(1990) Human Resource Development, Conceptual Analysis and Strategies, Sterling Publishers, India.
16. John H. Dunning & Tsai – Mei Uri, International Enterprises and the Global Economy (2nd ed.) (2007), Edward elagar Publishing, UK.
17. Narayanswamy, R.(2004),Financial Accounting – A managerial Perspective, Prentice- Hall, India.
18. McGrath, E.H. (2003), Basic Managerial Skills for All, Prentice Hall. India.
19. Robins Stephen P. &DeCenzo David A. (2007), Fundamentals of Management, Pearson Education in South Asia.
20. Singh, Ashok K., Personal Management in Public Enterprises-Storey, D.J., (1995), Understanding the Small Business Sector, Thomson Learning, Boston.
21. Stoner, Freeman, Gilbert,Jr., (2001), Management (6th ED), Prentice-Hall, India.
22. Thaduri, Balaraj.(2004), Entrepreneurship Development- An Analytical Study, Akansha publishing house, India.
23. Yudhvir Uppal,(1996) Economics and Management of Small Enterprises, Deep & Deep Publication. India.

Articles in Journals

1. Adner Ron, Match your innovation strategy to your innovation system, (2006), Harvard Business Review

2. Balje, S. and Waassdorp,P.(2001),Entrepreneurship in the 21st Century ,Netherlands.
3. Basant, R.,P.Chandra, and Sastry,T.(1999),for capabilities building and Integration with Global markets of small scale firms, Report for Department of SSI, Government of India.
4. Charcill, N.C and Lewis, V.C (1983), USA, The five stages of Small Business Growth, Harvard Business Review, Vol.61.
5. David A. Garvin and Lyncee C. Levesque, Meeting the challenges of corporate Entrepreneurship. (2006) Harvard Business Review.

15

Status and Challenges of Rural Women Micro-Entrepreneurs in Kohima District of Nagaland: A Micro Level Study

JAYANTA CHOUDHURY* & TIPUCHAL VALEO**

Women in India constitute around half of the country population. In the official proclamation, they are at par with men. But, in real life, the truth prevails otherwise. Our society is still male dominated and women are not treated as equal partners both inside and outside four walls of the house. In fact, they are treated as weak and dependent on men. As such, Indian women enjoy a disadvantageous status in the society. Our age old socio-cultural tradition and taboos arresting women within the four walls old their houses also make their conditions more disadvantageous. The scenario in rural India, is more acute where along with social discrimination, women have to share the economic crunches every steps. The situation becomes worse in the context of globalization where each and every matter they have to face

* Senior Lecturer & Coordinator, Centre for Rural Studies, Tripura University, Tripura, India.

** Student Rural Management & Development, Tripura University.

stiff competition and identity crisis. In this situation development of women as micro-entrepreneur has been recognized as very effective through out the world to tackle the twin problems.

The word 'entrepreneur' has been taken from the French language where it cradled and originally meant to designate an organizer of musical or other entertainments. Oxford English Dictionary (in 1897) also defined an entrepreneur in similar way as "the director or a manager of a public musical institution, one who 'gets-up' entertainment, especially musical performance." It was only in the beginning of the 18th century that the word was used to refer to economic aspects. In this way, the evolution of the concept of entrepreneur is considered over more than four centuries. Since then, the term 'entrepeneur' is used in various ways and various views. Women Entrepreneurs may be a single women or a group of women who think of a business enterprise, initiate it, organize and combine the factors of production, operate the enterprise and undertake risks and handle economic uncertainty involved in running a business enterprise. Again Microentrepreneurs may be defined as people who own small-scale businesses that are known as microenterprises. These businesses usually employ less than 5 people and can be based out of the home. They can provide the sole source of family income or supplement other forms of income. Typical microentrepreneur activities include retail kiosks, sewing workshops, carpentry shops and market stalls. (International Year of Microcredit 2005). Rural entrepreneurship means developing entrepreneurial activities through the value addition and processing of local raw materials and resources in rural areas. Therefore rural women micro-entrepreneurs are those women or group of women who start and manage their enterprises with optimal utilization of local resources in rural aresas as an option for their livelihood.

Development of Women Entrepreneurs- Recent Trends

With a view to develop better half of the society, the United Nations declared the decade 1975-85 as the decade for women.

The UNIDO Preparatory Meeting on the Role of women in industrialization in developing Countries held at Vienna during 6-10 February, 1978 identified several constraints such as social, attitudinal and institutional barriers, inadequate employment opportunities, inappropriate and inadequate training, insufficient information and so on which held women back from participating in industrial activities. The world conference of the united United Nation Decade for Women held at Copenhagen in Denmark on 30th june 1980 also adopted a programme aimed at promoting full and equal opportunities and treatment of women in employment and their access to non-traditional skilled trades.

The first National conference of Women Entrepreneurs held at New Delhi in November 1981 advocated the need for developing women entrepreneurs for the overall development of the country. It called for priority to women in allotment of land, sheds, sanction of power, licensing etc. The second international conference of women Entrepreneurs organized by the National Alliance of Young Entrepreneurs (NYAE) held in 1989, at New Delhi also adopted certain declaration involving women participation in industry.

Government of India has been assigning increasing importance to the development of women entrepreneurs in the country in recent years. The Sixth Five Year Plan, for example, proposed for promoting female employment in women-owned industries. The Government moved a step forward in the Seventh Five Year Plan by including a special chapter on Integration of women in Development. The chapter suggested – i) To treat women as specific target groups in all development programmes. ii) To devise and diversify vocational training facilities for women to suit their varied needs and skill, iii) To promote appropriate technologies to improve their efficiency and productivity, iv) To provide assistance for marketing their products and v) To involve women in decision-making process.

In her recent Industrial Policy 1991, the Government of India further stressed the need for conducing special entrepreneurship development programmes for women with a view to encourage women to enter industry. Product and process-oriented courses enabling women to start small-scale industries are also recommended in the Policy Statement.

Empirical Study

The present study was conducted among the purposively selected 80 tribal women entrepreneurs in Viswema village in Kohima district in the state of Nagaland with the following objectives:

i. To study the socio-economic condition of women entrepreneurs.
ii. To study present status of the enterprises.
iii. To find out various problems of enterprises run by women.
iv. To find out possibilities and way of further development of enterprises.

Results & Discussion

A. Socio -Economic Condition

Almost all of the women respondents belong to the tribal community and depend mainly on agriculture for the livelihood. Half of the entrepreneurs were from joint family (53%) and again half of them belong to below poverty line (BPL). About 36.25 percent women had passed class-X while 57.5 percent had completed their education between Class-X and BA. Majorities (46.25%) of women were between 25-30 years age groups and 22.5 percent of women were between 30 to 35 years of age groups. About 52.5 percent women entrepreneur were married and the remaining 47.5 percent were single. All of them were followers of Christian religion. Among the other occupation of the women entrepreneurs, most of them were housewife, mainly engaged in household activities and sometime go the field during harvesting. There were also some of the young women who continuing their study and running the enterprises in order to work independently and earn for themselves.

B. Enterprise Viability

Types of Enterprises

Majorities (45%) of women were engaged in traditional weaving. This was followed by 16.2 percent and 13.8 percent were engaged in tailoring and handicraft respectively and the remaining had choosing poultry, floriculture and garment shop are in growing stage. The art of weaving were practiced since time immemorial. Almost every household in this area are well known to the arts of weaving as it has become their culture of every women in every family.

Investment

Most of women entrepreneurs have made investment starting with low amount. About 32.5 percent of women had invested between Rs. 5,000 to Rs. 10,000 while 28.7 percent invested between Rs. 10,000 to Rs. 15,000. There were also few women (2.5%) who have invested in the entrepreneurs between Rs. 20,000 to Rs. 25,000 and contrasting to that 11.25 percent have invested more than Rs. 25,000 but not more than Rs. 50,000.

Source of Finance

Nearly 52.5 percent of women entrepreneurs of the sample survey had taken loan or help mostly from the family members /relatives at a reasonable rate or no rate of interest. A good numbers of women (22.5 percent) had to debt from the money lender. Only 15 percent of them received support from the bank as loan and rest 10 percent managed from the community society.

Utilization of Loan

The utilization of loan by the women entrepreneurs in sample survey was mostly used in purchasing raw materials. About 82.5 percent of women had utilized the loan in purchasing raw material from the market to produce it into finish product so that they can sell in the market in time. They were mostly from women who were engaged in weaving, handicraft and poultry. Remaining 17.5 percent of women had utilized the loan in purchasing of equipments mainly who were engaged in tailoring.

Training

Appropriate training for skill development, basic orientation of entrepreneurship or leadership training can play vital role to a successful develop entrepreneurship among the women. Since training provide them the knowledge of running the enterprise by equip them to manage the enterprise, keep records of the account of days to day activities, how to take risk and look to be a good manager as well as maintain friendly relationship with the customer. During study, it was found that about 16.3 percent and 26.25 percent of them had taken training for 6 month and for 1 year respectively for skill development while the majority of them (about 57.5%) had not received any training in running the enterprise.

Channel of Market

About 72.5 percent of women entrepreneurs used to sell their product directly without knowing the actual market price and some about 16.25 percent of them used to sell their product in weekly market. While some women who were engaged with enterprises like poultry, etc. (about 11.25%) used to sell their product at wholesale rate to the middlemen.

Employment Generation

Most of them were micro-enterprise and does not need any extra employment in running the enterprise as it can be simply manage by themselves or sometime by the family members. But during festive seasons and during winter the demand of the product is comparatively higher, so during such time they used to employed 1-3 women for 2 to 3 months and used to give them wage according to the number of product they made. Employment in their enterprises is not sustainable as the demand of their product very much occational, so they could not employ full time employee.

Monthly Profit

The profit of the entrepreneurs varies time to time. But

in an average, majority of the women entrepreneurs (37.5%) earned a monthly profit ranging from Rs.600-800/- and 32.5 percent women had a profit monthly profit of Rs.400-600/-. Whereas 17.5 percent of women earn a profit of Rs.800-1000/- and remaining 12.5 percent were able to earn very negligible amount (Rs.200–400). During festival season or during some occasion the demand of product increased, so during such season their earning also goes comparatively higher.

Monthly Saving

Most of the women utilize the amount of profit either for family needs or in purchasing material for further production. About 35 percent of women entrepreneur had a saving habit of Rs.100-250/- in a bank monthly for ulitizing in futures as well as in case of emergency.

Major Problems Faced By Women Entrepreneurs

Marketing

A major area of difficulty for women entrepreneurs was marketing. Marketing means mobility and confidence in dealing with the external world. Lack of market information, forced them to sell their products directly to customers and as well as in the weekly market at a very low price and even sometime product become damaged and results huge loss.

Raw Materials

Women Micro-entrepreneurs were facing problem in purchasing raw materials. The raw materials which are available in the market are of inferior quality and not upto the standard. So with such low quality raw materials, they were not able to make the product upto the expectation of the customers. As a result, they have to compromise to sell their product at a very low price with little profit.

Technical Know How & Design

Since most of the women did not received any opportunity for training, they are also lacking behind in the designing of their product. They still followed the old method of design which become thorny obstacle to face competitive market emerge as a result of globalization.

Household

As most of the women entrepreneurs were married, they had to take several household related responsibilities like cooking, fetching water, domestic chores, baby sitting etc. These activities some time pool them to concentrate in the enterprises. Sometime they become tired to balance between this two.

Financial

Credit is available for women through an abundance of schemes but there are still bottlenecks and gaps in commercial bank. The multiplicity of schemes is not adequately listed nor is there any networking among agencies. As a result, clients approaching one institution are not made aware of the best option for their requirements. Moreover with the complexity of the Rule and Regulations of the banks, they trend to take loan from the local moneylender which is easily available although have to pay charge with high rate of interest.

Recommendations

The following recommendations may be implemented in order to solve the problems faced by the women entrepreneurs.

i. More financial assistance should be provided to the women entrepreneurs for further entrepreneurial growth. There are several schemes like Self-Help Groups, Pradhan mantra Rojgar Yojana etc. for the development of women entrepreneurs. Necessary information has to be reached to the rural areas. Various audio-visual media should be used effectively. Local bodies, NGOs may play vital role here.

ii. State have to come out with financial inclusion policy for the women in general and rural women in particular.

iii. Encouragement should be given to those weavers, artisans and handicraft by giving them an opportunity to show their skilled in exhibition and fair within the state as well as outside the state for selling their product. Weaving cluster may be formed in the village level to solve the

iv. Training should be provided according to their activities since most of them have not taken any training to run the enterprise. EDP training, account training, skill training, improve design training may be provided

v. Banks have to come forward for creating women friendly environment to provide credit to the rural women entrepreneurs.

vi. The women entrepreneurs should be encouraged making the entrepreneurs insurance in any bank to cope up sudden risks.

Conclusion

Despite women contribution to various sectors, women have been neglected and are not being treated fairly in terms of wages, status and recognition. They are mostly confined within the four walls of their house. Our culture and tradition has forced them to work within the house as they are required to work within the kitchen, looking after the children and to look after the well being of their husband. Having various potential in generation of income, women were not treated fairly, but within the past decade, they have come out of the kitchen and are now running successfully in setting up their own enterprises. Some of them have even established all over the country as well as outside the country of their enterprise. Women have started to compete with their male counterparts in the business, and are even overrunning them in some of the enterprises. In comparison between male and female nowadays, we find women entrepreneurs are running more successfully than man enterprises as women are regarded as good manager, well organized, managing with limited resources, responsibility and commitment and are able to cater to different consumer preferences which are the main demands in the era of globalization. Thus women entrepreneurs will be the builder of society if they are provided with adequate knowledge and skill and training at an appropriate time with some physical and mental support. Such encouragement would help them to boost up their enterprises and be very much part of mainstream society and economy.

REFERENCES

1. Akhori, M.M.P. and S.V.S. Sharma (1978) : Small Entrepreneurship Development in North eastern India, SIET Institute, Hyderabad.
2. Arya, A. (2000). Indian women educational and empowerment, Publishing House, New Delhi. Choudhury, J (2005): Entrepreneurship Development through Science and Technology', TUI, Vol XII (4th issue), Sl. No. 46, Govt. of Tripura, pp. 42-49.
3. C.Hiremath (2002), Women in a Changing World, Pointer Publishers, Jaipur.
4. Choudhury, J (2006) : Poverty Alleviation through Self Help Groups : Issues of Sustainability in Tripura' in A.K.Sahoo (Ed.) Sociological Perspectives on Globalisation, Kalpaz Publication, New Delhi, pp. 141-149.
5. Dcvadas, R. P. (1999). Women and development, Centre for Women's Studies, Avinashilingam Deemed University.
6. Dodkey, M.P. (1999). SHGs and Micro credit sustaining rural women, Social Welfare, Vol. 45, No.12.
7. Gurumoorthy,T.R. (2000). Self Help Groups empower rural women, Kurukshetra, Vol. 48, No.5.
8. Joshi, S.C. (2002). Micro Credit not charity, Social Welfare, Vol. 48, No. II, 002.
9. Karmarkar,K.G. (1999). Rural credit and SHGs-Micro finance needs and concepts in India, Sage Publication, Delhi.
10. Upadhayay, N. & Choudhury, J (2006) : Social Mobilisation, Employment and Empowerment through SHGs- Tripura State Report in Taha (Ed.) Social Mobilisation, Employment and Empowerment through SHGs, NIRD, Hyderabad, 2006.

16

Women Entrepreneurship Development Through Self Help Groups: A Study in Tripura

MANOSHI DAS*

India is a society where the male is greatly revered. Therefore women, especially the young girls, get very little respect and standing in this country. The women of the household are required to prepare the meal for the men, who eat most of the food. Only after the males are finished eating, can the females eat. Typically the leftover food is meager, considering the families are poor and have little to begin with. This creates a major problem with malnutrition, especially for pregnant or nursing women. Very few women seek medical care while pregnant because it is thought of as a temporary condition. This is one main reason why India's maternal and infant mortality rates are so high. Starting from birth, girls do not receive as much care and commitment from their parents and society as a boy would. For example a new baby girl would only be breast fed for a short period of time, barely supplying her with the nutrients she needs. This is so that the mother can get pregnant as soon as possible in hopes of a son the next time.

* Research Associate, association for Research on People And Nature (ARPAN), Agartala, Tripura.

A significant development in recent years has been the mushrooming of community-based organizations and initiatives at the local level for women. Women's empowerment is a new phrase in the vocabulary of gender literature. The phrase is used in two broad senses i.e. general and specific. In a general sense, it refers to empowering women to be self-dependent by providing them access to all the freedoms and opportunities, which they were denied in the past only because of their being women. In a specific sense, women empowerment refers to enhancing their position in the power structure of the society.

Empowerment is defined as the processes by which women take control and ownership of their lives through expansion of their choices. According to the Country Report of Government of India empowerment means moving from a position of enforced powerlessness to one of power. It would promote women's inherent strength and positive self- image. It may be described 'as a process in which women gain greater share of control over resources- material, human and intellectual like knowledge, information, ideas and financial resources like money and access to money and control over decision making in the home, community, society and nation and to gain 'power'. The concept of empowerment has been the subject of much intellectual discourse and analysis. Thus, it is the process of acquiring the ability to make strategic life choices in a context where this ability has previously been denied.

The core elements of empowerment have been defined as agency (the ability to define one's goals and act upon them), awareness of gendered power structures, self-esteem and self-confidence. Empowerment can take place at a hierarchy of different levels – individual, household, community and societal and is facilitated by providing encouraging factors (e.g., exposure to new activities, which can build capacities) and removing inhibiting factors (e.g., lack of resources and skills).

UNDP (1994) defined empowerment as a process, which enables individuals or groups to change balances of power in social, economic and political relations in society. Empowerment represents sharing control, the enticement and the ability to participate, to influence decisions, as on the allocation of resources'.

The process of empowerment is sometimes viewed with concern by those in advantaged positions who may fear that raising the status of the disadvantaged can only be achieved by a lowering of their own level of power and privilege. This fear often translates into an even more repressive situation to maintain the status quo.

Entrepreneurship among women is an emerging recent phenomenon. It is the process of creating value by attracting together a unique package of resources to exploit an opportunity. Nowadays governments have identified the emerging features of micro enterprises as a new dimension and its results are more benefit to the economy. Micro credit programme will empower women by strengthening their economic roles, increasing their ability to contribute income to family and giving them experience and self-confidence in the public sphere, exposer to income earning activities. Women need credit for skill upgradation, training and entrepreneurial development. The impact of women empowerment would occur by the use of Participatory Learning Approach (PLA) for integrating women's own priorities and strategies in the mainstream of development. This study is aimed at stimulating an inquiry into the favorable circumstances for women to venture, motivational factors, socio-economic and managerial aspects of tangible and intangible benefits of the women micro enterprises in India. The study also represents physical and financial achievements of various institutions who extended support credit for women entrepreneurial development in the state.

In India small scale industrial units are owned both by men and women. Among scale industrial units owned by women entrepreneurs in India, Kerala tops the list with 1.39 lakh units, followed by Tamil Nadu with 1.30 lakh units. Tamil Nadu ranks second in the total number of small-scale units owned by women entrepreneurs in India. Lakshadweep has the lowest number of small-scale units owned by women entrepreneurs (67 units).

Table 1 : State-Wise Entrepreneurs Distribution of Small Scale Industrial Units Owned by Women Entrepreneurs

Sl. No.	*State/Union Territory*	*No. of SSI Units*	*Percentage to Total*
1	Kerela	139225	13.09
2	Tamil nadu	129808	12.20
3	Karnataka	103169	9.70
4	Maharashtra	100670	9.46
5	Andhra Pradesh	77166	7.25
6	Uttar Pradesh	72667	6.83
7	West Bengal	69625	6.55
8	Madhya Pradesh	68823	6.47
9	Gujrat	53703	5.05
10	Bihar	49443	4.65
11	Orissa	38233	3.59
12	Rajasthan	36371	3.42
13	Punjab	29068	2.73
14	Delhi	14383	1.35
15	Assam	11757	1.11
16	Manipur	10745	1.01
17	Chhattisgarh	10034	0.94
18	Haryana	9620	0.90
19	Uttaranchal	8804	0.83
20	Jharkhand	7865	0.74
21	Jammu and Kashmir	5742	0.54
22	Himachal Pradesh	3722	0.35
23	Mizoram	3700	0.35
24	Meghalaya	3580	0.34
25	Chandigarh	2243	0.21
26	Pondichery	1065	0.10
27	Tripura	863	0.08
28	Daman, Diu, Dadra and Nagarhaveli	213	0.02
29	Nagaland	179	0.02
30	Arunachal Pradesh	150	0.01
31	Andaman and Nicobar Island	110	0.01
32	Sikkim	98	0.01
33	Lakshadweep	67	0.01

Empowerment Through Self-Help Groups

In many developing countries (especially in South Asia), one strategy which has been found to be promising is participatory institution building in the self-help groups, often coupled with savings and micro-credit loans.

Self-help groups have been instrumental in empowerment by enabling women to work together in collective agency. Women's networks do not usually obtain business or political favours as they command few economic resources and frequently rely on time and non-monetized labour exchange. However, self-help groups, when combined with savings and credit, have enabled women to benefit economically by monetizing their contributions and in the process have empowered them to become agents of change. A related aspect is that self-help groups have facilitated the formation of social capital, where people learn to work together for a common purpose in a group or organization. The ability to associate depends on the degree to which communities share norms and values and are able to subordinate individual interests to those of larger groups. Out of these shared values comes trust, with the potential for social, economic and political change. However, these groups are often narrowly focused on micro-credit, which, although useful as an entry point, can also limit and confine these groups to very small-scale activities with limited impact beyond the immediate family.

The concept of SHG serves the principle "for the people, by the people, and of the people". The origin of SHG is not new but the present institutional practice is the brainchild of GRAMIN BANK of Bangladesh, which was founded by the economist, Prof. Mohammed Yunus of Chittagong University in the year 1975. This was exclusively established for the poor.

According to NABARD, Self-help group is a small economically homogeneous and affinity group of rural poor which is voluntarily ready to contribute to a common fund to be lent to its members as per group decision, which works for groups' solidarity, self-group, awareness, social and economic empowerment in the way of democratic functioning.

The efforts of government and its different agencies are ably supplemented by non- governmental organizations that are playing an equally important role in facilitating women empowerment. Despite concerted efforts of governments and NGOs there are certain gaps. Of course we have come a long way in empowering women yet the future journey is difficult and demanding.

SHGs Under Swarnjayanti Gram Swarozgar Yojana (SGSY)

The focus of development planning in India has been rightly on the alleviation of rural poverty since Independence. Rural India, however, continues to suffer from high incidence of poverty in spite of strengthening of antipoverty programmes in successive years from 56.44 percent of the population in 1973.74 to 37.27 percent in 1993-94. In absolute terms, however, the number of rural poor has remained more or less static. It is estimated to be about 24.40 crore persons. The adverse effect of such a large size of the poor on the country's development is not difficult to appreciate. Quite obviously, the situation needs to be redressed quickly.

The objective of the Swarnjayanti Gram Swarozgar Yojana (SGSY) is to bring the assisted poor families (Swarozgaries) above the Poverty Line by ensuring appreciable sustained level of income over a period of time. This objective is to be achieved by inter - alia organising the rural poor into Self Help Groups (SHGs) through the process of social mobilization, their training and capacity building and provision of income generating assets. The SHG approach helps the poor to build their self-confidence through community action. An interaction in group meetings and collective decision making enables them in identification and prioritization of their needs and resources. This process would ultimately lead to the strengthening and socio-economic empowerment of the rural poor as well as improve their collective bargaining power.

Objectives

SGSY is a self-employment programme of Ministry of Rural Development that aims at providing assistance to the BPL rural poor for establishing micro-enterprises through bank credit and government subsidy to acquire an income-generating asset. Self Help Groups (SHGs) are formed through a process of social mobilization, with their training and capacity building, infrastructure build up, technology, credit and marketing enabling them to take decisions on all issues concerning poverty eradication.

SGSY Has a Definite Objective of

- improving the family incomes of the rural poor and,
- providing for a flexibility of design at the grassroots level to suit the local needs and resources.
- bringing the assisted poor families (Swarozgaris) above the Poverty Line by providing them income-generating assets through a mix of bank credit and governmental subsidy.
- establishing a large number of micro enterprises in rural areas based on the ability of the poor and potential of each area.

The objective of the structuring was to make the programme more effective in providing a sustainable income through micro-enterprise development, both lands based and otherwise. In doing so, effective linkages have been established between various components such as capacity building of the poor, credit, technology, marketing and infrastructure.

THE STUDY

Objective of the Study

I. To study the socio economic condition of the women entrepreneurs under SHGs.

II. To review the functioning of SHGs and process of entrepreneurship development.

III. To find out the major challenges faced by women as entrepreneurs.

IV. To asses the out come of entrepreneurship development towards economic empowerment through

To fulfill the objectives and to collect information, stratified random sampling was followed to select SHGs and members who were start micro enterprise activities. For this study West and South Tripura district were selected purposively because in these districts the numbers of SHGs were higher. From the two districts, blocks were selected again based on the number of SHGs. From West District 3 blocks namely – Mohonpur, Jinania and Bisalgarh R.D. block were selected and from South district, Matabari and Kathalia R.D. blocks were selected. From each block, 20 SHGs were selected purposively. The groups who have completed 3 years and running Income Generation Activities were considered for the present study. Again from each group, 4 (four) members were randomly selected. Total 120 women SHG members from west district and 80 members from South district were studied. Therefore total sample size was 200 women SHG member. For this study, secondary data was collected from DRDA, West and South Tripura, studied blocks, related literature works, journals and electronic media like internet, website etc. For this study primary data was collected by interviewing the women entrepreneur. To collect the primary data a questionnaire was prepared which may fulfill the objectives of the study. The primary data was analysed through tabulation and graphical presentation.

Result & Discussion

A. Socio-Economic Background:

i. Most of the respondents in West district (around 45 percent) were literate upto primary school and few of them were Graduate. Almost same pictures were found in the South district.

ii. Aboutb38.33 percent members were from the OBC, followed by the SC community with 30 percent in the West district. In the South district 42.5 % members were from the OBC.

iii. Most of the SHG members were Hindu (90 %) and rests were Muslim in both the district.

iv. Around 85 percent SHG members were married and while 3.33 percent were widow in the West district while 95 percent were married in South district.

v. In West district 60.83 % members come from nuclear family where as in South district, 80 percent were from nuclear family.

vi. In West district 21.66 % members were house wife but 35 percent were housewife, followed by small business (25 %) and engagement in animal husbandry (22.5 %) in the South district.

vii. In the West district 33.33 percent SHG members earns between Rs. 500 and 1000 and few of them are earn between Rs.1000 and 2000. But in the South district most of the people earns less than Rs.500 and few of them earns above Rs.2000. In West district, per head income was more in compare to South district.

viii. In the West district 26.67 percent family's income was above 3000 and few of them i.e. 13.33 percent earns between Rs.1000 and 1500. But in the South district 30 percent people earns between Rs.1500 and 2000 and few of them earns above Rs.3000.

ix. In the West district, half of them were involve in other different organizations while in South district 85 percent SHG member are engaged in other organization like Panchayat, Nari-samity, etc.

B. Functioning of SHGs:

i. In the West district 40 percent members joined in the year 2003. In the South district 46 percent people are join in the year 2003.In the South district ratio of group forming is decreasing day by day in compare to West district.

ii. The amount of monthly thrift is more in South than the West district. In West district, most of the member's monthly thrift is Rs.30. On the other hand, in South district, among 80 members most their monthly thrift is above Rs.50.

iii. All of the group member's frequency of saving is monthly in both districts.

iv. Total 68 % and 85 % members contribute thrift in group from their own earning in West and South district respectively.

v. 42 percent taken loan once from their own group in West district while in South district, 80 percent took loan for more than two times.

vi. 45 percent members in West district utilised their loan in animal husbandry and few of them utilised in new assets. In South district, 35 %, most of them are utilise their loan in animal husbandry.

vii. Among the consumption purposes, 50 percent utilise their loan in health purpose in West district. In south district, most of them are utilise their loan in house repairing purpose.

viii. Among the total 26 members all of them utilised their loan for marriage purpose in West district. In South district, among the 12 members, most of them utilised their loan for education purposes.

ix. In West district 86.67 percent members had not taken loan under any scheme and those who are taken loan taken under the IRDP. But in the south district only 15 percent SHG member had early loan history.

x. In the West district 81.66 percent members have not taken loan under any other schemes except SGSY programme in last three years. Again in the South district also only 15 percent SHG member had taken loan.

xi. In the West district, among 22 loan borrowers, 36.36 percent members got loan within the one month of submission of application. But in the South district average time to get loan was nearly 3 months.

xii. In West district only 31.67 percent members felt that loan was adequate to start micro-enterprise. But in the South district most of the members (65 %) opined that the loam amount of loan was adequate to start business.

xiii. In west district among the members nobody depend on money lenders. But in the south district few members are still depend on money lender.

C. Entrepreneur Development:

i. In West district, 55.01 percent take small business as their new IGA. Some people are also taken agriculture (10.83 %), fishery etc. as IGA while 52.5 percent members had taken agriculture as their IGA in the South district.

ii. In West district, 73.33 percent and in South district, 50 percent members received training.

iii. They received training mainly from DRDA. In compare to two districts South DRDA is providing more training to the SHG members than the West DRDA. NGOs as training providers were more in South district than the West.

iv. In both districts most of the members received training for 2-3 days. In compare to two districts, West district SHG members have received less training for more than ten days.

v. In two districts most of the training was skill based. In compare to two districts providing general awareness programme and book keeping training was less in South district than the West.

vi. In West district 56.81 percent training method were apply in the classroom sessions but in the south district 75 percent training method are apply in the practical & exercise method. In compare to two districts south district are apply more practical & exercise oriented training method.

vii. Among the trained 128 SHG in the west district most of the members are not acquired the required skill for managing ME. In compare to two districts South district SHG members are more apply the training facility than the West.

viii. In the west district most of them i.e.97.72 percent members are trained under SGSY. In the South district 80 percent members are trained under SGSY. In compare to two district south district SHG members are more facilitate under other organisation then the West.

ix. In the West district most of them i.e.53.34 percent members received help from their SHG. In the South district 70 percent members also supported by their SHG. In compare to two districts West districts Govt. officials are more helpful than the West.

x. In west district among the surveyed 128 SHG members who get training, 79.55 percent SHG members are said that after completion of their training the authority have not provided any follow up support. 85 percent SHG members had not received any follow up support after completion of their training by the authority. In compare to two districts West district SHG members are more consulted by the authority.

xi. Among the surveyed 200 SHG members most of them are running ME since above three years. In West district 40 percent SHG are running since above three years and in West districts it is about 33 percent.

xii. Among the surveyed 200 SHG members most of them are not using any improved methods of production. Only in south district few members are using modern technology. In both the districts most of the members are running small business where modern technology is not that much important.

xiii. Among the surveyed SHG members, most of them are not getting any support in respect of improved methods of production. Only in South district few members are getting support from DRDA.

xiv. The channels of marketing of product which are producing by the SHG members have more than one channel of market. In both district main marketing channel of most of the members is wholesaler followed by different melas.

xv. Most of the members were dependent on middleman in limited extent. In West district dependency on the middleman of 72.5 percent of the members is limited, whereas in south district it is almost same. Most of the products of the member's are sail to the retailer or wholesaler, that's why their dependency on middleman is limited. But near about 30 percent members had to depend on middleman to large extent.

xvi. Among the members most of the SHG members are collect raw material themselves. In west district 83.33 percent members and in south district 75 percent members are collect raw material themselves. Few members are also depend on others family members for collect raw material in both districts.

xvii. In south district among total 80 surveyed members 55 percent members get the training. But in the West district nobody get the training, because the training agencies are not providing any training in this matter.

xviii. In the context of adopting modern technology for better designing of their product, in west district 60 percent and in south district 57.5 percent members wanted to adopt new technology. But most of them are not able to adopt new technology because they are not getting any support from the responsible authority.

xix. In West district 38.33 percent and in South district only 5 percent members are adopt new technology for better packaging of their product. Most of the SHG members are engaged in producing agricultural and farming product, where packaging is not necessary.

xx. Among the total 200 surveyed SHG members in two districts only 13 percent members are adopt level on their product. The percentage of members who are using level on their product is almost same in two districts.

xxi. Among the total 200 surveyed SHG members in two districts only 10 percent members are able to fulfill the market demand of their product. In west district any SHG members are not able to fulfill the market demand because market demand is higher in this district than the south district.

xxii. 75 percent SHG members wanted to continue of their production of both the districts. The SHG members are getting profit from their present enterprise so, they are interested to marketwise their product for long time.

xxiii. In the West district SHG members are getting more profit from their IGA than the South district.

xxiv. In West district, among 120 members, 55 percent SHG members and in south district 62.5 percent are generating additional employment of less the 5 days. Only few members are generating 11 to 15 day's additional employment in both the districts.

xxv. In West district, among 120members most of the SHG member i.e.60 percent and in south district 70 percent are generating additional income of less Rs.100-500. Only few members are generating Rs 2001 to 2500 day's additional income in both the districts. In compare to two districts, the members of the west district are generating more additional income than the South district.

Major Challenges

1. The SHG members are not getting proper market to sale their product, so, they have to depend on retailer or middle man.
2. In few block of South district, the Dala-Bandhus are not properly communicated with SHG members regularly. So, most of the members are facing various problem related to training, availability of raw material and market etc.
3. Some Self Help Groups are taken only the subsidy and running their enterprise with this limited capital. So they are not getting that much profit.
4. Due to lack of training some members are not able to maintain their official work and that's why they have to depend on their family member mainly on husband.
5. Though the quality of the product of the SHG members is good but due to poor packaging quality, their product is not that much selling in compare to other branded product of the market.

Recommendation:

1. Activity Cluster should be form by DRDA in all the blocks to solve the packaging, branding, quality of product, design even the training problem.
2. Banks should have to provide more loans to the SHGs.
3. More training regarding book keeping should be provided.
4. Marketing facility should be developed in the local area.
5. More skill and practical oriented training may be provided to all the members and training providing agencies have to take proper step regarding this.

6. Transportation facility in the rural area should be developed.
7. More skill based training is required for improvement of quality product. Various renowned institutes may be linked to provide training on particular IGA.
8. Awareness programme and information need to provide regarding sustainable use of local raw materials. Government has to arrange to supply scarce raw material to the SHGs through co-operatives.
9. Training should be provided to the SHGs to adapt new and modern design for making product. For improvement of design National Institute of Design, Ahmedabad may be linked.
10. Cluster for adapt packaging and branding technique should be made. Indian Institute of Pakaging, Salt Lake, Kolkata
11. Marketing facilities should be developed and for this Government has to provide permanent stall in local market to SHGs. Transportation facility should be developed in the rural areas for carrying out of their product. Advertisement is required for SHG product. DRDA West may form a product based website displaying the products with price etc. Activity cluster and federation must be formed for the economies of the scale.
12. Tie up with corporate sectors like ITC, Rural Hat, RCM chain business, NSIC etc. following the PPP mode! should be development. Rural Bazar approach of State Bank of India may be implementing on pilot basis.
13. Proper information regarding the prevailing market price may be provided to the SHGs. One session must be incorporate during all the EDP/MDP training on pricing policy. It will build the capacity for price fixation /coasting of product strategy among the members.
14. Banks have to give more loan to the SHGs in due time. Bankers should recognize the credit worthiness among the SHG members. Rural development department should organize exposure visit for the bankers in the successful micro-credit practitioners (may be in Bangladesh). This will not only boost up the confidence for lending but also will help in increasing confidence level and cooperation.
15. DRDA have to take proper care of SHGs and for this DRDA have to recruit new stuffs. Sufficient training (both BOP as well as skill based training) need to be provided to the SHGs.

Bibliography:

1. Aziz Ahmed (1999) "Women Empowerment: Self-help Groups at Gossaigoan, Assam", Kurukshetra, Vol-47(7).
2. B.K.Singh (2006) Women Empowerment Through Self-Help Group, Adhyayan Publishers & Distributors, New Delhi,
3. Baneee ,N (2004), Nari Bikash Sangha: Towards Empowerment, Indian Journal of Gender Studies, Vol-II (2): 179-203.
4. Chiranjeevulu (2003), Empowering Women through SHGs: Experiences in Experiment, Kurukshetra, 51(5): 16-19.
5. Choudhury, J (2005): Entrepreneurship Development through Science and Technology', TUI, Vol XII (4th issue), Sl. No. 46, Govt. of Tripura, pp. 42-49.
6. Choudhury, J (2006) : Poverty Alleviation through Self Help Groups : Issues of Sustainability in Tripura' in A.K.Sahoo (Ed.) Sociological Perspectives on Globalisation, Kalpaz Publication, New Delhi, pp. 141-149.
7. Gupta,A and etal (2003), Self-Help Group-A Friend of Poor, Political Economy Journal of India, Vol-12(1): 66-70.
8. Gurumoorthy, T.R (2000),"Self Help Groups Empower Rural Women ", Kurukshetra, Vol-48(5).
9. Hemalatha C and etal (2004), Marketing Channels of Select Products under SGSY-A Study of Four States, Research Reports Series, NIRD.
10. Karmakar,R and Ghosh, B(2002), Role of Women in the Self-Help Group: an Emerging Possibility to Cooperativization at Grass-root, Man in India, Vol-82(3-4):441-451.
11. Lakshmikantan, K.R (2000), Self-Help Groups in the Life of Rural Poor: A Pilihibit Case Study, Women's Link, 6(2):10-16.
12. Majumdar, C.B. & Choudhury, J (2008) : Women Empowerment through SHGs- a pilot study in Dukli Block of Tripura, Tripura University (Unpublished report)
13. Murgan & Dharmalingam, B (2000), "Self-Help Groups - New Women's Movement in Tamil Nadu", Social Welfare, Vol. 47(5), August
14. Promilla Kapur (2001), 'Empowering the Indian Women, Publications Division, Ministry of Information and Broadcasting Government of India.
15. Puhazendi, V and Satya Sai (2001) ,"Economic and Social Empowerment of Rural poor through SHGs", Indian Journal of Agricultural Economics, Vo.56(3).

16. Sarangi,P(2003), Self-Help Groups-An Experiment in Orissa, Kurukshetra February, Pp:30-32.
17. Shandilya(1996), Changing Status of Indian Women-A Myth or Reality", in Eds. Vir Dharam and Mahajan Kamlesh, Contemporary Indian Women, Politics, Awareness and Women's Movements, Vol-4, New Delhi.
18. Upadhayay, N. & Choudhury, J (2006) : Social Mobilisation, Employment and Empowerment through SHGs- Tripura State Report in Taha (Ed.) Social Mobilisation, Employment and Empowerment through SHGs, NIRD, Hyderabad, 2006.
19. Usha Sharma, 'Women Empowerment through Information Technology', Authors Press, Delhi,2003.

17

Forestry for Poverty Alleviation Through Micro-Level Economic Development: A Case Study from Tripura

A. K. GUPTA, IFS*

1. Introduction

Contribution of forestry sector in industrialization and other macro-level economics is well known and documented. However, due to a meagre contribution of forestry sector in the overall Gross Domestic Products (GDP), this sector is always considered second to Agriculture and other Primary sectors contributing more of tangible benefits. In this era of recession of global economy when most of the sectors contributing towards economic development the macro-levels, have gone dry, the economic development from the forestry sector has assumed greater importance in keeping the economic development paradigm afloat especially at the micro-level for the poorest of the poor having a direct bearing on the poverty alleviation.

I discuss contribution of forestry sector in mitigating the economic and social hardships of thousands of jhumia (shifting cultivator) families in the state of Tripura, in this

* Sr. Lecturer, Dept. of History, Dibrugarh University, Assam.

paper. It is seen that globalization for last almost two decades has only helped in introducing consumerism culture even amongst some of the most primitive communities in the State without helping them come out from the clutches of their existing subsistence economic status. The economy of the Jhumia communities is very closely linked with their culture and traditions, so much so that an economic consideration has also to equally cater to other two aspects as well. An economic package without consideration towards socio and cultural characteristics fails to produce desired results. It could be one reason as to why the globalization, as stand alone economic consideration, has failed to make any dent in the economic betterment of these communities, rather on the contrary, has proved counter productive for these communities.

It is in this context that forestry based economic package has rather proved a great success in enhancing both the economic concerns and socio-cultural needs of the jhumia communities. The benefits, though very meagre compared to the ones contemplated in the globalization-based package, yet, have succeed in breaking age-old inhibitions of the orthodox forest dwellers in accepting alternative economic packages in lieu of their traditional methods being used for subsistence economy.

Shifting cultivation, which consists of the alteration between a short phase of cultivation and a long period of fallow, is one of the main inducers of land-use change (Ruthenberg, 1976; Van der Wal, 1998). Agricultural plots are cultivated during a short period of time after which they are abandoned, and through processes of secondary succession become fallows. Simultaneously, new plots are established. In this way, shifting cultivation transforms homogeneous landscapes into mosaic landscapes with farm land, fallow lands of different ages, and mature vegetation. This kind of anthropogenic disturbance is very common in tropical regions; with at least 240 million people practicing it (Attiwill, 1994) it is the dominant food production system (Juo and Manu, 1996).

Shifting cultivation is the oldest cultivation system practiced throughout the tropics and subtropics (zones of high rainfall. moderate temperature, and steep slopes) dating back to the Neolithic Period (13000-3000 BC) (Sharma. 1976). In India, shifting cultivation is variously known as adiahik in Arunachal Pradesh. dawar in Madhya Pradesh, pantla by the Myrias of BastaI' in Madhya Pradesh. dahi. komon, pama dohi, or hrin/ia among the Bhuiyas of north Orissa. glldia or dllOn/iarchar in south Orissa. jhoom in Assam and Tripura. The Reangs of Tripura use hookni smong as a synonym for jhoom.

Shifting cultivation could be said to have evolved as a response to special physiographic characters of the land, economy and socio-cultural traditions of the cultivators. Two major ecological reasons for practising shifting cultivation could be poor fertility of fragile soils under tropical conditions with a tendency to decline further without modern soil conservation and irrigation measures, and low capacity of the soil to retain plant nutrients. Ganguly (1968) argued that unlike settled agriculturalists that use manure and fertilizers to augment soil fertility, shifting cultivators, who are not conversant with soil conservation methods shift to another fertile plot of land following loss of soil fertility on a particular jhoom plot. Shifting cultivation was a sustainable use of forest ecosystem while cultivators had plenty of forest areas available (Myers. 1990: Whitmore, 1975). However, current form of this cultivation accounts for about 61 per cent of total tropical forest destruction (Myers 1984, 1991: Westoby, 1989). Following large scale influx of migrant "shifted cultivators" (farmers without any background of traditional shifting cultivation) in the past 50 years, the traditional jhooming stands replaced with non-traditional jhooming , which in no way a sustainable utilization of forest ecosystem.

1.1 Jhooming in Tripura

In Tripura (23050' – 24032'N; 91010' – 92021'; 10,490 km2) shifting cultivation is deeply integrated into the social, cultural, and economic life style of many tribal groups that constitute about 31 per cent of the total population of the state. There are 19 different tribal communities of which 17 (excepting the Bhutias and the Chaimals) practice jhooming. Out of a total of 55049 shifting cultivator households all over the state, about 21,677 (39.3%) are entirely dependent on jhooming and the remaining 60.7% are partly dependent. The Tripuris (28%) and Reangs (25.6'%) tribes are two major jhumia communities. The majority (70.8%) of jhumias have only 0.8 to 2.0 ha of land per family for jhum, and only 6.1% had more than two hectares. About 223 km2 of forest (3.76% of the 'total forest area of the state) is cleared annually for jhooming that is higher than the National average at 2.26%. Differing in their socio-cultural and economic conditions, Gupta (2000) has identified two disparate jhumia communities: (1) traditional and (2) non-traditional jhumia communities and jhooming practiced by them as traditional and non-traditional jhumming, respectively. The basic methods of jhooming in Tripura, similar to other places, involve cultivation of an area for a short period, often only a year. After which it is abandoned for several years. Generally the slopes of the hills are reckoned suitable for jhooming. In a survey undertaken by the forest department in 2006, a total of 27, 278 jhumias have been enumerated in all the forest divisions across the state. The forest beats were taken as enumeration units and secondary records maintained in the Gram Panchayat/Village Committee offices were also consulted to supplement the primary data on jhumia populations.

As an inseparable part of their culture and tradition, this so called primitive cultivation method has been serving those tribal communities on economic and emotive (social, cultural and traditional aspects) fronts for ages. More of its emotional bondage than the economic contribution in the life pattern of the tribal communities has seen jhooming survive even the recent fast track developmental onslaughts. Yet, fast pace of development processes within and all around tribal communities have introduced certain non-traditional elements leading to the irrevocable loss of traditional trademark of jhooming (as an economically viable and ecologically secure cultivation practice). This altered (non-traditional) form of shifting cultivation (reduced per capita cultivation area; reduced gestation period; reduction in number of food and vegetable species cultivated in a given jhum plot; increased use of chemical manure; etc.) has become almost untenable on all fronts (social, cultural, traditional, economical and ecological) for tribal communities.

Jhooming cannot survive in the long term because increasing population in the absence of an abundant supply of land is bound to shorten the jhum cycle, bringing about continuous deterioration in soil fertility and ecological conditions. Studies conducted in the Philippines, Gambia, Malawi, Zambia and in India (Ganguly, 1968; Saha, 1970) reveal that carrying capacity of jhooming plots is very low-about six persons per sq. km. In view of current demographic, economic, and land use patterns in Tripura, it may be too ambitious to attempt at reverting back to traditional jhooming. Therefore, the best solutions may lie in finding suitable alternatives (Gupta, 2000) as complete replacements to the jhooming. One such alternative was to settle the jhumias on the settled agriculture. Three groups were considered for this process. The first group consisted of those people who became entirely dependent on jhoom cultivation after their timber business was lost due to partition of Bengal. The second group consisted of people with jhoom cultivation as main occupation and these were less dependent on other forest resources. The third group was consisting of marginal farmers who used to practice jhoom only to supplement their family income from other resources.

While it may not be possible to reverse the development processes, it may however, be possible to redefine the mechanics of shifting cultivation to cushion up its adverse impacts on the socio-economic and cultural life style of the tribal communities and on the ecology of the area. Alternately, it may also be possible to introduce enabling changes in the shifting cultivation practice to match the contemporary socio-cultural, traditional, economic and ecological needs of different stakeholders.

The State Forest Department (SFD), through its various programmes and schemes, has been trying for past many years to address the socio-economic concerns of the jhumia families by providing forest based income generating opportunities. The department is also attempting at increasing the forest safety net for these jhumia families and other rural poor by protecting and adding on to the existing forest ecosystem through afforestation and reclamation of degraded forest areas.

2. Resettling Jhumia Families: A Holistic Economic Development Model

The Forest Department has taken up the task of re-settlement of those Jhumia families who have voluntarily started settling down all along the National highways. The site chosen by them all along the highways due to availability of certain basic amenities as compared to interior forest areas that used to be their abode so far.

A total of 23 such villages comprising of 3,800 families in all the 4 districts in the state have been taken up for settling jhumias by providing them different livelihood facilities (both forest-land & non-forest-land based). Each family in the regrouped village has been made part of a given Joint Forest Management Committee and Micro-plan for each committee has been prepared. Two major activities undertaken in each village relates with creation of both basic infrastructure and income generating facilities. In this model of Jhumia rehabilitation within the re-grouped forest villages, technical and financial assistance is being provided by eleven (11) line departments by introducing enabling provisions in the micro-plans. The monitoring and evaluation of this scheme is done through a State Level Steering Committee (SLSC) under the chairmanship of the Chief Secretary having members drawn from each concerned line department. The Forest Department has been made the Nodal department. Other line departments involved with this project have nominated one officer each to liaise with the concerned forest officer-in-charge for technical assistance. A copy of the Micro-plan for each re-grouped forest village has been given to all concerned line departments for incorporating proposed activities in their respective Annual Plans.

The Forest Department as the Nodal Department has prepared a comprehensive project to meet the basic infrastructure and livelihood needs of regrouped jhumias. Total project outlay is Rs. 36.8 crores for five years. The project stipulates involvement of 11 line departments [Forest (Nodal Department), Fisheries, Animal Resource Development

Department, Industries & Commerce, Rural Development Department, Tribal Welfare Department, Health and Family Welfare Department & Health Directorate, Agriculture & Horticulture, Power, Information, Culture and Tourism, and Education] to provide their specific technical and financial inputs to addressing following main objectives:

- Meeting economic, social and cultural concerns through infrastructural and income generation related activities.
- Reducing honeycombing of forests. It is understood that the jhum plots.
- Providing secured living environment to the jhumia families due to proximity of regrouped forest villages to the markets and main towns.
- Arranging for basic amenities and infrastructure facilities, such as, health, education, sanitation, power, safe drinking water, etc.
- Providing multiple income generating livelihood options.
- Helping them to stop jhumming practice by leading a settled life.

This project has effectively started working from the last quarter of FY 2005-06 and has almost completed three years of operation by the end of FY 2008-09.

2.1 *Operational Mechanisms*

- Joint Forest Management Committees (JFMCs) have been created in each RGV. In some RGVs, there are more than one JFMC depending upon the number of families.
- The flow of funds and expenditure modalities has been adopted on the pattern of existing Forest Development Agencies (FDA).
- All concerned line departments have been providing technical and financial assistance to the concerned forest division for given RGV. As stated earlier, each line department has incorporated activities to be taken up in the RGVs as integral part of their Annual Plan of Operation.

- Forestry and non-forestry activities have been undertaken in each of the regrouped villages within the purview of the Forest Conservation Act, 1980.
- Main emphasis has been given on the creation of basic infrastructures (schools, housing, health facilities, safe drinking water facilities, power, and surface communication, etc.) and sustained non-forestry and non-land based alternative and additional income generating options.
- Many activity based self help groups from amongst the existing JFMCs have been constituted to sustain the income. The revolving fund has also been encouraged in each SHG for facilitating self-entrepreneurship and self-management of funds for generation of livelihood options well beyond the project period.
- Micro-plans have been prepared for each JFM Committee where all the families in a given village are the members. This Micro-Plan contains details on different components & activities for different departments including the requirement of funds for the purpose of undertaking such activities. Wherever required, the details on technical inputs required from each department have also been mentioned in the Micro-plan. The Micro Plans have been prepared through a well defined Participatory Rural Appraisal Process ensuring involvement of local people both during the formulation and execution of activities in listed regrouped forest villages.
- A State Level Steering Committee under the chairmanship of Chief Secretary ensures that inputs (both technical and financial) from each concerned department are timely and effectively provided.
- The Chief Project Officers (CPO) have been appointed from the concerned forest division for focussed attention on regrouped forest villages. The Tribal Welfare Department has also deputed two officers in each district to work under the supervision of CPOs specifically for regrouped forest villages. Apart from

the above, each department has notified one officer as the Nodal officer for coordinating with the CPOs in connection with the technical and financial inputs to the regrouped villages from the concerned department.

- The involvement of eleven (11) line departments, mainly for providing infrastructure and non-land based income generating options has ensured quality in the technical inputs and timely availability of funds. This has resulted in full collaboration and coordination among different departments. This change in attitude is also resulting in much higher outputs of line departments in other field based activities. It is probably for the first time that so many departments are contributing to the same cause through their respective technical inputs apart from funding contribution within a given project area. This integrated approach is what is actually needed for changing the status of families from below poverty line (BPL) to above poverty line (APL). The compartmentalized working approach of different line departments has thus given way to a coordinated approach. This approach has reduced the possibilities of duplication of efforts by different line departments within the same project area.

2.2 *Criteria, Indicators, Current Status (Achievements)*

Based on different criteria and indicators for each activity, following (Table 1) achievements (current status) reflect the success of this scheme in providing economic and socio-culturally viable alternatives to the jhumia communities in the state:

Table 1: Criteria, Indicators, Current Status

S. No	*Criteria*	*Indicator*	*Current Status*
1	Education to 3-6 age group children through ICDS centers	100% coverage of all children	Average coverage is ~60-70%.
2.	Education facilities to 6-12 age group	100% coverage	Average coverage 80-85%

	children in schools		
3	Setting up of activity based SHGs	15-20 families/SHG for all the families	65-70% families involved as SHGs
4	Capacity Building (CB)	• CB should commensurate with the type of IGAs in a given village. • Should commensurate with types of SHGs. • Should lead to enhancement in social and economic conditions.	
5.	Forest based activities	• Short rotation crops (mucana, jatropha, pepper etc.) • As food value • Value additions possible • 0-5-1.0 ha per family • Water harvesting strutures	• Only ~35-40% families covered with required area under plantation • WHS- satisfactory progress
6.	Man-days	15-18 man days/ family/month	Not achieved in full
7	Water bodies	• Additional income • Water recharge • Aid in agriculture productivity • Pisciculture • Scope to form SHGs	~90% achievement on an average
8.	IAY houses	• At least one for each family	~60-62% achievement
9.	Anganbari centre	• As per requirement (at least one in each village)	• Satisfactory achievement in having the centre • Poor performance in all the villages on account of proper facilities and running of those centers.
10.	Community Halls/ Market Sheds/ roads/Schools	• As per requirement in the village • Help in	• The performance in all the villages is satisfactory

		confidence building • Meeting social need of the inmates • Aid in transporting products for sale in away markets for better price	
11.	Electrification	• Connections to the villages through LT/HT • Domestic connections to each family	• LT/HT laying is completed in about 85% villages • Domestic connection progress is not satisfactory
12	Drinking water facility	• To meet day to day requirements of each family • To meet up supply of water during pinch periods	• ~90% achievement on an average • Absence of electric connectivity in some villages is responsible for digging of deep tube well etc.
13.	Fund	• Contribution from each department as per the agreed arrangements	• Mainly forest and RD contributing funds • Fishery department is providing help in kind
14	JFM	• To cover each family	• 30 JFMCs created in 23 villages • Plantation area is far short than required • Scope to expand area under plantation exists. • Resources to be allocated to each family in JFM. • Activity based SHGs to be formed
15	Drinking water facility	• To meet day to day requirements of each family • To meet up supply of water during pinch periods	• ~90% achievement on an average • Absence of electric connectivity in some villages is responsible for digging of deep tube well etc.

2.3 *Major Achievements:*

The achievements of the Project can be seen against following work items:

2.3.1 *Creation of Infrastructures*

S. No.	*Infrastructure/Facility*	*Number/Km./Families*
1	Aanganbari Center	62 Nos.
2	Schools	44 Nos.
3	Road	158.2 km.
4	IAY houses	1125 Nos.
5	Community Halls	13 Nos.
6	Market Sheds	27 Nos.
7	Training Centers	7 Nos.
8	Electirc Lines taken to	20 villages (643 families)
9	Solar Light	515 families
10	Drinking Water Facilities	242 Nos. (RCC wells; Mark I, II, III tubewells; Kuchha Wells; Deep Tube Wells; Water Tanks; Masonary Well; Ring Wells; Pump Sets; etc.)
11	Supply of school uniforms	418 Nos.
12	Vegetable mini kits	212 Nos.
13	Agarbatti Implements	51 Nos.
14	Supply of mosquito nets	98 Nos.
15	Fingerlings	1,90,500 Nos.
16	Betel leaf suckers	261 families
17	Ginger	41,000 Kg. (1512 families)
18	Drum sticks around homestead	712 Nos. (15 families)

2.3.2 *Creation of Income Generating Assets*

S. No.	*IGA Facilities*	*Quantity/ Families covered*
1	Plantations of short rotation crops	3100 ha area and 3.02 lakhs seedlings of different species. On an average it has provided as asset equivalent to 0.76 ha per family
2	Check dams	266 Nos. (252 ha area). These check dams are helping in S & M conservation. Many pisciculture based SHGs have been formed with the technical and financial assistance from the Fishery Department. The SHGs are earning profits selling fish in the open markets.

2.3.3 *Capacity Building of Target Families*

S. No.	*Type of Capacity Building*	*Nos./Family Covered*
1	Training courses in different income generating aspects	3100 individuals (tailoring, pisciculture, duckery, piggery, agarbatti making, agarbatti rolling, etc.)
2	Training courses	204 Nos.
3	Formation of SHGs	321 Nos. (duckery, nursery, pisciculture, plantations, handloom, jatropha, musical band, tailoring, weaving, agarbatti making, agarbatti rolling, etc.
4	Revolving fund with SHGs	Rs.3,15,500 (till March 2009)

2.3.4 *Generation of Man-Days*

S. No.	*Year*	*Man Days (in lakhs)*
1	2005-06	1.81
2	2006-07	3.30
3	2007-08	3.65
4	2008-09	3.85

2.4 Fund Allocation and Expenditure

- A total of 254.3 lakh has so far been allocated for the activities pertaining to 23 RGVs from all the sources.
- Of the total fund received so far (254.3 lakh), maximum contribution has been from the Forest Department (52.9%), followed by Rural Development Department contributing 27.1% and remaining 22% contributed by all other line departments.
- A total of Rs. 301 lakh has been spent so far since 2005-06, which is only 8.2% of the total Project budget (Rs. 36.8 crores).

3. Conclusion

Quite oblivion of the concept of globalization and its all encompassing effects across the length and breadth of the globe, the jhumias in Tripura are much more comfortable in ensuring that they are able to meet their both ends. This is being achieved through inputs not at the macro-level, but at the micro-level addressing not only the economic considerations but also their socio-economic aspirations. This scheme has helped in building capacity of many beneficiaries in different fields of activities, which would ensure the sustainability of their economy in face of any upheavals at the macro-level. This is because their economy is based on all such local factors at the micro-level which can be controlled by them themselves. Moreover, social and cultural parameters are also taken care of by this participatory approach of forestry management which would provide solidarity and protection from the extraneous factors, to which the macro-level economics are more prone to.

The Forest Department has achieved a great deal in resettling tribal jhumia families in regrouped forest villages. This unprecedented success can be gauged by one simple fact that all the 23 villages continue to exist and the number of families have increased therein. Initial outflow of few families from these regrouped villages in favour of their old habitations for practicing jhum cultivation has now stopped altogether and replaced by non-jhum based (alternative) income generating options.

The success of this scheme in 23 villages has prompted other Jhumia families to request for such arrangements. A number of applications have been received by the forest department from many Jhumia families across the state for setting up new Regrouped Forest Villages on the similar pattern. Encouraged by the initial success of this innovative approach, the department is planning to extend this model embracing entire Jhumia populations across the state, especially those families who are residing deep inside the forest areas.

The success of this scheme proves a point that integrated and holistic approach is all what is needed in convincing and re-settling Jhumia families on alternative (non-jhooming) livelihood options for their holistic development comprising of economic as well as socio-cultural needs as well.

REFERENCES

1. Attiwill, P.M., 1994. The disturbance of forest ecosystems: the ecological basis for conservative management. *Forest Ecol. Manag*. 63, 247–300.
2. Ganguly, J. B. (1968). *Economic Problems ofJhumias of Tripura*, Bookland Private Ltd., Calcutta.
3. Gupta, A. K. (2000). Shifting cultivation and conservation of biological diversity in Tripura, Northeast India. *Human Ecology*, Vol. 28 (4), pp. 605-628.
4. Juo, A.S.R., Manu, A., 1996. Chemical dynamics in slash-and-burn agriculture. Agric. Ecosyst. Environ. 58, 49–60.
5. Myers, N. (1990). 'The World's Forests and Human Populations: The Environmental Interface'. In Churchill, E. (ed.), *Human Demography and Natural Resources*. The Population Council, New York, U.S.A.
6. Myers, N. (1984). The Primary Source: Tropical forests and our future. W.W. Norton, New York.
7. Myers, N. (1991). Tropical Forests: Present status and future outlook. In Myers, N. (ed.), *Tropical Forests and Climate*. Kluwer Academic Publishers, London, U.K., pp. 3 - 32.
8. Ruthenberg, H., 1976. Farming Systems in the Tropics. Clarendon Press, Oxford, UK.
9. Saha, S. B. (1970). Socio-Economic Survey of the Noatia Tribes. Unpublished report of the Tribal Welfare Department. Government of Tripura, Agartala, Tripura, India.
10. Sharma, T.C. 1976. The Prehistoric background of shifting cultivation. *J. Shifting Cultivation in North East India*, Meghalaya.
11. Westoby, J. 1989. Introduction to World Forestry: People and Their Trees. Basil Blackwell Ltd., Oxford, U.K.
12. Whitmore, T. C. (1975). *Tropical Rain Forests of Far East*. Clarendon Press. Oxford, UK.
13. Van der Wal, H., 1998. *Chinantec Shifting Cultivation and Secondary Vegetation*. BOS Foundation, Organization for International Forestry Cooperation, Netherlands.

18

Physico-economic Sustainability of Rubber Plantation—A Case Study on Bishalgarh Subdivision of Tripura State

SUNIL KUMAR DE*, SAUMI RAY* AND TULIKA PAL*

Abstract

The present Rubber plantation is a growing economic sector in the state of Tripura. Most of the tilla side slopes of the west district of Tripura are being converted into rubber gardens because of its economic values at the cost of overall natural environment. Deforestation, destruction of indigenous plant and animal lives, increasing soil erosion, erratic nature of rainfall as well as overall climate change are the expected bad effects of such plantation in the long run, which in turn affects the socio-economic environment. The present article aims at highlighting the physical and socio-economic sustainability of rubber plantation citing an example from Bishalgarh subdivision (Bankumari Rubber Plantation Centre) of state of Tripura.

* Department of Geography and Disaster Management, Tripura University, Suryamaninagar - 799130, Tripura West.

Introduction

The expansion of rubber plantations began in the early 1950s as post-revolutionary governments aimed to modernize and industrialize the agricultural systems in minority dominated rural regions of South-East Asia (Liu, *et al* 2006).

Rubber is one of the major plantations which shares a major part of the total economy of the state of Tripura. More than 33,000 ha of land of the state were under rubber plantation by July 2006 out of which about 16,000 ha was under production. With increasing population demand the area under rubber plantation has gradually been increasing at an alarming rate. The amount of economic profit from such plantation is season bound. Relatively it gives a good return to the producers immediately but in the long run it suffers from sustained profit in the state because the yield rates of rubber in Tripura are much lower than national average and Bishalgarh, being a subdivision of the state, cannot be an exception.

For creating land for such plantation, all categories of vegetation (both indigenous and planted) are cleared along the tilla-side slopes. Contour terracing is the next step for such plantation. This deforestation activities as well as such unscientific contour terracing enhances the possibility of soil erosion (Ong, 2009). Moreover, rubber leaves take long time to decompose with the soil, do not allow the undergrowths to be grown within the gardens and thereby increases the possibility of soil erosion. The liquid sap collected directly from the tree for processing latex produces several toxic chemical effluents (Serum). Solid latex requires huge amount of energy to separate water from it after coagulation. Vulcanization of latex into rubber also produces effluences that are highly toxic to the environment. For monocrop plantation like rubber often natural forests are cleared and timber is often stalked and burned. This results the killing of vast majority of forest species including those which are living in the soil like micro-organisms. These animals are directly exposed to the sun, rainfall and cannot survive or withstand the fluctuating heat and moisture levels. Once rubber trees are planted re-growth of any other vegetation or undergrowth is impossible until the seeds are completely depleted away from the soil or the canopy is closed (Jason, 2004).

Climatologically this plantation is not healthy, too. The category of vegetation absorbs huge amount of moisture from the soil as well as from the atmosphere causing dry atmosphere and erratic nature of rainfall for which the overall natural climate of the area and at large the whole region is under threat.

Although the plantation looks like a profitable one in the short run, but the overall deterioration of the natural environment in terms of climatic change, destruction of indigenous plant and animal lives will put not only the state but also the whole regions under severe threat in the long run (Liu, 2006). The present study aims at highlighting such problems with some documentary evidences keeping in mind about the broader interest of the society.

Location of the Study Area

For the present study a rubber garden, viz. Bankumari Rubber Plantation Centre (23^{0}41′N and 91^{0}19′E) from Bisalgarh subdivision of the state of Tripura has been selected, because rubber cultivation in Bisalgarh subdivision is practiced widely covering about 17% of the total area. The present garden in maintained by TFDPC. Other gardens in the subdivision are controlled by TRPC , TTAADC and some private owners.

Bankumari Rubber Plantation Centre comprises an area of 70 h and located at an elevation of 40 m from mean sea level. This garden falls under North Charilam tahasil of Bishalgarh subdivision (Fig. 1).

Sustainability of rubber plantation: examples from Bishalgarh subdivision, Tripura

Physical sustainability: from field observation

Since rubber plantation is deciduous in character that is why during field observation in the month of February, 2009 it was found that all of the trees were devoid of leaves while the ground surface was fully covered with dry leaves. There is almost no vacant place from where the bushes or

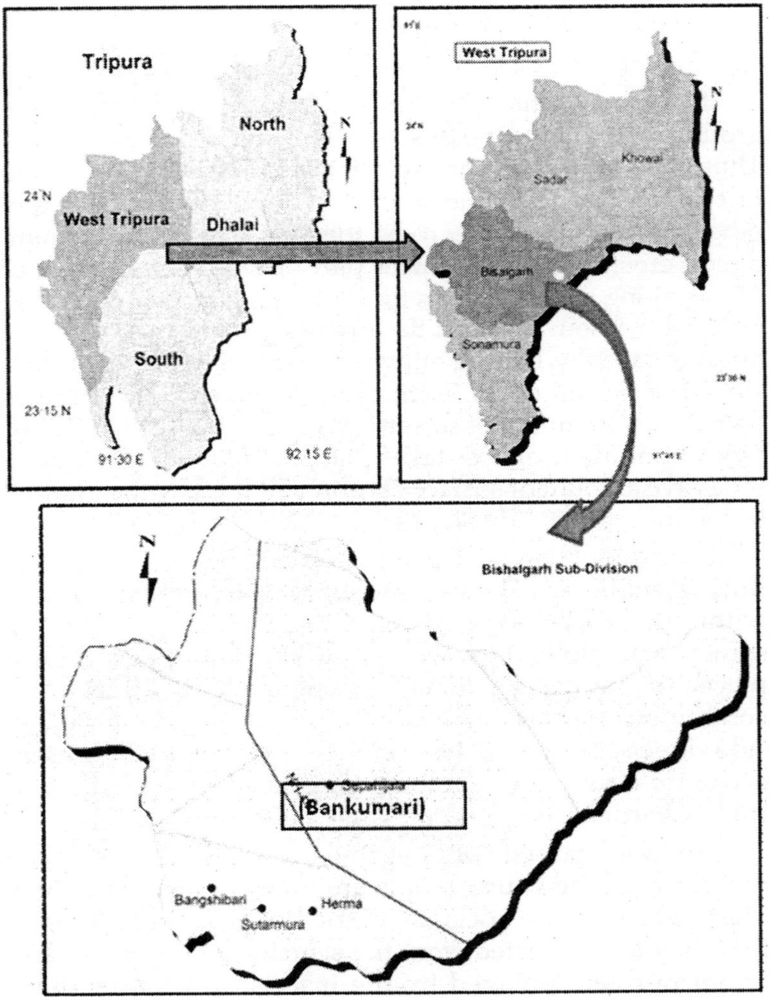

Fig 1. Location map of the study area

undergrowth can be grown up. From the biological point of view the cellulose of the leaves take long time to decompose or to mix with the soil but small veins of the leaves remain unchanged like skeleton (Greggio, et al, 2008). Moreover, they enhance the acidity of the soil (Plate: 1) through such decomposition and enhance the possibility of soil erosion. An example of such event is clearly visible from the rubber garden of Bankumari in Bishalgarh subdivision of Tripura.

a. In terms of increasing the acidity of the top soil cover

b. In terms of increasing the possibility of the soil erosion

The roots of the rubber plants spread laterally over the ground surface and posses very less soil holding capacity. Thus, they have hardly any role in increasing the compactness of top soil cover. As the secondary roots do not have any other sub-veins or smaller roots, they allow enormous amount of soil erosion from the lower part of the roots. In most of places along the slopes it is found that the roots are existing nakedly without any soil base which proves their less soil holding capacity. During rainy season relatively it seems that since the topsoil cover is concerned with three four layers of leaves, the amount of soil erosion can be less. But in reality, huge amount of soil loss takes place along the slopes due to excessive amount of surface run-off and thereby the gradual reduction of tilla side slopes.

It is noticed that the laborers are cleaning such dry leaves during winter season and gathering them in some places within the garden for burning. This practice is going on in some places along the lower part of the tilla slope but most places of the garden remain unchanged. As a result the contour strips those are made for plantation along the tilla side slopes have totally been eroded away and their present existence is very difficult to notice especially in Bankumari rubber garden.

From the gardens of Bangshibari, it has been observed that shoot of the young plants are whitewashed with lime. These practices are specially carried over young plants so that they are protected from the scorching rays of sun and might not get damaged by the insects. In these gardens degraded lands having slope greater than 15^0 are cut into terraces inside the tilla face and they are prepared in such a manner so that 1 m gap lies in between two terrace respectively. These are so because the inward inclination of the terrace helps in water restoration making the slopes suitable for plantation. Since these gardens have been raised recently, the process of soil erosion does not spoil the surfaces yet, but due to lack of proper maintenance the contour strips the slopes will be unable to maintain their original form making the slopes smooth and degraded.

Again it has been observed that sometimes other mature trees are cut down for the purpose of smoke house where with the help of black smoke produced by these woods creosote are deposited over the sheets making the rubber sheets ready for 'bell' (50 kg sheets required to make one bundle). These bells are then exported to near off factories for further processing. Here the gardens are not treated properly, which is well observed from the absence of the cover crops namely Purerium, Mucena and Mimosa. These are artificially planted around plant points so that they could stop soil erosion, generate nitrogen fixation in soil and also can suppress weeds that may cause damage to the plants specially the immature ones. Normally trees should be given about four weeks rest for sustaining latex production. It is observed that proper procedures of latex collection are overlooked for excessive profit making attitude of the owners, e.g. during winter months tapping is practiced when the yield of latex remain very poor because of the lack of both soil and atmospheric moisture. Furthermore extraction of latex randomly during this period often leads the plants in the verge of extinction. Hence if these problems are not addressed specially in the gardens of soil erosion and proper necessary measures are not taken immediately, the path of sustainability could not be achieved and one day will come very soon when all the gardens or the planted areas will convert into degraded land once again like before.

Economic Sustainability—From available Database Analysis

Gradual Change in Cultivated Area

Bishalgarh subdivision is credited with the maximum area under rubber plantation, 5127.15 ha. The plantations here are looked after by TFDPC, TRPC and private entrepreneurs are also there. In Bishalgarh TFDPC comprises 926.03 ha and TRPC and private entrepreneurs are also there. In Bishalgarh TFDPC comprises 926.03 ha and TRPC covers 722.31 ha. TFDPC covers only BANKUMARI RUBBER PLANTATION CENTRE while TRPC encompasses the gardens of BANGSHIBARI, SUTARMURA and HERMA

PLANTATION CENTRES. The areas of both TFDPC and TRPC are given below:

Table 1. Areal coverage of Bankumari in Different Years

Years	*Centre*	*Area (h)*	*No. of beneficiaries*
2001	BANKUMARI	76.58	27
2003		19.36	12
2007		70.20	20
2008		70	13
Total		236.14	70

Source: TFDPC Report (unpublished).

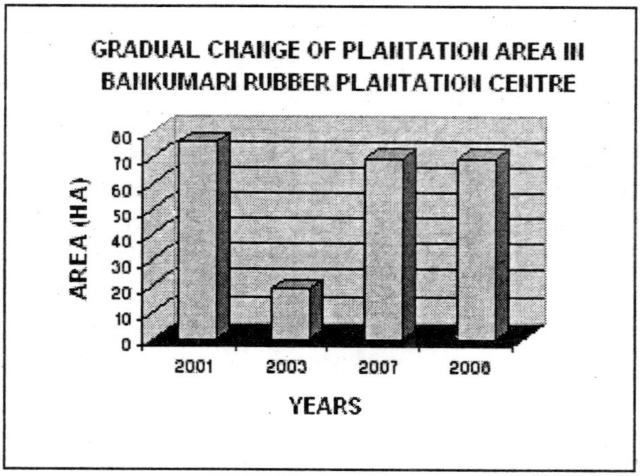

Fig 2. Plantation area of Bankumari in different years

In the year 2001, the area was 76.58 ha when forest areas were reclaimed that was covered by Sal and raised by TFDPC. The areas were actually taken under lease from the beneficiaries the number of which was about 72. In 2003, the area decreased due to poor maintenance, resulting the reduction of the plant points within the garden. In 2007, the area further increased due to restoration of proper management, plantation, processing etc. Thus the beneficiaries were benefited as 2/3 rd of the output was given to them and the remaining was manufactured for sell by TFDPC. In 2008, although the output remained constant, the plant points are decreasing to a greater extent (Table 1, Fig 2). The present scenario is not in the favour of sound plantation as a result of which many plots were handed over to the private entrepreneurs, TTADC etc. Thus the total area is 236.14 ha from 70 beneficiaries.

Production

Production of 5 years has been analyzed from the data given. It has been observed that the production was 35034 kg in the year2004-2005. In the year 2005-2006 the production decreased to 32976 kg followed by 32850 kg in the year 2006-2007. In the next year 2007-2008 the production is gradually decreasing at an amount of 32650 kg whereas in 2008-2009 the production is reduced to 27712kg respectively. Thus we can identify the gradual decreasing trend from 2004 onwards. This gives a clear idea about the sustainability of the gardens which are far from satisfaction (Table 2, Fig 3).

Table 2. Production of Bankumari in Different Years

Year	*Centre*	*Production (kg)*
2004-2005Y	BANKUMARI	35034
2005-2006Y		32976
2006-2007Y		32850
2007-2008Y		32650
2008-2009Y		27712

Source: TFDPC Report (unpublished).

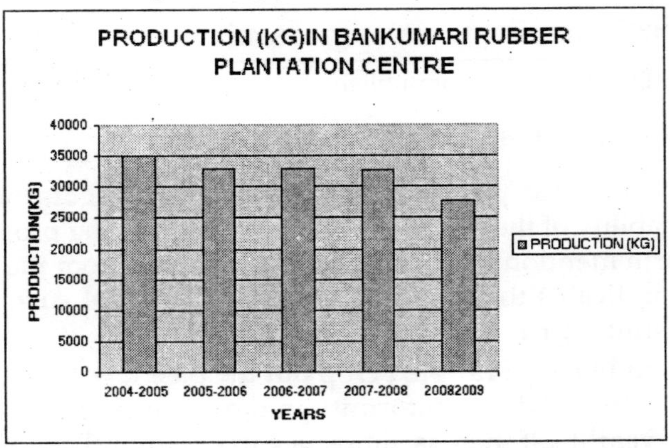

Fig 3. Production in different Years

Workers Strength

Bankumari plantation however shows a negative picture. The overall scenario reveals that the area remains more or less constant rather it deteriorates from 76.58 ha in 2001 to 70 ha in 2008. Since both area and employment opportunity are inter-related, hence with the shrinkage of area, the workers strength gradually decreases, which has come down from 12177 in 2004-2005 to 8582 in 2008-2009. Hence it is proved that either the plantation has not yet achieved the path of sustainability or it may be in the verge of extinction (Table 3, Fig 4).

Table 3. Area and workers Strength of Bankumari in different years

Years	*Area (h)*
2001	76.58
2003	19.36
2007	70
2008	70
Years	Labours
2004-2005	12177
2005-2006	14588
2006-2007	13806
2007-2008	14346
2008-2009	
Upto DEC. 2008	8582

Source: TFDPC Report (unpublished)

Problems Related to the Sustainability

Apart from the physical and economic aspects of the sustainability of the rubber plantation the following problems are worth mentioning those were investigated from the field which indicates the question of sustainability of such crop in the study area.

1. Rubber is a rain-fed crop but the past few years have witnessed no uniformity in the pattern of rain. This year itself there is almost a gap of 6 months between

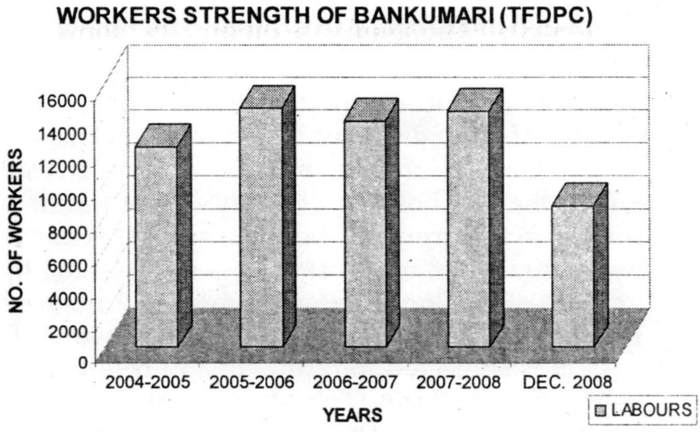

Fig 4. Workers strength in Different Years

rains. Excessive rainfall reduces the number of tapping days that affects the productivity and production of latex as experienced by the farmers. During monsoon months it is found that latex of mature trees gets blown away from the collecting channels and fall down the ground instead of the collection pan due to cyclones and norwesters. Oral surveys reveal that due to the increasing quantity of rubber plantation the average temperature of the state has increased for the last few years. Rubber is basically a tropical tree thrives in the undulating lands in almost all the districts of Tripura, locally known as "tilla"-"lunga" topography. In Bishalgarh subdivision this type of topography is also prevalent but with less altitude and moderate slopes.

2. Sometimes the leaves produced by shedding often creates great problem by making the ground sodden and soggy as the leaves do not get easily mixed up with the soil resulting the growth of different types of pests and insects. This creates problem while extracting latex by the tappers.
3. The soil of the overall state including the study area is very loose and fragile as the available phosphorus and potassium levels are low with high concentration

of nitrogen. The available organic carbon status of the soil is of medium range.

4. It is very important to state that the roots of trees are branched in different direction instead of deeply penetrating downward into the soil as a result of which the soil holding capacity is low but at some places on the ground where the soil cover is binded by the branched root resulting somewhat negligible amount of erosion. The remaining portion where the ground cover is not protected by the network of root system is subjected to rapid erosion resulting micro columnar structures. This structure is mainly due to erosion of sandy particles enriched with iron contents and residual resistant portion stand out as a columnar structures.
5. It is noted that the formic acid prescribed for rubber plantation which is organic in nature and some dishonest cultivators use Sulphuric acid for coagulation which is inorganic in nature, resulting deleterious effect on the environment. Illegal felling is predominant by the dishonest residents and planters as well and is widely practiced almost in every garden for the lure of rubber woods which has gained its status recently.

Conclusion

Rubber plantation is no doubt a great economic source of the state of Tripura. At glance the plantation has helped a lot in improving the ecological balance of the state that was under severe threat due to widespread jhumming. Rehabilitation of the tribal landless cultivators have improved the situation and relatively generated supplementary benefits like prevention of soil erosion and development of watersheds etc.

On the contrary mass scale plantation of rubber destroying the indigenous categories of environment friendly vegetation with economic value, may be lower than that of rubber, will create different problems both in terms of physical and socio economic environment. Naturally the sustainability of rubber plantation will be in vein in the long run.

In the short run this plantation is suitable for stabilizing the economy of the rural state of Tripura, but the cost of overall environmental degradation will be unbearable in the long run. Thus, along with this plantation alternative agricultural practices should also be incorporated to replace this plantation very slowly keeping in mind about the poor class of population, those are directly or indirectly dependent on it.

REFERENCES

Greggio, T.C., Assis, L.C. and Nahas, E (2008). Decomposition of the rubber tree (Heavea Brasiliensis) litter at two depths. *Chilen Journal of Agricultural Research,* 68: 128-135 (April-June, 2008)

Jason, W.C. (2004). World agriculture and the Environment : A commodity - by - guide tom impacts and practices. Island Press, 340-345.

Liu, W., Hu, H., Ma, Y and Li, H. (2006). Environmental and Socioeconomic Impacts of Increasing Rubber Plantations in Menglun Township, Southwest China. *Mountain Research and Development*, 26 :3; 245–253

Ong, D.J. (2009). Turning forest reserves into rubber plantations. *The Star*, 18 March 2009